D0205702

The Code of Cuenca

THE MIDDLE AGES SERIES

Ruth Mazo Karras, General Editor
Edward Peters, Founding Editor

A complete list of books in the series
is available from the publisher.

The
Code of Cuenca

Municipal Law on the Twelfth-Century
Castilian Frontier

Translated and with an Introduction by
JAMES F. POWERS

PENN

University of Pennsylvania Press

Philadelphia

Fairleigh Dickinson
University Library

MADISON, NEW JERSEY

KKT
6331
.A17
C 8413
2000

Publication of this volume was assisted by a subvention from the Program for Cultural Cooperation Between Spain's Ministry of Education and United States Universities.

Copyright © 2000 University of Pennsylvania Press
All rights reserved
Printed in the United States of America on acid-free paper

10   9   8   7   6   5   4   3   2   1

Published by
University of Pennsylvania Press
Philadelphia, Pennsylvania 19104-4011

Library of Congress Cataloging-in-Publication Data
Cuenca (Spain)
   [Forum Conche, English]
   The Code of Cuenca : municipal law on the twelfth-century Castilian frontier / translated by James F. Powers.
      p.   cm. — (The Middle Ages series)
   Includes bibliographical references and index.
   ISBN 0-8122-3545-2 (alk. paper)
   1. Cuenca (Spain)—Charters, grants, privileges.   I. Powers, James F.   II. Title.   III. Series.
KKT6331.A17 C8413 2000
348.46'47023—dc21   00-020261

To Lorraine

Contents

Introduction

Background and General Content of the Code

Fueros play an extremely important role in the development of medieval Hispanic law. Conceptually, they derived from the older Germanic tradition of the *bannum*, a grant of exceptions or freedoms from standing royal directives that apply to the realm. As they evolved during the southern expansion of the Christian kingdoms, they were increasingly awarded to individuals, institutional entities, and municipalities from the eleventh through the thirteenth centuries. Powerful nobles with territorial authority and institutions, such as the military orders, acquired the right to issue them in the lands which they held. Towns often received such grants as a settlement incentive to bring people to the frontier, where they assured the permanence of conquest and settlement by their presence. Until the mid-twelfth century, Castilian *fueros* remained similar in length to the charters being granted to towns by the contemporary monarchs of England and France. The latter twelfth century in Iberia witnessed a remarkable increase in the length and detail of these documents, especially in the kingdoms of Castile and Aragon. By the end of the century they began to emerge in some cases less as a collection of royal exemptions and privileges and more as extensive municipal law codes. These later *fueros extensivos* included a considerable body of local customs and practices either written by the townsmen themselves or dictated to the royal redactors who compiled the final version drafted for the king.[1]

The Muslim-founded town of Cuenca had briefly been in the possession of the Leonese-Castilian monarchy in the late eleventh and early twelfth centuries, but succumbed to Almoravid reoccupation after the battle of Uclés in 1108. Its position as a supply base for Almohad expeditions against La Mancha led King Alfonso VIII of Castile (1158–1214) to besiege it for several months during 1177. In this endeavor Alfonso VIII received aid and a personal visitation at the site of the siege by King Alfonso II of Aragon (1162–96). The Aragonese monarch had recently established a settlement in Teruel to the east of Cuenca on the other side of the Iberian Cordillera and had an interest of his own in Cuenca. The two kings were in the process of mutually determining their respective future spheres of conquest, and the assault on Cuenca provided an opportunity for assuring that their mutual progress would be peacefully determined. Cuenca capitulated to Alfonso VIII on 21 September 1177.[2] Within two decades of their acquisition, both Cuenca and Teruel received extensive *fueros* from their kings, codes remarkably similar in content and with a length exceptional for contemporary European municipal law.

The *Forum Conche* or *Fuero de Cuenca* is a remarkable body of municipal law originating in the Central Middle Ages in the Hispanic kingdom of Castile. The forces that contributed to its formation provided a uniquely balanced background for the creation of the largest urban code in its contemporary world. A developing but not overpoweringly dominant monarchy, a fluid military frontier that required settlers to populate and aggressively defend it, and the concurrent emergence of a blossoming legal and institutional tradition common to late twelfth- and early thirteenth-century Europe all played a role. Possibly the most important factor lay in the intense competition provided by an equally precocious neighbor, the kingdom of Aragon, where a similar municipal code, the *Forum Turoli* or *Fuero de Teruel*, appeared at roughly the same time. Both of these codes clearly seem to have been themselves influenced by a growing tradition of local custom in the Iberian Cordillera that they shared, a tradition informed by the long-term Muslim residents who were conquered by the expanding Christian kingdoms that took Teruel and Cuenca in 1171 and 1177 respectively.

As a result, we have an extraordinarily lengthy description of life in a frontier town, a kind of window into their lives as Heath Dillard has termed it,[3] a window both revealing and yet distorting in the insights it offers. Nonetheless, we see residents participating in local government for their town, electing and serving as municipal officials, whose duties are described in detail. Cuenca also possessed a quasi-legislative body, the *concilium* or *concejo*, a town council of the wealthiest citizens not unlike the older Roman curia which served the civitates of the Empire. Here as well we find a two-tiered judicial structure which provided appellate review with the power to render sanctions that ranged from small fines to death sentences. The king interfered with none of this activity. He did place royal officials in the area: the *merino* as district supervisor and the *Señor* as the specific representative of the throne in the town. The *Forum Conche* carefully regulated what powers these functionaries possessed in Cuenca. We lack the detailed history that would tell us just how well these original arrangements worked in reality, but the code suggests a balanced relationship between crown and town, with an unusual amount of independence for the *vecinos* or citizens of the latter, especially as compared to contemporary England.

The creation of a bishopric in Cuenca occurred by 1183, when the new bishop became a suffragan of the archbishop of Toledo. Almost certainly the office of bishop of Cuenca thus preexisted the granting of the extensive *fuero* to Cuenca, and yet little reference to that figure appears among its laws. He receives mention as the lawful owner of a palace (I, 8), and as the grantor of a special dispensation permitting a clergyman, archdeacon, or archpresbyter to serve as bondsman for a citizen. Otherwise such service was not legal because city officials did not ordinarily have jurisdiction over the clergy in Cuenca (XIX, 4). Indeed, the religious receive attention only when they undertook their infrequent tasks in civic life: priests have a part in the conduct of ordeal of hot iron for women (XI, 45–46); they have a potential role as bondsmen (XIX, 4 and 10), competent trial witnesses (XX, 12); and they can be drawn into judicial procedures both through being challenged with a layperson and through challenging a layperson themselves (XXI, 5, 6, 10). Monastic clergy appear only once, and then in a negative position. No sale of real estate could be made to them, on the grounds that their order forbade them to sell land to the town (II, 2). One can find evidence for the involvement of the bishop, clergy, and nearby military order of Santiago based at Uclés in the life of the town in the royal, municipal and cathedral archives, but the *Forum Conche* envisioned the Church as an entity separate from the town, with a limited role to play in the community.

With the placement into tangential situations of the crown and the clergy, two very important forces in twelfth-century Europe, the code of Cuenca focuses primarily upon the citizenry, their relationship to and their expectations of each other, and the structures that assure stability in town life, economy and security. While the specification of the rights and mutual obligations of citizens is often scattered throughout the code, one can observe an effort by the redactors to group categories of laws into consecutive chapters and sections of the *Forum Conche*. A certain amount of repetition appears in the citation of the laws from one area of the code to another. This appearance suggests a degree of haste by the redactors, which probably resulted from attempting to write down a considerable amount of previously unrecorded custom into a comprehensive whole in a comparatively short period of time. Some earlier scholars have suggested that the Cuencan code was copied from the already extant *Forum Turoli*.[4] But given that the ordering of the laws demonstrates rather little in the way of parallel structure between the two municipal codes, I believe that the redactors of the *Forum Conche* recorded local customs similar to those of neighboring upland Aragon, rather than simply copying Teruel's laws. Despite the apparent haste and repetition, the code of Cuenca reveals a notable effort to group laws into coherent topics in consecutive chapters. The repetition results largely from citing various laws as they apply from one section of the code to another.

The first chapter offers a general summary of the laws of the town. Thereafter, laws dealing with property, its types, its public or private status, and the means of protecting it are discussed (II through VIII). Chapters IX and X discuss the rights of inheritance of property and the making of a proper will. Chapters XI through XIV deal with homicide and personal injury. Chapters XV through XIX cover the process of acquiring bondsmen and obtaining sureties, with the noteworthy exception of Chapter XVI, one of the most important in the entire code. That chapter examines municipal officers and delineates their method of election and their municipal duties. Chapters XX through XXIX elaborate trial and appellate procedure, including the role of witnesses, the rules of judicial combat, and the four levels of the appellate structure. Chapters XXX and XXXI detail the extensive military obligations of the citizens both in offensive conflict and in defensive security procedures. Chapters XXXII through XXXIII deal with the sale and fiscal guarantees of estate sales. XXXV through XXXVIII examine the treatment of animals and the rights of hunters. Chapters XXXIX and XL discuss the rights and obligations of herders and hired workers. Chapters XLI through XLIII, the final chapters, take up an assortment of problems, including the relationship of hosts and guests, the specification of craftsmen and the proper practice of their trades, and an assortment of regulations that have no coverage in the earlier laws. These are general categories, and as noted above, law pertaining to particular sections can be found scattered in other sectors, doubtless an endeavor by the redactors to provide cohesion for the entire code through cross-linkage.

Municipal Government

Since the *Forum Conche* would be granted to a number of other towns in the Iberian Cordillera, La Mancha, and upper Andalusia during the course of the thirteenth century, we can learn a great deal from its extensive detail regarding the life and activity of these frontier townspeople during this crucial period of the Reconquest. The town council, an assembly of citizens who owned houses in the town and dwelled in them for a portion of the year, provided the central authority of the town. The council's size (possibly 300–500) prevented it from performing the daily management of the municipality, so once a year in late September or early October the council elected a variety of municipal officials to perform the tasks appropriate to the municipal executive branch (XVI).

Foremost among these was the *iudex* (Romance *juez*), in effect the mayor. He headed the town council, functioned as the chief judicial officer to whom legal complaints were first presented, and had theoretical command of the militia in wartime. He played a far more important role in the Cuenca charters and their copies than in any of the other Hispanic municipal *fueros*. The *alcaldus* (employed in this book in its Romance *alcalde*, since it was not originally a Latin word) held second place in importance after the *iudex*. The Council elected one of these from each parish (Latin *collacio*, Romance *colaçion*) in the town, a number that varied as Cuenca grew in population. The *alcalde* is the most frequently cited municipal official in the *fueros* of the twelfth and thirteenth centuries. In addition to their more typical religious function, the parishes functioned politically as town wards, and the *alcalde* constituted the ward boss or alderman for his district. Jean Gautier-Dalché has argued that these parishes may go back to areas under the control of particular mosques during the Muslim era.[5] In addition to assisting the *iudex*, the *alcaldes* met with the *iudex* each Friday to hold a judicial court, the court of appeal from the decisions of the *iudex*. If citizens had a political or legal grievance, their *alcalde* was likely to be the first person they would seek out. As with the office of the *iudex*, the *alcaldes* were expected to have a judicial capacity, a notion strengthened by the fact that *alcalde* is derived from an Arabic word meaning "judge," suggesting a component of Muslim custom that had been integrated into the *Forum Conche*.

A number of lesser officials also carried out governmental tasks. The municipal notary and clerk, the *escribano* (Latin *notarius*), maintained the town's official records and its *padrón* or census list, including entries by royal officials as well as those of the council, the *iudex*, and the *alcaldes*. It is noteworthy that the Latin word *notarius*, which is ordinarily translated as notary, is here rendered in Romance as *escribano*, which is usually translated as scribe. The *iudex* and the *alcaldes* employed a number of bailiffs, called *andadores* (Latin *apparitor*), who performed a good deal of the legwork in the judicial structure. The code obliged one to be present at the court of the *iudex*, and all of them had to be present at the Friday court of the *alcaldes*. They carried messages and instructions from these city officials, collected pledges from citizens involved in litigation, and served as jailers when the *iudex* incarcerated individuals. The *sayón* (Latin *sagio*) functioned as town crier, announcing the meetings of the town council, articles lost and found, and such other things as the *alcaldes* wished him to proclaim. He also served as porter for the meeting of the Friday court of the *alcaldes*, and occasionally as executioner. One special official provided for order in the marketplace of Cuenca.

The *almotacén* (Latin *almutazaf*), another office derived from that of a similar Muslim official, controlled the general running of the markets in the town. He vouched for the accuracy of all weights and measures used in the markets and inspected them each week. He had responsibility for keeping the streets and public places clean. All complaints regarding these matters came first to him. All these municipal officials received wages, portions of fines, percentages of sales, or shares of war booty as reward for their services. The comparative independence of Cuenca as a frontier municipality is reflected in the power of these officials, along with the restrictions placed on the authority of the royal servants noted above.

With regard to the origins of these municipal officials, pitfalls await anyone who attempts to pursue them exclusively on the basis of Castilian evidence. The only general study of municipal government for the eleventh through the thirteenth centuries, that of María del Carmen Carlé, restricts itself to the Leonese-Castilian *fueros*.[6] From that work one could form the impression that most of these officials originated in the Cuenca code, since she finds earlier references only to the *iudex*, the a*lcaldus*, and the s*agio* occurring in the *fueros* of Palenzuela (1074), Nájera (1076), and Sepúlveda (1076).[7] Little is said in these references regarding the precise duties with which these officials were charged. However, our knowledge gains considerable perspective when we examine the Aragonese charters of the early twelfth century. The positions of *iudex*, *alcalde* (still close to its Arabic form), and *saion* appear with an ever growing body of functions attached to them in Calatayud (1131), Daroca (1142), Molina de Aragón (1152–56), Estella (1164), and Alfambra (1174–76).[8] In addition, Daroca, Molina, Estella and Alfambra chronicle the appearance of the other municipal officials that will later appear in the *Forum Conche*.[9] The existence of a number of Muslim-derived municipal officials in the Forum Conche may well be explained by the survival of Islamic minorities who remained in larger numbers in the conquered towns of Aragon as compared to Castile.[10] Their presence and role became a part of the Cordilleran traditions which influenced the codes of both Teruel and Cuenca.

The Municipal Economy

While there is clear evidence of municipal commerce and its regulation in twelfth-century Cuenca, the economy of the town differed from its counterparts in France, England, and even Italy. The municipality included a considerable portion of the rural areas around it, and the boundary stones of its jurisdiction or *alfoz* reached as far as twenty-five kilometers or more from the town itself. Perched on a sharply rising ridge on the flanks of the Iberian range carved out by the deeply eroded valleys of the Júcar and Huécar Rivers, the town occupied a secure defensible position. The area enclosed a patchwork of landed jurisdictions controlled by various nobles, the military orders of Santiago and Calatrava, and the Church. Nonetheless, Cuenca's economic control incorporated a number of villages and hamlets in its *alfoz*, and much of this economic activity lay specifically under the town council's rights to make trade rules. The regulation of various craftsmen and the supervision of the marketplace by the *almotacén* and municipal council agents called *corredores* (Latin *venditor*) suggest a lively trade and merchant activity on a local basis (XVI, XXIX, XL, and XLI), but they constituted only a portion of the municipal economic resources. In fact, the municipal economy consisted of a balance among municipal commerce, agriculture, and livestock raising, the latter unusual for Europe in the period. References to sheep and cattle appear in over half of the forty-three chapters of the code, and there are allusions to other animals, such as dogs and fowl, as well as mention of dovecotes and beehives. Citizens had ready access to public and private grazing land for their livestock, although grain fields, orchards, and vineyards remained closed to them. Finally, the attention devoted by the *Forum Conche* to the collection and auctioning of military booty indicates a considerable amount of income from that bellicose resource.[11]

Protection and Transfer of Property

As in most twelfth- and thirteenth-century documents, property receives a great deal of attention. With the conquest of Cuenca in 1177, the possibility of possessing the newly available land seized from the Muslims who died or emigrated after the occupation provided a major incentive for settlers to move to the town. A land-dividing commission established in the wake of conquest granted the original holdings (II). However, the frontier maintained a fluidity that allowed new citizens to come and go, sometimes leaving their land vacant for a time. Some who received grants awarded at the time of the conquest may not have taken up immediate residence, allowing latecomers to acquire and develop the still vacant lands.[12] This could become a problem when the original grantees appeared on the scene to claim their conquest share. Laying down an orderly scheme of property acquisition, transfer, and abandonment clearly became a major priority, given the portion of the code devoted to it (especially

II, VI, VII, XXXII, and XLIII). Property was divided into immovable (real estate), movable, and animate, the first and third categories receiving the most attention. Chapters IX and X discuss transfer of property through wills and provide the format for writing a proper will. Some lands remained under the control of the council, such as springs, gypsum beds (for plaster), and stone quarries sufficient for the cutting of millstones. Mills, however, remained privately owned, although several restrictions governed their placement and use (VIII). The farms of the district produced orchards and grapes as well as grain, and laws dealt with their maintenance and protection.

Urban property received attention because of the closeness of citizens' holdings to each other and the problem of one structure encroaching on another. The height of houses and the use of shared walls were regulated, along with proper drainage, the covering of privies, and the building of structures that bordered on the streets (VI and XLIII). In the countryside, land holdings had to be properly surveyed and provide proper access to those needing to pass through. Real estate purchases had to be made at certain times and under certain conditions, and regulations regarding the renting and subletting of property can also be noted (VII and XXXII). The role of bondsmen and the provision of sureties demonstrates remarkable sophistication in property transfers. The existence of an investing class able to serve as bondsmen to guarantee these transactions is particularly interesting, since they also offer this service in cases of civil and criminal justice (XV–XX, XXVI, and XXVIII). All this suggests the probability that these practices had evolved over some time, finding written expression for the first time in Castile in the Cuencan code.

Law, Order, and the System of Justice

The task of maintaining law and order in the municipality fell primarily upon the *iudex* and the *alcaldes*. Aided by the other municipal officers, especially the chief of the marketplace, the *almotacén*, they enforced the laws specified by the code, and it was to them that complaints were brought. They exercised their functions passively most of the time, an important exception being during periods when the town's militia took to the field or when enemy raids were likely. In these times of threat a sundown curfew prevailed and individuals found on the streets without a light were arrested and held for identification by the town council (XXX). In peacetime, complaints had to be brought to an *alcalde* or to the *iudex*. Victims of a crime or their kindred, creditors with an uncollected debt, and individuals suffering injury or damage to their property contacted the appropriate official to begin the legal process. The *iudex* or *alcalde* dispatched a court officer, the *andador*, to respond to the complaint and collect any sureties from the parties involved. Thereupon a remarkably complex court process began before the *iudex*. If the individual wished to be represented by a lawyer (Latin *advocatus*, Romance *abogado*), the counselor had to begin to represent his client at this point and no later in the progress of the case. If the *iudex* failed to settle the dispute, the matter moved to the Friday court of the *alcaldes* (XXIII–XXVII). The great portion of the code devoted to bringing matters to the door of the *iudex* and to the Friday court of the *alcaldes* seems to imply that issues were settled at this level, but the plaintiff could appeal to the town council for a reading of the municipal *fuero* as it applied to the present case. Beyond this, aggrieved parties could take cases to the court of the king, within certain guidelines (XXVII). Since the code mentions lawyers with comparative infrequency and warns of their casuistic ways, readers are led to conclude that individuals pleaded their own cases more often than not. It was also possible to resort to the judicial duel to settle matters (XXII), which is more fully described in the *Forum Conche* and the *Forum Turoli* than in any other contemporary sources in Europe.

The sanctions applied for conviction of law-breaking vary considerably according to the level of the violation. Fines ran the gamut from a few silver coins (Latin *solidi*, Romance *sueldos*) to three and four hundred gold coins (Latin *aurei*, Romance *maravedís*), the equivalent of ten good horses or an expensive house. Presumably only the wealthy could pay the latter. The fines were distributed among the municipal officials as fees, to the plaintiff in successful suits, and on occasion shared with the royal representative, the *Señor*. The accused had to give sureties in advance garnered from bondsmen to guarantee payment of fines if the defendant lost the case. The case had to be proven in the courts for the sanctions to take effect, and defendants often possessed the option to secure a number of citizens who would swear in their behalf that they were innocent. Their numbers varied from one to twelve, depending on the seriousness of the crime. If the case was proved, however, such compurgators had no role.

Some penalties physically damaged the miscreant. Chapter XI cites instances when public whipping was sanctioned, primarily against women in cases of child abandonment and concubinage, although a married man could be whipped with his concubine. One might also include the ordeal of hot iron, exclusively applied to women as a judicial procedure, which might leave the hand burned. Permanent damage resulted from several forms of mutilation. A citizen could lose his ears for theft of bathhouse equipment, marketplace theft, or theft during a military campaign (II, XVI, and XXX). The *escribano* who altered records could lose his thumb; injuring someone during a fair or failing to complete payment of a homicide fine could cost one's right hand; loss of one's tongue and eyes also appear as sanctions (I, XIV, and XVI). These disfigurements also identified an individual who fled the town and attempted to reside elsewhere behind the anonymity of a fluid frontier.[13]

Individuals faced capital punishment for serious crimes, usually associated with homicide or treason. The most frequently cited form consisted of hurling the guilty party from the high cliffs readily available on the nearby Júcar and Huécar gorges. In towns that later received Cuenca's *fuero* but had no adjacent precipices, death by hanging became the normal equivalent. Certain categories of homicide led to this form of termination: a noncitizen killing a citizen; an employee killing an employer; assaulting an individual who later died; killing a surety bondsman; or killing a member of the town council during a revolt. Capital acts of treason included harming the king, selling or giving food or weapons to the Muslims (presumably in time of war), pillaging a battlefield before combat had concluded, or, in the case of a noncitizen, walking the streets at night without a light during military curfew. Also subject to capital punishment were the disloyal trading expedition leader operating in Muslim lands and the court officer lying to the town council about the king's decision in a legal case. A citizen who gave his son as a military hostage without the town council's permission was thrown from the cliffs (although if he used his daughter he was burned at the stake). Some sexual crimes fell into this capital category, such as bigamy, dishonoring a woman in a bathhouse or stealing her clothing from that place, or violating a religious woman.

In some instances, the guilty, especially women, could be burned at the stake. The man who violated or abducted a laywoman was executed in this manner, and if the woman had acquiesced to the abduction she was burned with him. Conviction of sodomy bore the same sanction, and in general homosexuality was condemned by a society keen on increasing its frontier population. Women who killed their husbands, committed bigamy, aborted their children, practiced herbal medicine or witchcraft, or cast a spell were liable to this fiery disposition. The same punishment prevailed for a woman caught in flagrante delicto with a Muslim or Jew or convicted of being a procuress. Any woman compelled to endure the ordeal of hot iron and failing to heal properly faced execution by fire. Those who publicly wished the king dead or who sold a Christian to Muslims or Jews were burned. Finally, theft committed at the time of a fair or theft of something worth five or more gold coins could lead to this form of execution.

Another rarer from of execution consisted of burial alive beneath the body of one's victim. Killing a fellow townsman during a fair or during a military campaign led to death in this manner. This penalty ensued also if someone killed a guest in his house or during a journey in which the other person depended on him for survival, interesting because these also constitute significant crimes in the Muslim world and may indicate a point where local custom is influenced by the persistence of Islamic law.[14] If the convicted party could pay the fine for homicide of three to four hundred gold pieces to escape death in a capital case, he usually faced obligatory exile from the community. The willingness to apply capital punishment in so many instances, along with the mutilation sanctions, suggests some of the incipient violence and the wish to constrain it on this military and cultural frontier.

Women in the Code of Cuenca

Given that women's lives are totally integrated into the code, it would seem somewhat artificial to single them out for particular attention. However, as Heath Dillard's now standard work on women in frontier León-Castile demonstrates, women held an unusually strong position in the Iberian Reconquest as compared to their twelfth- and thirteenth-century contemporaries in the remainder of Europe.[15] They could own property, inherit it, and maintain control over their possessions during marriage and in the event of their husband's death, when property was divided among heirs (IX and X). Contemporary documents in the cathedral archives verify this practice.[16] Nothing in the *Forum Conche* prevented them from owning and running shops and trading enterprises, and evidence from other towns clearly indicates that they did.[17] In the military sphere, women were prohibited from entering combat and inheriting military equipment (XXX). Central to their position was their role as lifegivers and childrearers. These tasks assured the continuity of the population and property accumulation. Aborting their children constituted grounds for execution, and to abandon them even to their father led to a public whipping and forced reestablishment of custody.

A woman's personal reputation and her honor were connected directly to her value as a wife, mother, and property holder. A good example of the threats to their personal honor faced by these townswomen can be observed in the laws relating to the public bathhouse (II). As I have argued elsewhere, these bathhouses existed as survivals of Muslim social life and had been used by the Christian conquerors with a certain amount of concern.[18] Restrictions required that women bathe in them only on certain days of the week, and the possibility that men might intrude to insult or rape women could lead to men being executed. The concern for a woman's shame or dishonor loomed so great that even to steal her clothing invited a one-way visit to the town's cliffs. Since women's marriageability and future status as heir producers held enormous value on a thinly-populated frontier, Cuenca's laws fiercely protected their honor, as the sanctions against its violation clearly indicate. The loss of that honor through becoming mistresses, prostitutes, procuresses, or sorceresses quickly led to their marginalization and possibly to their death. In defense of themselves and their honor, they could hire champions for judicial combat, although they could not personally participate in such duels (XXII). Through their life, work, and family position, women held a central position in the life of the town, as the code's extensive treatment of them clearly indicates.

Jewish and Muslim Minorities in Cuenca

Historians have long debated the impact of the Reconquest on the relation-ships among Christians, Jews, and Muslims regarding the nature of the resul-tant frontier society that became their milieu. Two primary themes have emerged with advocates on both sides of the Atlantic: one emphasizes the conflictive impact that tended to marginalize the Jewish and Muslim peoples in Christian Spain; the other emphasizes the existence of a multicultural society with important elements of interaction, called by Américo Castro *convivencia*. It should be pointed out that the two views are not necessarily mutually exclusive, and Cuenca's code provides ample fuel for both lines of argument.[19] Chapter I welcomes Jews and Muslims as well as Christians to settle in the town with full citizenship. Some of these minorities might have dwelled in Cuenca prior to Christian conquest and remained to accept the rule of the king of Castile. The code contains Muslim legal influences, names officials with roots in Islamic tradition, and refers specifically to the three religions collectively on several occasions: they can serve as bondsmen and offer sureties; they possess full trading rights during fairs; they can all obtain rights as sellers (*corredores*) in the municipal marketplace; and they are all collectively warned against overpricing grain and taking weapons from the city, unless they do so for military purposes. Yet clear lines of division exist among the three groups, along with significant indications that these lines are not to be crossed.

Jewish citizens made up a special legal caste in the Spanish kingdoms, in that the kings held custody over them as royal property (XXIX). The homicide and injury fines they paid went to the king, not to the community. Since Jews could take weapons from the town for combat purposes, we can assume they probably served in the militia. They had their own particular section of the marketplace, the *alcacería*. They had their own equivalent of the *iudex*, called the *albedí*, and the right to elect Jewish *alcaldes*. In litigation with their fellow Christian citizens, Jews possessed special privileges. Both the *iudex* and the *albedí* had to be involved in such litigation, along with both a Jewish and a Christian *alcalde*. Both Jewish and Christian testifiers had to be present, the Jews swearing on the Torah, the Christians on the Bible. But these same privileges also emphasized Jewish separateness. Jews and Christians could not participate in judicial combat with each other, possibly because of the potential volatility of the situation, but more probably judicial duels required the taking of oaths, working on the assumption that God intervened to determine the winner. In the bathhouses Jews bathed on Fridays and Sundays, not on the Christian days. If one entered on the day of the other, he and his heirs received no legal recompense if he were injured or killed. If Jews or Muslims were surprised in intimate acts with a Christian woman, both the man and the woman were burned at the stake. Social interaction seems largely to have taken place in commerce, and in a more limited manner in municipal government and in the militia. But even in warfare, the town structured militias into parish units, a specifically Christian structure, and Jews may have been separated into distinct divisions. True social interaction requires contact and interface, and the above barriers were unlikely to have fostered real integration.[20]

Muslims held a position distinct from both Christians and Jews in many respects. While they shared some of the privileges and responsibilities of Christians and Jews cited above, they bore the burdens of sharing a religion held by the royal and municipal enemies to the south. For decades after the conquest of the city, Cuenca faced an active threat from the Islamic principalities, often aided by reinforcement from North Africa. After the Castilian disaster at Alarcos in 1195, Cuenca was subject to two years of intensive raiding as a part of the Tajo River campaigns launched from Al-Andalus, before a truce eased pressures in the following decade. Muslims seized during these combats were traded to the Islamic states for Christian prisoners, or retained as slaves in the *alfoz* of the municipality. Indeed, the *Forum Conche* sharply distinguishes between free and unfree Muslims. Muslim slaves were divided up along with other military booty, granted to city officials as a part of their salaries while the rest were put up for auction, and had few rights in the code. Owning or hiring Muslim slaves made the owner or hirer responsible for any harm they caused by their actions. In such cases, owners were obligated to pay their fines or hand them over to the plaintiff. Christians could not be enslaved in Cuenca, and while Jews were technically owned by the king, the ruler protected them and provided comparatively benevolent and distant overlordship. One need only look to the history of slavery in the United States to observe the impact of this unfree condition on African-Americans. Even after the Muslims gained their freedom, it was difficult for them to achieve ultimate Muslim integration into the larger community once they had endured direct ownership by their neighbors.

Yet a case for integration and *convivencia* exists. As noted above, free Muslims existed, settled Cuenca and its territories, and possessed rights similar to those of Christians and Jews. Chapter XI has several laws that indicate this. The same fines and sanctions that protected the lives of all citizens specifically protected them. They served in the municipal militia, even as unit commanders, and received special rewards for the capture of enemy Muslim settlements. An especially interesting law permits a Christian who has fathered a child by another person's Muslim slave to take that child into his household if the father redeems it. That illegitimate child is then entitled to a full share in his will along with the legitimate siblings. If the owner converted a slave to Christianity, the former slave became a servant with the implied right to pass his goods to his own children (IX). Thus, either by converting or by gaining their freedom, Muslims captured in war could become citizens of Cuenca with substantial rights. However, important exclusions continued to exist. Like Jews, Muslims caught in intimate acts with Christian women were burned along with their partners. Fears regarding the lustfulness of Muslim men toward Christian women noted in Chapter XI probably contributed to such sanctions. Nonetheless, whether by the long-enduring enmity, fear for Christian women (X, 39), or religious differences, even free Muslims appear to have remained a people apart. Moreover, they appear to have lacked the right to elect an *albedí* or an *alcalde* of their own, unlike the Jewish citizens.

Warfare and the Municipal Militia

One remarkably well-developed area of activity for Cuenca and other frontier towns of the era can be seen in its military service laws. Chapters XXX and XXXI contain extensive references to the military requirement that fell on every household, demanding either mounted or foot soldiers, depending on their wealth and status. Chapter I contains a law (15) stating that the town's militia only joined the royal forces if the king personally commanded, and then only within the boundaries of its own territory. These restrictions could not have prevailed for very long, as their combat record will attest. While no time limit is set on the length of this service in any given year in the Cuenca charters, a maximum of one to two months is cited for other towns in the later twelfth and thirteenth centuries.[21] Moreover, we know that the Cuencan militia participated in campaigns that could easily have taken that long. In 1211 and 1213, their forces joined armies led by their founder Alfonso VIII as a part of expeditionary forces consisting primarily of municipal militia contingents, the first of which struck at Játiva and the Mediterranean coast, over a hundred miles away. In 1225 Cuenca's militia, headed by local leader Alfonso Téllez and Bishop Lope of Cuenca, led other town militias in an independent foray against Valencia and Murcia, yet further distant. They also served in the force besieging and taking Córdoba in 1236.[22] No urban forces in Europe were operating anywhere near as far from home at that time, and these were by no means the longest campaigns made by Iberian municipal armies in the twelfth and thirteenth centuries. More than any other reason, this military capability explains why the kings granted the extensive freedoms and independence to towns such as Cuenca.

Offensive campaigns provided the most comprehensive and predictable aspect of their military role. For these forays, Cuenca organized its forces into units based on its parishes, placing each of these under an officer called the *quadrellarius* (Romance *cuadrillero*), who was charged with camp security and the taking and distribution of booty for his parish unit. The laws deal with the appointment of scouts, organization on the march and in encampments, and the dispatch of mounted raiding parties while in the field. The *Forum Conche* specifies the manner of recruiting the militia and legitimate use of substitutes and provides a code of conduct while on campaign and in battle, including restraints on the taking of booty, the care of casualties, equipment requirements, and the rights of wives at home while the army was away. An ample body of law covered the taking of booty, its distribution and its use for paying the royal fifth share of the spoils (another Muslim tradition), and the compensation for injuries and losses of animals and equipment. The management of the auction process by which the booty was converted into shares receives lengthy attention. The focus on the entire booty process informs us about the vital role played by these revenues in the municipal economy, and the incentive the townspeople felt regarding the undertaking of independent campaign activity to attempt to enhance these resources despite the attendant risks of battle.[23]

Another far less predictable area of military service centered on the defense of the town. Here the municipal enemies possessed the initiative and usually sought surprise as part of their plans. The town's livestock grazing in the *alfoz* provided an attractive lure for Muslim raiders, just as Cuenca's raiders targeted such mobile booty in its own raids. The Muslims as well, were fully capable of launching a major expedition and the possibility of a large-scale attack on the town and a siege of its walls always loomed. Chapter XXXI offers a body of laws addressing this problem, providing for the rapid assembly of a defensive force, called the *apellitum*. Summoned by horn blasts, church bells, smoke signals, and individual messengers, the muster gathered around the town standard or joined it in the field. The mission of these forces focused on meeting the enemy before they seized much booty or approached the walls of the town. These laws also survey the need for vigilance in the countryside as well as on and inside the municipal fortifications. From the perspective of the king, this defensive system filled a need if anything greater than that provided by the offensive campaign capability. The settlers maintained the security of their territorial zones on a day-to-day basis, even before a royal force gathered to maximize the defensive efforts, making it costly for campaigning enemy forces to move in the fluid frontier without paying a price. If the colonists of Cuenca and the other frontier towns had rendered only this service, it would have constituted an invaluable contribution worth granting their liberties in exchange.

The Question of Law Versus Actual Practice

The question must certainly arise in the mind of any historian concerning how much of the material contained in the *Forum Conche* represented actual practice on the part of the citizens of Cuenca. Law constitutes the statement of an ideal, not necessarily the real conduct of individuals, as modern automobile speeding regulations might indicate. Moreover, we lack a wide variety of surviving court cases that might better illuminate the extent to which these laws were actually followed. One can note, however, the growth and evolution of municipal law in earlier *fueros* to suggest the emergence of many of the precedents of the laws of Cuenca and Teruel. Moreover, the widespread adaptation of the *Forum Conche* by other towns flanking the Iberian Cordillera, La Mancha, western Castile, and upper Andalusia indicates that this collection of laws had a pragmatic utility that other towns could copy and modify to their particular needs.[24] This aspect of universality avoids many of the doubts as to its actual use that might be raised by a single application of the code at one place. In addition, the writing down of so much customary law that lacked clear precedent in prior royal awards to Castilian towns indicates that many of the specifications denoted local practices already a part of custom to which Alfonso VIII was giving royal recognition. The most likely explanation for the Castilian king's motivation to take this step consists in his awareness that Alfonso II of Aragon was taking similar steps in the creation and granting of the *Forum Turoli* to Teruel, just across the Cordilleran frontier. While students of these codes must take care in their assumptions regarding the literal application of the codes, the concept that they indicated a viable representation of civic life on the Hispanic frontier merits a certain amount of trust.

The Surviving Manuscripts in Latin and Romance: The Manuscript Tradition and the Question of Dating

The archival history of Spain provides an often tragic record of documentary survival, with civil wars, fires, and occasional unprofessional archivists taking their toll on the precious documents we still have available to us. The earliest versions of the Latin *Forum Conche* come down to us in two manuscripts, one from the mid-thirteenth century in the Escorial Library and the other in the Bibliothèque Nationale, Paris, variously dated from the early thirteenth century to the fourteenth century. The earliest Romance versions survive in a complete version in the University of Valencia library called the *Codice Valentino*, dated from the later thirteenth to the early fifteenth century, and a fragmentary version from the fourteenth century in the Municipal Archive in Cuenca.[25] The Latin version of Cuenca's charter was adapted by the towns of Moya, Consuegra, Alcázar, and Villaescusa de Haro, of which only the last manuscript has survived.[26] The Romance version was adapted by yet more municipalities in the thirteenth and early fourteenth centuries, namely Alarcón, Alcaraz, Alcázar (in both thirteenth- and fourteenth-century versions), Baeza, Béjar, Huete, Iznatoraf, Iniesta, Villaescusa de Haro, Andújar, Úbeda, and Zorita de los Canes. The Fuero de Plasencia also demonstrates a strong influence from the Cuencan code. Most of these *fueros* have received modern published editions.[27]

The Escorial manuscript of the Latin *Forum Conche* has been published in an outstanding edition by Rafael Ureña y Smenjaud, compared in column presentation with Romance copies of the *Codice Valentino*, the Cuencan archival fragmentary version, and the *Fuero de Iznatoraf* (an early adaptation of Cuenca's code). An edition of the Paris Latin manuscript appeared in the early

1900s, edited by George H. Allen. More recently an edition of the *Forum Conche de Cuenca* in modern Spanish was published by Alfredo Valmaña Vicente.[28] While I have seen the various versions in their manuscript form, my translation has been based on the published Latin edition of Ureña, compared with Ureña's Romance version, the Latin edition of Allen, and Valmaña's modern Spanish version. I have not included the *Forum Turoli* or *Fuero de Teruel* among the charters influenced by the code of Cuenca. Published editions of the two Teruel charters also exist.[29] There exists a school of Castilian scholars who argue that Cuenca provided the original *fuero* from which Teruel's *fuero* was copied, initiated by Ureña himself. An equally determined group of Aragonese scholars counter with a case that priority belongs to the Teruel code, from which Cuenca may have derived its contents. My own experience with the laws assembled in these codes leads me to conclude that a Cordilleran or Extremaduran thesis of contemporary generation of these two codes offers the most likely solution. The customs are strikingly similar on both sides of the Iberian Cordillera in Castilian and Aragonese Extremadura, probably collected at roughly the same time by the redactors of Alfonso VIII and Alfonso II with the objective of establishing a new template for municipal law in these regions. I should note that in the course of my own research on the military, dueling, and bathing legislation, the most interesting precedents lie on the Aragonese side.[30] Indeed, one might make the case that the *Forum Turoli* merits at least as much a translation into English, save that it influenced only two other town *fueros* and had nothing like the spread or the longevity of impact of Cuenca's code.

The Problem of Dating the Code of Cuenca

One problem becomes clear when considering the pattern of surviving copies of the *Forum Conche* and *Forum Conche de Cuenca*: the originals of neither manuscript survive. What does survive cannot be dated any earlier than the mid-thirteenth century, if then, based on paleography. Since a number of municipalities received copies of Cuenca's charter in New Castile, La Mancha, and upper Andalusia in the reign of Fernando III (1217–52), Cuenca's *fuero* had certainly been granted to the town by then.[31] One model argues that, despite the preface to the *Forum Conche* that makes Alfonso VIII (1158–1214) the grantor, Cuenca may only have received a short charter in his reign, similar to that granted to Zorita de los Canes in 1180, although no such earlier version for Cuenca has survived. This argument also notes that the florid rhetoric of the preface seems precocious for the last decade of the twelfth century.[32] This does not preclude the possibility that the preface was added to a later copy of the code, the laws of which were completed in the late twelfth century. Moreover, as we shall see, the prologue constitutes a double-edged sword as a device for dating the *Forum Conche*, particularly regarding its content rather than its rhetoric. At any rate, the code can be placed in the time frame between conquest of the town in 1177 and the death of Alfonso VIII.

Several factors persuade me to consider a twelfth-century date for the original *Forum Conche* in something close to its current form. One is the closeness in time of the granting of the *Forum Turoli* to the town of Teruel, almost certainly granted by Alfonso II of Aragon (1162–96) before his death. The closeness in content between these two unprecedented codes warrants the assumption that they are contemporary and draw from similar bodies of customary law in Castilian-Leonese Extremadura.[33] While they are not so close in relationship as the code of Cuenca is to one of its copies granted to other Castilian towns, the parallels are nonetheless striking. Alfonso II and Alfonso VIII experienced periods of close cooperation during their reigns. As noted above, Alfonso II joined the Castilian king's siege of Cuenca in 1177, and the two worked out a series of frontier treaties between them that foresaw the expansion of the Christian frontier to the conquest of Valencia and beyond. The coincidental, if not co-planned, determination to grant large territorial codes to two of their recently conquered frontier municipalities (Teruel was taken in 1171) is worth considering as a possibility, if not a certainty.

The coincidence theory takes on ever greater weight when one considers events in the contemporary kingdom of Leon to the west. Here, too, the desire to create a new, larger format of municipal law led King Alfonso IX (1188–1230) to grant an extensive *fuero* to Ciudad Rodrigo in the last decade of the twelfth century, similar to that of Cuenca in length but not in its laws. The situations could also be compared in that Ciudad Rodrigo was recently founded as a town to provide a bulwark against neighboring Portugal. Here, too, neighboring Christian kingdoms competed for settlement and land in Leonese Extremadura against the Muslim states and with each other. While the original charter granted to Ciudad Rodrigo does not survive, versions were given to seven towns along the Leonese frontier with Portugal and the Muslim south between 1209 and 1243, copies of which did survive to be published in edited modern editions.[34] The incidence of yet another initiative in large-scale municipal codes emerging at the end of the twelfth century by another peninsular Christian monarch, considered in the light of Teruel's *fuero*, suggests that creating an extensive code for Cuenca had a deep context in late twelfth-century Spain. By the end of the century, King Alfonso IX of Leon was betrothed to Berenguela, the daughter of Alfonso VIII of Castile, and the awareness of each monarch's policies on the part of the other appears a reasonable assumption. Indeed, Spain was approaching the crest of a legal renaissance for which this era of extensive municipal codification of law was the harbinger. To move the origins of the *Forum Conche* later into the thirteenth century requires the movement of much of the Peninsular context with it.

In his lengthy edition of the codes of Cuenca in 1935, Ureña y Smenjaud placed the date of Alfonso VIII's grant between 1189 and 1190.[35] The first part of the dating bracket, based on the controversial prologue, mentions the name of Alfonso VIII's son Fernando. Since we know that Prince Fernando was the king's firstborn son, and that he was born in Cuenca on 29 November 1189, few have any problem with accepting this as the *terminus a quo* for the *Forum Conche*.[36] The *terminus ad quem* of Ureña's time bracket presents more problems. He bases it on a document in Cuenca's municipal archive dated 17 January 1190, which gives a number of rural estates to the town. Since the place names cited within that concession are not mentioned anyplace in the code, Ureña presumes that this grant must have followed the issuing of the *Forum Conche*.[37] Unfortunately, the listing of numerous areas within the *alfoz* of Cuenca almost certainly in the possession of the town, but not mentioned in the code, must be quite long. This weak argument from silence is therefore not particularly persuasive. Beyond the additional assertion that the wording in the prologue suggests that Prince Fernando's birth was quite recent, Ureña's case has left scholars with ample reasons for arguing that composition of the *Forum Conche* belongs in the following century.

But the Prologue contains tantalizing pieces of evidence that Ureña did not exploit. First is the reference to the possibility of renaming the city Alphonsipolis and making it a place of royal residence. Possibly the king intended to make Cuenca a forward base in the assault on the Almohad south, a plan terminated by the disastrous loss at Alarcos in 1195. For whatever reason, Alfonso's project for Cuenca did not last long and is not likely to have been referred to much after 1195. More interesting is the reference to the Hohenstaufen prince Conrad. Here it is noted that "Don Conrado, illustrious descendant of the Roman Emperor, and Don Alfonso, King of León, are happy to have received the weapons of combat and his backing, a reminder of his goodness and of having kissed his hand." The Conrad referenced here is the fourth son of Frederick I Barbarossa, Konrad von Rotenburg. Conrad had recently been betrothed to Alfonso VIII's eldest daughter Berenguela in 1187, later confirmed by a treaty between Alfonso and Frederick formally consenting to their marriage, dated 23 April 1188.[38] In late June 1188, Alfonso held a session of his court at Carrión de los Condes. On 4 July eighteen-year-old Conrad joined him there, going through the knighting ceremony alluded to in the preface of Cuenca's code. In addition, Alfonso declared Conrad to be the future heir to Castile should the king die without male progeny.[39] But the birth of Prince Fernando in November of 1189 placed grave doubt on this potential Hohenstaufen opportunity, unless Conrad had bided his time waiting to see if Prince Fernando predeceased his father (as Fernando actually did in 1213). Indeed, Conrad himself died in 1196. The matter was resolved long before that, however, by the Church. Since Berenguela and Conrad were cousins, the issue of consanguinity soon emerged. The contemporary historian Rodrigo Jiménez de Rada notes that Cardinal Gregory, dispatched to Iberia in 1191, and the Primate Archbishop of Toledo Gonzalo Pérez jointly issued a document annulling the marriage of Conrad and Berenguela. While the document does not survive, Bishop Gonzalo passed away in the late summer of 1191, so the annulment had to be accomplished that year.[40] Beyond that, Conrad died at the age of twenty-six in 1196, and it is certainly unlikely that he would have been cited after that.

This raises considerable doubt that the preface could have been written much after 1191. The reference to Conrad would have been fatuous and unlikely in such a document, certainly by 1197, when Berenguela married the other knighted person mentioned in the prologue, King Alfonso IX of Leon. If the prologue truly belonged later in the thirteenth century, as Juan Gutiérrez Cuadrado has argued in his edition of the *Fuero de Úbeda*,[41] why would its author attempt to place it artificially in this time frame of 1189–91 with nothing else to guide him? There are, after all, no other particular chronological references to indicate the precise dating of the *Forum Conche*. Moreover, the argument from the excessively flowery rhetoric for the period contained in the prologue wants more analysis than Gutiérrez Cuadrado offers to make a convincing case. The poet Horace, from whom the rhetorical quotations derive, represents an author reasonably well known during the Twelfth-Century Renaissance. Joseph O'Callaghan has demonstrated that Italian legal jurisprudence penetrated Castile to a considerable degree during Alfonso VIII's reign.[42] In the absence of a better case than heretofore offered, Ureña's assumptions regarding the chronology of the prologue, and probably of the *Forum* also, stand up reasonably well, if not for the reasons he presented.

Additional evidence for dating the laws of Cuenca in this period exists in contemporary documents.[43] While land sales constitute a large category of surviving medieval documentation, not many have come down to us from

Cuenca during the last two decades of the twelfth century. But some of those that do survive cast light both on the questions of the *Forum Conche*'s origins and on its actual usage as a guide to conduct. The first group relates to the acquisition of properties by the military order of Santiago, based at nearby Uclés, including six documents dating from the years 1184–86, prior to the granting of Cuenca's code.[44] Another group of seven documents dealing with land sales to a cathedral canon spans the years 1193 to 1194.[45] The *Forum Conche* indicates specific conditions for property sales in widely separate parts of the code. Among them: the day of sale should be Saturday or Sunday (VII, 12); the seller of property must provide a surety bondsman (II, 4; XXXII, 2); five witnesses should be signatory (VII, 13); and the document must ratify that the buyer has already paid the price (VII, laws 12 and 13). What does a comparison of the two sets of documents reveal regarding these regulations and the conformance of either group to the code's norms?

The group dating between 1184 and 1186 offer little in the way of conformance to the requirements of the future *fuero*. Only one carries a day date, and that day is a Friday (the remainder are dated by month and year); only two of the six mention a surety bondsman; one of the six has an insufficient number of witnesses; and one of the six indicates the price has not been paid yet. By contrast, the 1193–94 group in the cathedral archive conforms rather more closely to the specifications of the *Forum Conche*. All seven documents have day dates; of these, four were made on Saturday or Sunday, while two of the others may have been affected by adjacent religious feasts.[46] All seven mention surety bondsmen, six of the seven list five or more witnesses, while the witness list from the seventh seems to be missing, and all seven indicate that payment has already been made. Most important, all seven include a phrase missing from the first set of documents. That phrase is "according to the *Forum Conche*," a clear indication that the code of Cuenca exists and is being followed. Considering that the requirements adhered to by these documents are spread throughout the *fuero*, one can infer that a great portion of the code we possess had already been written and abided by, at least in the case of real estate transactions. Since the first of these documents to mention conformance to the code is dated 14 March 1193,[47] a strong case can thus be made for the awarding of the *Forum Conche* between 29 November 1189 and 14 March 1193. In that event, it can be described as law of the twelfth century.

The impact of the *Forum Conche* lasted well beyond its period of initiation. As already noted, copies of the code were granted to a number of towns through the reign of Fernando III to his death in 1252. Subsequently, Alfonso X el Sabio tried to restrict its spread and attempted to revoke the copies given to Alarcón, Requena, Baeza, and Béjar in favor of his own *Fuero Real* format. The *Fuero Real* drew on Visigothic and Roman traditions of law as well as a model derived from a group of charters based on *fueros* given to Toledo. The four towns persisted in their resistance, and Alfonso X yielded to their reaction by restoring the Cuencan model to all four by 1272.[48] At least one Cuenca copy was awarded in the fourteenth century, indicating a continuing appeal for this gathering of customary law in the regions of eastern and southern Castile. Beginning in the reign of Alfonso XI (1312–50), however, a royalist reaction to these untrammeled municipal privileges set in, witnessing the restriction of these freedoms steadily through the era of the Trastámara dynasty to the Renaissance despotism of Fernando and Isabel at the beginning of the modern era. The closing of the Reconquest thus withdrew the ambiance which had given rise to the age of such frontier municipal liberties. But the *Forum Conche* nonetheless records the fact that they existed.

Conclusion

It is the hope of this translator that this edition of the *Forum Conche* will find a wide audience among those interested in the history of Spain, the evolution of medieval law, the development of municipal life in the twelfth and thirteenth centuries, and the interaction of Islam, Judaism, and Christianity in the medieval West. This translation makes available to English readers for the first time a large body of urban custom from south of the Pyrenees, and the contents constitute a true landmark in the development of towns in the Mediterranean world. It must be utilized with the same caution appropriate to any other code of law as a statement of ideals, however locally based, and not as a certain guide to actual practice. Nonetheless, the code's pragmatism, extraordinary detail, and widespread popularity as a body of law in Castile from the twelfth to the fourteenth century at least suggests that it may well have been based on genuine custom and was therefore not without some influence in the daily life of Spanish townspeople who lived under its rules. The code evokes a sense of adventure and exuberance that puts us in touch with the world of the Reconquest frontier in Iberia, a world not unrelated to that of the English-speaking builders of world empire and the frontier society of the American plains.

Notes on the Translation

Some words of introduction are necessary with regard to the methods and approaches applied in translating this extensive law code into English. It suffers, as must all translations from one language to another, from the inability to bring a body of text written in a different era and culture into modern English with perfect accuracy. Nothing can ever replace the authenticity of the original read by an individual with a solid knowledge of the language and the historical ambient from which it emerged. It is equally true that a society's law often diverges from its actual practice, and therefore is to be employed with great discernment in trying to understand how that society functioned. I have attempted here to present the code in clear modern English in a manner appropriate to the way in which modern English or American laws would be written. That has not always been an easy task. To convey the essential content in an edition intended for the modern reader and the modern classroom, I have deemed it necessary to take some liberties with word-for-word accuracy in order to convey a modern sense of the whole. While it is primarily the surviving Latin editions I have endeavored to translate, occasional resort was made to early Romance versions for purposes of clarity and supplementation. My use of the term Romance indicates the contemporary form of Spanish in use during the later middle ages prior to the classical Castilian that evolved during the Golden Age of the sixteenth century.

Gender invariably constitutes a problem for the modern reader, since this code was the product of a male-centered society, but one in which women played important roles. I initially thought to avoid this problem by utilizing the plural form in many places where the text employs the singular, enabling me to translate the subject as gender-neutral "they." Ultimately this created so much awkwardness and potential inaccuracy that I abandoned the effort. Since women possessed some remarkable freedoms in twelfth-century Cuenca, the male singular is often intended to apply to women as well. But the code did not assume women as the primary agents in its laws, and it would not be appropriate to suggest otherwise to the reader.

Verb tenses provide another area of difficulty. The king was the grantor of the code, and speaks in the first person (singular or plural) present indicative. Otherwise the present indicative, the normal usage in modern English-language law, is comparatively rare. Far and away the most common usage is the description of the practice or action under discussion in the future or future perfect tense, followed by the resultant action or the applied sanction in the present subjunctive. While I have retained the subjunctive usage in all but a few instances where it made for an awkward English translation, the present indicative has been substituted for the future and future perfect as it would be in our law codes. This provides for a far more readable and familiar text, and I do not believe that it does violence to the intended meaning of these laws. Participial and gerundive forms have been translated as they are.

THE CODE OF CUENCA

Poem and Prologue

*God Unity and Trinity, protect us according to your pious custom.
Beginning without beginning, end without end.*

*God is the beginning of all things, Founder of the Species; Light True and
Beauteous and Day of Days.*

*The present volume has as its author the honor of the world, Alfonso,
flower of kings, the scent of virtue.*

*This torch of kings, splendor of the world, standard of the law, hammer of
the unruly populace, shield of the patriotic, he crushed the armies of
the Muslims, he subjected their kings, annihilated their kingdoms,
their powers, their dwellings, their gods; he overwhelmed Christian
kings by acts of war, imposing laws on the places beneath his rule.*

*Thus he vanquished the Navarrese, thus the Leonese, thus he subdued the
Aragonese, thus also the Portuguese.*[1]

Here begins the Prologue[2]

Let those study who enjoy it, and the oven of their intellect bakes in medita-
tion the interweaving of speech with the ornaments of words. Let those worry
who know how to beautify their poems with elegant literary embellishments.
I, on the other hand, inclined more toward the useful than the sweet, not
concealing my stupidity, nor including myself among those who went before,
banish the pomposities and the six-syllable words and I don't compare myself
foolishly to the great writers, agreeing with that famous sentence: "It is right
that each should measure himself by his own rule and standard" [Horace,
Epistulae 1.7.98]. Therefore, rejecting the showy circumlocutions of prologues,
I cite the phrase, "I made an effort to be brief" [Horace, *Epistulae* 2.3.25], since
succinct brevity has to be demonstrated, lest the noted statement lack sense.
Therefore, as the thought of Flaccus advises, "He gains everyone's approval
who mixes the pleasant with the useful" [Horace, *Epistulae* 2.3.343].

The memory of men is fragile and insufficient for a multitude of things and for this reason one has proceeded with the sagacity to put the laws of legal statute and civil rights in writing. After meditative selection [these laws] sprouted from royal authority to calm the discord between citizens and inhabitants; thus some could crush villains by the greatest possible cunning, since they are protected by royal guarantee, and cannot subsequently be weakened by fraudulent subterfuge.

For this consideration, then, I, Alfonso, proclaimed king by the grace of God, the most powerful of the Hispanic kings, notice of whose immense greatness and concordant fame resonated far and wide, from the rising of the sun to the bounds of the earth, under whose domain the kings are happy to be subjected, under whose government the laws are pleased to be administered; I, the guide of those who take pride in the Hispanic kingdoms, codified the summation of the judicial institutions in behalf of safeguarding peace and the rights of justice between clergy and laity, between townsmen and peasants, among the needy and the poor; and I codified it, ordered it written with much care so that any question or discussion, as much in the petition as in the judicial action (as much for the cause as for the accusation), which occurs between the citizens and the inhabitants, removing all appeal, except those which later on excluded the laws, and having torn the veil of the sham, could determine under the judgment of the justice, once imputed and discerned, the cause of both parties to the tenor of the written laws and the use of the custom "in which rests the right and the norm of the language" [Horace, *Epistulae* 2.3.71–72], the reason of each part having been expressed and versed, so let the law be defined under the supervision of the knighthood.

Thus, [this is] a king of such renowned authority, that from sea to sea the kings [who are] enemies of the name of Christ fear his name only, since they have experienced his power and have been crushed by him many times; [of such renowned authority that] Christian princes serve him as the first [lord], and from whom Don Conrado, illustrious descendant of the Roman Emperor, and Don Alfonso, king of León, are happy to have received the weapons of combat and his backing, a reminder of his goodness and of having kissed his hand.

After laying siege and after many tasks, tormented by numerous difficulties and distressed by the enemies within, nine months having passed, he made his entry into the city of Cuenca, preferring it to the others, since he chose Cuenca as Alphonsipolis, he preferred it for his residence, and he adopted its citizens as his favorite people, in order to strengthen its prosperity, freedom, and distinction among the others he had liberated from the captivity of Babylon and from the yoke of the Pharaoh with the weapons of his royal power, once he suppressed the filth of its idolatry.

Therefore, so that so great a prerogative of dignity should be known, he conceded high rank to the inhabitants and settlers of Cuenca, as much to those already there as those to come; by this code of freedom, the tenor of which concerns matters of public affairs and its sentences, which are examined in justice with meditating decision and granted by royal agreement, he confirmed it forever with the seal of the royal effigy.

Happy is that marriage certainly when Law and Justice join in uniform alliance, so that when the Law instructs that one should be cleared, he is cleared by the Law, and that which it determines should be condemned, is condemned by Justice, which sufficiently favors definition by both. Thus Law is that which permits the honest and prohibits the opposite; Justice, on the other hand, is the virtue that concedes each one his rights, punishes the culprit, and acquits the innocent.

Disposing these things continually for the honor of Holy Mother Church and for the increase of the Catholic faith, which in the district of Cuenca remained overwhelmed in an extraordinary way, for God Living and True, to whom to serve is to rule and whose yoke is soft and his load light, they serve in freedom, and just as they obey the Commandments of a single God, they also obey the orders of a single king and prince.

Therefore, I Alfonso, king by the grace of God, together with Leonor my wife the queen, and our serene son Fernando, whose birth distinguished the above city with serene and pleased look, grant to all the inhabitants of Cuenca and to their successors this summary of dignity and prerogative of freedom; and so that for posterity it could not be broken, I confirm it with the guarantee of our seal and with our royal protection.

CHAPTER I
Concession of the Code and Outline of Its Privileges

First of all, I give and grant to all inhabitants of the city of Cuenca and to their successors, Cuenca itself with all its district; that is to say, with its mountains, springs, grass, rivers, saltworks, and mines of silver, iron, or any other metal.

1. Those who hunt or cut firewood within the district of Cuenca

If a citizen of the city finds a stranger hunting in the district of Cuenca with hunting birds, dogs, nets, or crossbows; or finds him fishing, cutting wood, making firewood, gathering salt, iron, or other metal, or seizing hawks, then he may capture him without any penalty. The trespasser then remains a prisoner until he is redeemed with money.

2. The stranger who injures a citizen

A stranger who injures or kills a citizen in self-defense should pay the penalty for the offense he has committed, in accordance with the code of Cuenca. But a citizen who injures or kills a stranger in self-defense should pay no penalty.

3. The nobleman who causes violence in the city or its district

If any nobleman or gentleman causes violence within the district of Cuenca and is injured or killed as a result, no penalty is incurred [by the one who injures him]. Therefore, I order that no penalty incurs when anyone hurts or kills someone, in Cuenca or within its district, who enters an inn by force or appropriates anything violently. But if the nobleman or the *miles* injures or kills a citizen, he should pay the penalty of the offense he has committed, according to the code of Cuenca.

4. No strangers may graze their livestock within the district of Cuenca

I command that, if strangers enter the district to graze sheep, mules, or cows on the grass of Cuenca, the council keeps one-fifth of these animals and throws the perpetrators out of the district of Cuenca without their incurring a penalty.

5. Refusing citizenship to settlers within the district

The council reserves the right to deny settlement privileges to anyone it does not approve of, without risk of subsequent fine.

6. No citizens to pay tribute

Anyone owning a house in the city that is occupied by family members is free of all taxes in perpetuity. This exemption does not include the levies for the upkeep of the walls of the city and for fortifications and towers in the lands under the city's control. However, a mounted knight owning a horse worth fifty *menkales* or more is exempt from fortification taxes and he passes that right to his heirs.

7. All settlers get equal penalties

Those counts, *potestates*, *milites*, or *infançones*[1] who come to live in Cuenca, from my kingdom or any other, will abide by the same penalties as the rest of the settlers, concerning death as well as life.

8. Only the king and the bishop may possess palaces

I command that there be in Cuenca no more than two palaces; namely, that of the King and of the Bishop. All other houses, rich and poor, noble and commoner, have the same rights and the same obligations.

9. *Montaticum* and *pedaticus*

The citizen of Cuenca does not pay *montaticum* [woodland usage tax] or *pedaticus* [market tax] anywhere on this side of the Tajo River.

10. Privilege of the settlers

I likewise grant to all settlers this prerogative: whoever may come to live in Cuenca, whatever condition he may be, whether Christian, Moor, or Jew, free or servile, should come in safety. He need not answer to anyone by reason of enmity, debt, bond, inheritance, *mayordomia, merindadico*,[2] or any other thing he may have done before the conquest of Cuenca [1177]. But if he had an enemy before the conquest of Cuenca, and he encounters his enemy while living here, both parties should designate bondsmen, according to the code of Cuenca, so that they remain in peace. He who does not want to designate a bondsman should leave the city and its district.

11. The stranger who commits a homicide in Cuenca

Any man from another village [not within the territory of Cuenca] who commits a homicide in Cuenca, let him be hurled from the city cliffs; and he cannot be reprieved by the Church, nor the Palace, nor a monastery, even though his enemy was killed before or after the conquest of Cuenca.

12. Citizens are buried in Cuenca

Any citizen who dies or is killed in Cuenca may be buried in Cuenca.

13. The stranger who commits a homicide within the district of Cuenca

No penalty is incurred [by those who kill] a stranger who injures or kills someone in the villages or within the district of Cuenca, or who goes with an armed gang, and who is injured or killed there. But if the stranger himself injures or kills someone, he should pay double the penalty of the offense that he has committed and the same for the resultant damage. In addition, if residents are present but refuse to lend aid to their fellow citizen, each one who did not help should pay one hundred *aurei* to the *iudex*, to the *alcaldi*, and to the plaintiff.

14. Advising or assisting a neighbor's enemy

Any citizen who welcomes, advises, or assists the enemy of his fellow citizen at home should pay a fine of one hundred *aurei*.

15. The council does not go on the *host* with anyone but the king

I also concede that the Council of Cuenca does not have to go on the *host* beyond the borders [of their kingdom], and then only with the King, and with no other.

16. There is only one *Señor* under the king in Cuenca

Likewise I grant that, under the king, there is only one *Señor* [royal representative in the city], one *Alcayat* [royal castellan],[3] and one *Merino* [royal regional official].

17. Citizens and Jews may not be *telonearii* nor *merinos*

No *telonearius* or *merino* should be a citizen of Cuenca or a Jew.

18. The *alcayat*'s house held as security

Whoever becomes *alcayat* in Cuenca, before he receives rents from the city, he should pledge his house as security to the council, and the *iudex* should receive it. If the *alcayat* or some of his associates injure or punish anyone, the *iudex* takes sureties on the house until the complainants are satisfied, in accordance with the code of Cuenca. If the *alcayat* refuses to give his house as security, he should not be accepted by the council nor should he receive rents from the town.

19. The *iudex* and sureties for penalties involving the Palace

The *iudex* is responsible for accepting sureties to cover the penalties of crimes committed by citizens against men of the Palace; likewise, he accepts sureties for crimes committed by men of the Palace against citizens. Nevertheless if the *iudex*, because of complaint from the Palace, refuses to accept sureties from a citizen who finds a bondsman, then the citizen is free of the sureties without any penalty.

20. The Palace does not give guarantees for a citizen

The Palace never provides guarantees for a citizen. Of those monetary penalties to which the Palace has a right, the council receives a quarter of each one; the Palace, another quarter; the plaintiff, another quarter; and the *iudex* and the *alcaldi*, the final quarter. The plaintiff receives his corresponding quarter of the monetary penalty first, which the *iudex* can equally withdraw and obtain his share of the legal disposition.

21. Pecuniary penalties the Palace can claim

The Palace should not receive a quarter except in the case of the penalties for homicide, breaking into a dwelling, and violation of a woman. When, for example, the penalty for homicide is imposed, the Palace receives its portion if the owner of the house is killed, wounded, or injured by illegal weapons. Except for these [aforementioned] insults, infractions, or challenges, the Palace should not receive anything.

On the other hand, the monetary penalties for other infractions belong to that individual whose bread a person eats or in whose property he dwells, and to no other, except the individual's son and his tenant. Then, in effect, whoever who has rented a house is owner of his place, *señor* of his things, and father of his children.

All penalties for theft belong to the Palace; thus, if someone is convicted of theft, he has to pay the Palace the ninth portion [of the value of the object stolen]. The plaintiff receives double the value of the item stolen. The Palace also receives a portion of the penalties imposed by the following offenses: forcing or violating a *señora*, assaulting a *señor* with illegal weapons, breaking into a dwelling, blows or injuries to a *señor*, causing disturbance in the market and in the council, and use of illegal weapons, if they are wielded in the market, in the council, or in the remainder of the city, with intention of injuring someone. The Palace also receives a portion of the penalties imposed for injuring a *señor* with weapons, as a part of a faction, in challenging the *iudex*, the *alcaldi*, or the *notarius*, if they are wrongly challenged or insulted, when present in the tribunal or outside it, due to the case they are judging before the door of the *iudex* or in another place. The Palace also receives a portion of the penalties imposed for the unjust imprisonment of a *señor* and for assault on a *señor*, as much in the open air as in another place.

All these penalties should be divided into four portions, except that of theft, which belongs wholly to the Palace. The plaintiff should receive the first quarter portion and same portion of the juridical arrangements; the council, the second quarter; the *iudex* and the *alcaldi*, the third quarter; and the Palace, the fourth. The *iudex* and the *alcaldi* should receive the council's portion, and the same from all the councils, except the executive council, since the council should form these. The *alcaldi* should do all the others, as aforesaid. But if in those councils any damage ensues to the council because of their fault, the *alcaldi* should restore double all the losses.

22. Citizens not to be detained by the *Señor* of the city or the *alcayat*

No one, not even the *Señor*, may detain a citizen in prison because of a penalty over which the Palace has jurisdiction; only the *iudex* has that right. Not even the *Señor* may detain a citizen, although this is waived in the instance of a penalty or debt over which he has some right. However, the *iudex* should hold the citizen under house arrest until the person pays the required sum.

23. Purchasing a Moor for exchange with a captive Christian

Whoever purchases a Moor in Cuenca to be given in exchange for a captive Christian should pay the owner of the Moor the price the Moor cost him, plus ten *aurei* as profit, and the owner should surrender him; after the Moor is attested, regardless whether he is sold or undersold, after receiving the agreed-upon price, the owner of the Moor should release the Christian from captivity.

24. Those who come to this city with goods

Of those who come to Cuenca with goods, whether Christian, Jew, or Moor, none can give sureties unless they be debtors and bondsmen. Anyone else who takes his sureties should pay one hundred *aurei* to the council and double the value of the sureties to the plaintiff who complains.

25. Granting of fairs

For the benefit and honor of the city, I also grant fairs that are to begin eight days before the celebration of Pentecost and last until eight days after this feast. Whoever comes to these fairs, whether Christian, Moor, or Jew, should come safely. Whoever impedes them or causes any damage should pay for the king's portion a fine of one thousand *aurei*, and to the plaintiff double the value of the damage done. If he is unable to pay the charges, let him be hanged. Whoever kills a man will be buried alive beneath the dead person. If he injures someone, he will have his hand cut off.

In summary, during the fairs, whoever injures a man, let him have his hand cut off; whoever kills another, let him be buried alive beneath the dead person; he who robs should pay one thousand *aurei* in fine to the king, and double the damage that he had done to the plaintiff. He who cannot pay let him be hurled from the city cliffs, and likewise he who steals anything let him be hurled from the city cliffs.

CHAPTER II
Statutes Regarding Property Holdings

1. Properties and their disposition

I also grant that whoever possesses real estate holds it fixed and sound, and it will always be his to do with as he pleases. Consequently, he can give, sell, change, lend, or pledge it, or leave it in his will, whether he be healthy or sick, regardless of residing in Cuenca or elsewhere.

2. No sale of real estate to monks

No one is permitted to give or to sell real estate to monks or to those who have renounced the world. Since their order forbids them to give or sell real estate to us, so the code and custom forbid us to do the same for them.

3. Work done on real estate

All work that anyone does on his real estate is approved and sound, so that no one should oppose or should prohibit him from doing the work or construction that he wants, be it a bath, an oven, housing, a mill, an orchard, a vineyard, or any similar thing. If someone challenges the owner's right to the property but is defeated in the case, he should pay ten *aurei* to the landowner of the property and to the *iudex* and to the *alcaldi*;[1] also, he should pay the expenses double, according to a declaration under oath by the defendant and by another citizen.

4. The plaintiff in a real estate dispute provides a bondsman in advance

Whoever sues someone else for a property should first of all provide the defendant with a bondsman. The latter should pay the fine of ten *aurei* that has been cited, and double the court costs, in case the plaintiff loses the case.

5. Those who occupy another's property

Whoever occupies another's property and loses the case for it should pay ten *aurei* and deliver the property over to the plaintiff with all its fruit and completed work. The plaintiff should receive one half of this fine and the *alcaldi* the other half.

6. Two litigants who argue the same case

If two litigants claim a property and each one says that he ought to possess it by award of the land-dividing commission, the one who worked it

first should defend it and affirm with two members of the commission or with
two citizens that he obtained it through assignment of the commission and
that it therefore belongs to him.

7. Those who encroach on another's work

For this reason we commanded that he who has worked first on a property occupies it and proves his right to that property, since whoever encroaches on another's work has to pay ten *aurei*. If a person defends his right
to the property but cannot prove it, he should abandon the property, paying
the cited fine of the ten *aurei*. But if he can prove his claim he retains his
property.

8. The witnesses to a property dispute

In a property dispute [in which the property] is worth up to twenty
menkales, if the witnesses confirm ownership, they should be believed; if the
property is worth twenty *menkales* or more, the witnesses can be challenged, if
it pleases the plaintiff. If the witnesses are wrong, they should pay double the
value of the property. If the witnesses do not want to respond to the judicial
challenge or they are not approved, according to the inquiry, those who
defend their right to the property should then lose it, together with the fine of
ten *aurei*.

9. Those who introduce the same motive

If both claimants say that they obtained the property through a distribution share of common land and that, also, they worked the plot first, the
current possessor of the property should occupy it and prove his right to it.

10. Those who introduce similar motives

If each party says that he is the one who owns it, the current occupier
takes the position of defendant and proves his right.

11. The property of patrimony

Whoever has real estate by right of patrimony or kind of inheritance does
not have to respond to claims, as long as he can prove that the one from whom
he inherited the holding obtained it in peace and that no one demanded it
from him. If, however, the deceased had been sued because of a prior claim on
the holding, and did not fulfill the law of the code by responding, the heir has
to respond, according to the code of the city. If he defends it judicially and ultimately loses the case, he has to abandon the real estate and pay the cited fine.

12. Those who invade another's work

Whoever encroaches on another's land or begins to work it to give himself a claim for a legal challenge loses the right to the property and should pay the ten-*aurei* fine. This is established so that those who work it do not kill each other over it, in case neither of them wants to yield in favor of the other.

13. The plaintiff summons his adversary, as stated in the code

If someone sees another working on a property that he considers to be his, he should not enter the property but rather should take sureties daily for it until he goes with his rival into the presence of the regular or the substitute *alcaldi*. These *alcaldi* charge the parties to survey the property. They also decree that in three days both individuals should come to a hearing before the church door and there choose two citizens as surveyors. The one who does not present himself by the end of the allowed term should pay his adversary five *solidi*.

14. How a property should be surveyed

When a property is surveyed, the plaintiff should survey it, marking its perimeter foot by foot; if those who work the land leave at that time, the plaintiff enters onto the property with no penalty. We say "at that time" because, if the defendant leaves it later, it should not be allowed, but rather the plaintiff should be sent away from the property and pay a ten-*aurei* fine.

15. Those who occupy a property in presence of surveyors

If the man who works the property occupies it in the presence of the surveyors, the plaintiff should summon him before the tribunal of the *alcaldi* on the following Friday, and there each one should obtain his right.

16. The claimant of real estate who does not come before the tribunal within the term

If one of the litigants does not come before the tribunal within the established term, he should lose the case. If it is the defender who does not present himself or, although present, is defeated in the judgment, he should leave the property and pay the ten-*aurei* fine.

17. Rural villagers who litigate for a property

If the litigants are rural villagers, the plaintiff should summon his adversary before the door of the *iudex* within three days, and the *iudex* should charge the litigants to survey the property, fixing them a term, as has been said above.

18. The kind of work that grants the right to occupy real estate

The present holder who works the land with a plow or a hoe that works the earth from furrow to furrow has the right to defend a property; no other kind of expropriation is legal at all.

19. Those who see someone working on their property but do not present a demand before nine days

If someone finds a farmer working on his property but does not prosecute this until the farmer completes his work, and the latter can prove it, then the farmer should not be sued for the completed work. If a farmer plants someone else's field, his claim to the property may be defeated at law and he may have to return it together with the ten-*aurei* fine, as has been said repeatedly. However, in this case, I command that the owner of the real estate should not have a right to any of the farmer's crop. But if he plants a vineyard, builds a house, or completes another similar work, and he subsequently is defeated at law in his claim to the property, he should abandon these additions to the owner together with the above fine. Nevertheless, after the owner receives the fine, the farmer should be reimbursed for the completed work, according to appraisal of two *alcaldi* or two citizens. If the farmer prefers it, however, the plaintiff should be required to perform an equal amount of work in a similar place.

If the farmer cannot prove that he finished his work before a claim against him was made, then the plaintiff should swear with a citizen, and the case should be prosecuted within nine days, counting from the day on which he saw the work. Then the farmer of the real estate should respond to the challenge, as has been said. But if the farmer is unable or unwilling to get the matter judged, he should lose his work, as has been said.

20. Those who have real estate

Whoever holds a property in tenth, fiftieth, or similar lot distribution, and he denies it, or if he holds it and prosecutes another for it, should pay double its value along with the ninth [of the crop], if the sworn *alcaldi* can prove it.

21. Incorrect appraisal of real estate

If someone appraises a property for less than twenty *menkales* that he requires to avoid going before the king or for fear of the judicial challenge, the *alcaldi* should appraise it, if it is located in the city. But if he is in a rural village, two citizens should appraise it; if it is worth more than twenty *menkales*, they should go to the king or retain it, if necessary.

22. Real estate lacking access

The sworn *alcaldi* should visit all property that does not have an entrance or an exit to establish if it is a field of work, such as a vineyard. If so, they should make an access in the location that causes the least amount of harm, and this access should stand.

23 Those who impede a road

Whoever impedes, changes, or closes a road that the *alcaldi* have pointed out should pay ten *aurei*, since such access and exit that the *alcaldi* designate or grant should be permanent and unalterable.

24. Where new settlers should build

The settlers who come to Cuenca or to its villages should build where the council of the locale permits them. If by chance the council of a village does not want to designate this, the *iudex* of the city and the *alcaldi* should give them a plot to build on near the rest of the houses and in the most convenient zone. However, if someone sells his house later and wants to construct another, he should be forbidden unless he builds on the plot bought with his money.

25. Freshly plowed ground

Ground that is freshly plowed outside the limits of public land or the boundaries of real estate is held securely under the law.

26. Frightening or driving away draft animals

Whoever drives away from a field or a plot the mules or oxen that are working or threshing, or impedes them in pursuing their work, should pay double the value [presumably of the work not done]. He should pay as much for the mules as for the oxen, whenever the plaintiff can prove the charge. Otherwise, the accused swears with two citizens and he should be believed.

27. Those who kill yoked mules or oxen

Furthermore, anyone who kills yoked oxen or mules should pay fifty *aurei* and double the damage that has occurred.

28. Penalty for impeding workers

Whoever drives workers from a property or prevents them from working should pay thirty *aurei* for each worker, if it can be proved. Otherwise, he should swear a judicial oath with two of four designated residents of his parish and he should be believed.

29. How the buyer on the property should be introduced

Whoever sells a property in its entirety, be it in the city or in a village, should introduce the buyer to some representative portion of the property, in behalf of all of it. The buyer should then take possession and this is ratified if it has taken place in the presence of suitable witnesses. Thus, if someone sells only one farm and retains any other, he should introduce the buyer only to the property under negotiation, surveying his own perimeter before a witness; and the new owner should take legal possession.

30. Boundary litigation by the councils of the villages

If the councils of the villages contest their boundaries, the *iudex* and the *alcaldi* should examine and survey each of the boundaries, according to the previously positioned boundary markers. If the council agrees that it has placed its boundaries within the limits of another, it should pay ten *aurei* and leave the occupied boundary together with the produce and the assets. The ten-*aurei* fine should be allotted to the *iudex*, the *alcaldi*, and the council that has been encroached upon, as it is stated in the code.

31. Ovens and bakers

The baker should heat the oven, place the bread in it, and, when it is cooked, remove it. The ovens should cook up to thirty-two loaves of bread. The baker has right to one-fourth of the rent of the oven. If the baker, male or female, does not arise every morning to heat the oven, he or she should pay double the damage that ensues for this reason, according to the judgment of the owner of the oven. And if he heats the oven badly and for this reason damage ensues, the baker should pay double the fine. The baker who changes a woman's turn at the oven also should pay five *solidi*, one half to the plaintiff and the other half to the *almutazaf*, and in addition double the value of the damage caused.

32. Concerning the bathhouse, and the testimony of women

Men may use the common bathhouses on Tuesdays, Thursdays, and Saturdays. Women may enter on Mondays and Wednesdays. Jews should enter on Fridays and Sundays. No one, neither woman nor man, should pay more than an *obolus* entry fee. Servants and children of citizens should enter free of charge. If a man enters any part of the bathhouse premises on the women's day for bathing, he is liable for a fine of ten *aurei*. He should pay the same fine for spying on women in the bath on those days. However, if a woman enters a bathhouse on a day reserved for men, or is found there at night, and because of this the woman is publicly dishonored or harmed in some way, she should have no right to bring charges of a kind sufficient to exile the offending man. On the other hand, if a man commits these acts against a woman on the women's bathing days, or steals her clothing, let him be hurled from the city cliffs. Officials can gather testimony from women at the bathhouse, at the bakehouse, at the fountain and river, and also at the spinners' and weavers' workplaces. Female witnesses should be wives or daughters of citizens of the city.

If a Christian should intrude in a bathhouse on the Jewish bathing days, or if a Jew should intrude on the Christian bathing days, resulting in either person attacking or killing the other, no formal accusations should be accepted from either of the persons or their relatives.[2]

The bathhouse manager should provide bathers with all bathing necessities, such as water and the like. Failing to provide these necessities will make the manager liable to a fine of ten *solidi*, five to be paid to the *almutazaf*, and five to the complainant. Anyone stealing bathhouse equipment should have his ears cut off; if bathers' belongings are worth up to ten *menkales* or more, then let the thief be hurled from the city cliffs.

CHAPTER III
How Grain Fields Should Be Guarded

1. How grain fields should be guarded

If the owner finds his grain fields damaged, the harvest watchman should restore all damage if the offender does not come forward. If the harvest watchman finds a horse or mule, an ox, a donkey, or a pig during the day, the owner of the land should receive for each animal an *almud* of the class of seed that is sowed on the land; for every twelve goats or sheep, he should receive an *almud*; for each goose, he should receive also an *almud*. However, if the damage is caused at night, and the owner can prove it, he should receive a *fanega*; otherwise, the suspect takes an oath with any other citizen and he should be believed.

2. The month from which grain fields should be evaluated

From the first of May until the grain fields are harvested, the owner should receive [for any damage to his field] the one he prefers, the fine for an offense or the valuation of the damage.

3. Refusal to value grain fields

If the owner of the livestock does not want to appraise the grain fields in the company of their owner, he should pay their value as declared under oath by the proprietor, if the latter subsequently proves it with a witness.

4. The owner of grain fields

The owner of grain fields has to take an oath concerning the damage suffered and accept the payment for the same. Hence, the owner of the grain fields deserves this payment, and if the perpetrator does not know where to take it, or does not have clear responsibility, then it is the harvest watchman who has to pay the damage.

5. Duties of the harvest watchman

The harvest watchman has to swear to have sureties in hand for the resultant damage, and the owner of the grain fields has to collect the payment of the same. But if the owner cannot confirm it, the suspect should take an oath with another citizen for the damage caused by day, and with two citizens for that caused at night.

6. Those who flee with sureties

If the herdsman or anyone else flees with sureties but remains within reach of the harvest watchman or the owner of the grain fields, then they may recover the sureties without incurring a penalty. But if they are unable to find him, the owner of the fields should take the sureties, set at double the value of the damage, at the livestock owner's home, in the presence of any other citizen.

7. The owner of livestock who defends sureties

If the owner of livestock demands sureties simply because of the mere act of doing it, he should pay the resultant damage and, also, five *solidi* to the *iudex* and to the plaintiff.[1]

8. The herdsman who defends sureties

If the herdsman who guards the livestock defends the sureties against the harvest guard or against the owner of the fields, he should pay five *solidi* and take sureties in the house of the owner of the livestock for the resultant damage, as has been said.

9. Those who believe that sureties are taken wrongly

If the owner of livestock believes that sureties have been taken unjustly, he should affirm it holding the sureties in hand. The harvest watchman, for his part, should swear, having the sureties in hand, that he has taken the sureties justly for the damage which the stock owner's livestock did.

10. Taking stray livestock to the owner's corral for which the herdsman defends sureties

When the owner of the grain fields, or the harvest watchman, finds an animal in the grain fields, and the herdsman or the owner of the livestock refuses to offer the sureties, the owner of the fields should lead the livestock to his corral without any penalty. And if someone seizes the animal, he should pay double its value.[2]

11. Refusing to give livestock as sureties

If the herdsman, or the owner of the livestock wants to give the best sureties that he possesses during transhumant migration, and the harvest watchman or the owner of the grain fields does not want to accept them and encloses the livestock, the encloser should pay double.

12. Stripping someone while taking clothing as sureties

Although the laws above have settled that the harvest watchman, or the owner of the grain fields should take sureties from those who cause any damage, nonetheless, it remains prohibited that either the harvest watchman or any other should leave someone naked. Those who do this should pay five *aurei* and return double the value of the clothing removed. Therefore, if those who have caused any damage are wearing only enough clothing to cover themselves, one should not disrobe them, but rather take sureties at their home, as said before.

13. Livestock without a herdsman

Whoever finds any livestock without a herdsman in his grain fields should lead such animals to his corral and give public notice immediately. The owner should pay for the resultant damage when he reclaims the animals. But if, once proclaimed, no one reclaims the livestock, they should remain enclosed for three days and then released to graze in the field until their owner appears, at which time he should pay the resultant damage and recover his livestock.

14. Failing to give public notice of captured livestock

But if the owner does not give public notice of livestock he has found, and he keeps the animals in his corral for a night, then he should return double their value. But if, even if proclaimed, any of the livestock starve to death or die of thirst or under any other circumstances, the owner should present the hides of the cattle to its owner and swear that it did not die through his fault. He should accept the amount of the damage caused by the animals and deliver the hides to their owner.

15. Carrying off livestock from uncultivated land

If someone says that the harvest watchman or the owner of the grain fields carried off livestock from uncultivated land and not from the grain fields, the harvest watchman should swear that he did this because of the damage that it caused and he should be believed. The owner should take a similar oath under such conditions and he also should be believed.

16. Those who hurt or kill the harvest watchman with illegal weapons

Whoever injures the harvest watchman with illegal weapons, in addition to the sureties, should pay double the penalty for what he has committed, if the watchman can prove it; otherwise, the alleged perpetrator should swear as the code establishes. Those who injure the watchman without such weapons should pay double the penalty for what they have done; otherwise, they are cleared as the code establishes.

17. Those who make a path through another's field

Whoever makes a path through another's field should pay ten *solidi*. Those who hunt with a hawk near another's field should pay ten *aurei*.

18. Those who steal grain stalks in another's grain field

Whoever uses his fingernail to steal a handful of stalks from another's grain field should pay no penalty if he only does it once; then, if he is found twice in the same grain field, he should pay five *solidi*.

19. Those who reap grain stalks with a sickle in another's grain field

Those who steal grain stalks with sickle, long knife, or another tool, rather than with their bare hands, should pay one *aureus*.

20. Those who reap or uproot another's field

Whoever reaps or uproots another's field, against the will of its owner or without his knowledge, if it is by day, should pay the *iudex*, the *alcaldi*, and the plaintiff sixty *menkales* and double the resultant damage. If this is done at night, he should pay these fines double and also restore double the damage. If the accused denies his guilt for the damage done in daytime and cannot prove it, he should swear a judicial oath with two citizens and he should be believed;

for the damage caused at night, follow the procedure as in the case of theft, if he denies his guilt and cannot prove it with witnesses.

21. Those who set another's grain field on fire

If someone deliberately sets another's grain on fire in the field or in the small plot, he should pay three hundred *solidi* if it is proved; otherwise, he should be cleared as in the case of theft.

22. Those who confess to a fire in a grain field

Those who admit they caused the blaze and affirm that it happened by chance and not on purpose, should swear to this with twelve citizens and they should be believed. If they cannot complete this requirement, they should pay three hundred *solidi*, as said before.

23. Sureties not redeemed before the feast of Saint Michael

No one should be required to take responsibility for damaged grain fields after the feast of Saint Michael [September 29]. If sureties have not been withdrawn by that date, neither the harvest watchman nor the owner of the grain fields responds for them.

24. Those who set their own or another's stubble on fire

Whoever sets his stubble on fire should pay whatever damage that occasions, according to declaration of those harmed under oath. Whoever sets another's stubble on fire or cuts another's straw should pay for it, according to declaration under oath of its owner, and also the damage that ensues as a consequence of the blaze.

25. Livestock that causes damage in a plot

If another's livestock causes damage in a plot, the owner of the livestock should pay for it or take an oath, according to what has been said regarding the grain fields. However, until the herdsman of the livestock appears, each one should guard his plot and should not evaluate the amount of the damage that occurred there. After the arraignment of the herdsman, the owner should get the amount of the damage, as has been said. However, for the hen that goes to the plot, no one should demand any payment.

26. Duties of the guard of grain fields

Whoever is a guard of grain fields should swear faithfully that he will guard them faithfully from the first of March until the middle of July.

27. Paying the guard of grain fields

The guard of grain fields should receive an *almud* as pay for his work, of which measure half is in one kind of grain and half in another, for all those fields that yield a *kaficius* or more. From all the fields that yield less than a *kaficius*, he should receive half an *almud*.[3]

28. Those who sue for an established holding at harvest time

If two sue for a sowed property at harvest time, in order that the harvest will not be lost for the duration of the judgment, the *alcaldi* should require them to designate two responsible intermediaries for each side. These men should gather the harvest and guard it for the one who reclaims the established holding.

29. The occupation of plowman

The plowman should reap and thresh and consult about the work with his landlord. If they hire a journeyman in common, the plowman should contribute part of the expenses in proportion to that which he receives for the product of his work. When they hire a journeyman in common, the owner should allot two men and an animal; one of these men should reap in the company of the plowman and the other should carry the grain with the animal, which eats from the common land. Also the owner should allot for a woman who will sweep the land together with the wife of the plowman. Once the grain is gathered, the plowman should roof a building in order to stock the necessary straw for the oxen along with those he himself works. He also should provide enough food for four trips to the stable for the oxen. In all these things the plowman should provide everything necessary, except the wood, which the owner should supply. All this being fulfilled, he can leave his *señor*, if he desires it.

When the plowman does not plow, he should gather, break clods, or do any other tasks particular to agriculture, in agreement with the orders of his *señor*. The owner should also provide the plow and the yoke with all its apparatus and feed for the oxen. The plowman, for his part, should take care of the oxen with all the farming implements, by day and night, until he leaves his *señor*. Also, the plowman should give his *señor* one share of everything he obtains or secures during the military expedition, or in another place, as well as the fruit which he has sowed.

30. Maintenance of the plowman

The *señor* should give his plowman for his maintenance four *kaficia*, half and half; an *almud* of salt, a string of garlic, a string of onions, two *solidi* for sandals, another two for cheese, and a share of all fruit of the field, according to the pact that has been made with his *señor*. The unripe barley and the mixed fodder are excluded, since of these things the plowman does not have to receive anything.

CHAPTER IV
Care of the Vineyards

1. Care of the vineyards and fidelity of the guard

The guard of the vineyards has to swear faithfulness from the day on which he is placed in charge of the vineyards until all grapes are gathered. If someone shows him his vineyard in the presence of two citizens and then discovers that it has been damaged at the time of vintage or before, he has to hold the guard responsible for repairing all damage that has occurred by day; for damage happening at night, the guard does not have to respond. But if the damage happens at night and the guard does not inform the owner of the vineyard about it until three days later, the guard should pay for it. Similarly, he should pay for damage caused during the day if he does not give sureties or show the damage to the owner. If the owner of the vineyard says that the damage did not occur at night, but rather by day, and damage of one *aureus* has occurred, the guard should swear and should be believed. For values higher than one *aureus*, the guard should swear with any citizen and should be believed; and if he is unwilling or unable to swear it, he should pay the damage.

2. The guard should swear to having sureties in hand

For all the damage the guard might be judged responsible, swearing that he has sureties in hand, he should be believed, up to the amount of five *aurei*. For five *aurei* or more, he should affirm it with any citizen in order to get his payment.

3. Those who defend sureties by the guard of the vineyards

Whoever secures sureties by the guard of the vineyards outside the town should pay an *aureus* and take them at the home of the one whom he defends. But if the guard has no house, he should provide a bondsman; later the guard should be summoned before the door of the *iudex* and there obtain his right, in accordance with the code.

4. Those who injure or kill the guard of the vineyards

Those who injure or kill the guard of the vineyards, because the vineyards are involved, either by day or at night, should pay double the penalty of the offense they have committed, if it can be proved. Otherwise, clear the suspect or the accused according to the code. If by chance the guard injures or kills someone in another's vineyard, he should not have to pay any penalty nor depart from the city as our enemy.

5. The owner of the vineyard has to prove damage done by livestock

If the owner of the vineyard is able to prove damage caused by livestock, he should receive his compensation; if he cannot prove it, the suspect should swear with a citizen for the damage caused by day; for damage caused at night, he should swear with two citizens.

6. How the owner of livestock should compensate for the damage they cause

If an ox or another animal causes damage in a vineyard by day, his owner should pay five *solidi* for every three vines; for twelve sheep or six goats, the same. But if it be a lesser number of sheep or goats, he should pay according to the number of damaged vines. If it should be a dog or a pig that causes the damage in a vineyard, its owner should pay five *solidi* for each damaged vine. However, his owner should not pay any fine for the dog that is controlled by a hooked staff; if this staff measures two elbows long and an elbow of bend, then instead of a fine, he has to whip the dog, but not kill it. If the animal is not controlled by a hooked staff, the dog's owner should kill it in the vineyard. But if he cannot hold onto it, the owner of the dog should pay the fine, as has been said. If an ox or other animal enters a vineyard, even though it does not cause any damage, for the mere act of having trampled the vineyard upon entering and upon leaving, the owner of the animal should pay five *solidi*.

7. The owner of the vineyard chooses between the fine or the appraisal

For all damage that had been caused in a vineyard, its owner should choose between the fine or the damage appraisal, whichever pleases him more.

8. Those who enter into a vineyard without permission of its owner

If someone enters into a vineyard without permission of its owner or of the guard from the first of January until the vineyards are harvested, he should pay five *solidi*, even though he seizes nothing in there. If he seizes grapes or any another fruit by day, he should pay ten *aurei*; if at night, he should pay twenty *aurei*, if it is proved. But if not proved, he can be cleared by the oaths of six citizens for the damage caused by day. For damage caused at night, the procedure is the same as in the case of theft.

9. Those who cut off another's vine

If someone cuts off a vine in another's vineyard, he should pay five *aurei*; for a vine branch, one *aureus*; for any other vine shoot, five *solidi*.

10. Those who cut off another's entire grapevine plant

If someone cuts off another's entire grapevine plant, he should pay ten *aurei*; for a vine branch, five *aurei*; for any other vine shoot, five *solidi*. Those who remove a sprout from a vine also should pay five *solidi*.

11. Those who sell unripe grapes

Whoever sells unripe grapes before the vineyards are harvested should pay an *aureus*, whether he be a Jew or a Christian. The plaintiff and the *almutazaf* should receive this fine, as it is in the code.

12. Those who seize roses in a vineyard

Whoever seizes another's roses, iris, wickers, thistles, or canes in a vineyard should pay an *aureus* for each one of these things, if it can be proved. But if not, he should be cleared as in the case of theft.

13. Those who seize another's sumac

Those who seize another's sumac should pay ten *aurei*, if it can be proved; but if not, clear them as in the case of theft.

14. Demarcation of the vineyards, done once per vintage

All the vineyards should be enclosed, as has been said above, from the first of January until the vintage. From then until the first of the following January, if an ox, a horse, a donkey, or a pig enters into the vineyards, its owner should pay an *almud* of wheat.

15. No one has to respond to sureties after the feast of Saint Martin

Likewise, starting from the feast of Saint Martin [November 11], no one should respond for the damage to the vineyards which had been caused earlier, even if he possesses sureties for such damage.

16. The vineyard that does not have an exit

If any vineyard does not have an exit, it should have a passage for a furrow from those other vineyards which are nearest to the road, for which no penalty is imposed [by the owners of those vineyards].

17. Salary of the guard of the vineyards

The salary of the guard of the vineyards should be four *denarii*, paid by everyone who possesses a vineyard in the area of his custody. And those who possess many vines should pay the same as those who have few.

CHAPTER V
Demarcation of Orchards

1. Demarcation of orchards and their custody

If the livestock of someone enters into another's orchard, its owner should pay the damage that has been done and a fine of one *aureus* if this happens by day. But if it is at night, he should pay two *aurei* and double the value of the damage that has been done if he is declared guilty. Otherwise, the owner of the livestock should swear alone for the damage caused by day and should swear with a citizen for the damage caused at night, and he should be believed. If someone causes damage in another's orchard by day, he should pay one *aureus* and the value of the damage that has been done; but if he causes it at night, he should pay two *aurei* and double the value of the damage he has caused, if he is declared guilty. Otherwise, for damage done during the day, he should be cleared with the help of one citizen, and with the help of two for damage done at night.

2. Those who retain water in order to irrigate

If anyone irrigates an orchard, linen, hemp, or other crop whatsoever, and after its use does not return water to the canal or the river, and it causes any damage, he should pay double the value of the damage and in addition a ten-*aurei* fine if he is declared guilty. If he is not found guilty, he should swear with two citizens and he should be believed.

3. Those who seize water in the time of another

Whoever seizes water in the time of another, cuts him off from it, exercises any violence in the process, or retains water wrongly should pay two *aurei* if he is declared guilty. If he is not found guilty, he should swear with two citizens and he should be believed. Those who for that reason wound or strike someone, should pay the fine of the city.

4. Those who injure or kill a gardener at night

Whoever injures or kills a gardener in his own orchard at night should pay double the penalty of the offense that he has committed. But if it is the gardener who injures or kills someone in his orchard at night, he should not pay any penalty or leave the city as our enemy.

5. Pay of the gardener

The gardener should be given two *kaficia* as payment, half of one grain and half of another. Also, the owner of the orchard should contribute the seeds, an animal to ride, and the fodder for the animal. The gardener should cultivate the orchard and should get as much of its fruits as he had agreed with its owner.

6. Water that flows in any real estate

If water flows in an orchard, vineyard, or other real estate, it should flow through the adjacent properties, and through the most convenient locations, until it drains into a stream or into a place where it should harm no one.

7. Those who do not want to receive water

If any of the adjacent holders do not want to receive water, they should pay ten *aurei* and double the value of the damage.[1]

8. Enclosure of a property that borders with another

Whoever possesses an orchard, a vineyard or a grain field that borders on any pasture or public land and does not enclose it with fence, wall, or barrier does not receive any payment or fine [in the event of damage to his land] for that. Those who place a fence, barrier, or wall should make it sufficiently high so that no livestock can pass over it to the cultivated area.

9. Those who do not want to fence their borders

If someone does not fence his borders, as has been said above, whether the area is cultivated or not, he should pay one *aureus* and double the value of the damage, if for that reason damage ensues to others. The owner of the livestock, on the other hand, should not pay anything.

10. Those who destroy another's fence

Whoever breaks another's enclosure should pay five *aurei* and double the damage that ensues from this, if it can be proved; but if not, he should swear with two citizens and he should be believed.

11. The tree that is planted on another's property

If a tree is planted on another's property, the owner of the real estate has the right to a fourth portion of its fruit. If a tree spreads its branches over the property of another, the owner of the property has the right to a fourth portion of the fruit which drops on his property. But the owner of the property should keep the tree free from damage.

12. Those who cut down another's tree

If someone cuts down another's fruit tree, he should pay thirty [*aurei*] if he is declared guilty; if he cuts off a branch, ten [*aurei*] if he is declared guilty; but if not, he should be cleared as in the case of theft.

13. Those who strip bark from another's walnut tree

Whoever strips bark from another's walnut tree or other tree should pay ten [*aurei*] if it can be proved; but if not, he should swear with one citizen and he should be believed.

14. Those who cut off a branch of a fruit tree

If someone cuts off a branch of a fruit tree, he should pay five *solidi* if it can be proved; but if not, he should swear alone and he should be believed.

15. Those who seize fruit from a tree by day or at night

If someone seizes fruit of a tree by day, outside the vineyard, he should pay ten *aurei* if it can be proved. But if not, he should swear with six citizens and he should be believed. He should pay more for the damage caused at night, namely twenty *aurei* if it can be proved; but if not, he should swear with twelve citizens and should be believed.

16. Those who seize leaves from another's mulberry tree

Whoever seizes some leaves of another's mulberry tree by day, should pay one *aureus* if it can be proved; but if not, he should swear alone and he should be believed. He should pay more for the damage caused at night, namely two *aurei* if it can be proved; but if not, he should swear with two citizens and he should be believed.

17. Those who cut down a non-fruit tree

If someone cuts down a tree that does not give fruit, he should pay five *aurei* if it can be proved; but if not, he should swear with one citizen and should be believed.

18. Those who cut down an oak or an evergreen oak

Whoever cuts an oak or an evergreen oak for the acorns should pay the same fine as that for a fruit tree.

CHAPTER VI
Aggression with Illegal Weapons

1. The penalty for those who confine another with illegal weapons and other additional offenses

I command that anyone who confines another with illegal weapons should pay three hundred *solidi*, and for each individual confined, he should pay another three hundred *solidi*.

2. Those who break into another person's house

Whoever breaks into another person's house should pay five hundred *solidi*, and for each person there is in the house, he should pay another five hundred *solidi* and also double the damage caused. If he injures or kills one, he should pay double the penalty of the offense he has committed, along with the other fines. The collaborators of the housebreaking should pay these fines and pecuniary penalties, as many as there are, if it can be proved with witnesses; but if not, each [accused] one can be cleared by twelve citizens and he should be believed. But if one of those cannot fulfill this requirement, he should pay as has been said.

3. What constitutes breaking into a dwelling

It should be known that one breaks into a dwelling only [when] he enters there with intention of injuring, and he in fact injures; or he enters angrily with illegal weapons, even if he does not come to injure anyone; or he enters or remains within against the prohibition of the house's owner.

4. Those who set a house on fire

Whoever sets another's house on fire should pay five hundred *solidi* if it can be proved; otherwise, he should swear with twelve citizens or he should respond to the challenge [by combat]. If he burns a person within the house, he should pay four hundred *aurei* and he should depart as our enemy if it can be proved; otherwise he should clear himself with as many [groups of] twelve citizens as persons who have been burned in the house and he should be believed; or he should swear by himself only and respond to the challenge [by combat]; this should remain at the election of the plaintiff.

5. Those who set a forest on fire

This same we say on the subject of one who sets a forest on fire.

6. Those who enter into the house of another person in spite of the prohibition of its owner

Whoever, against the prohibition of the owner, enters that person's house should pay the penalty as for housebreaking. If the owner of the house injures, kills, or throws out violently the one who persisted in entering, he [the owner] should not pay any penalty for this nor depart as an enemy. In the same way, whoever is at the home of other people and does not want to leave in spite of its owner's order should pay as a housebreaker of a dwelling. And if the owner of the house throws him out violently or injures or kills him, he should not pay any penalty for this nor depart as an enemy. But if he who persists in staying injures or kills the owner of the house or some of his [household], he should pay double the penalty of the crime that he has committed [i.e., the injury or the homicide].

7. The wrongdoer or debtor who, being in a house, does not want to give a bondsman

If one has committed a crime or is a debtor and, being in any house, refuses to provide a bondsman, relying on the code of inviolability of houses, the owner of the house should throw that one out, or he should give the plaintiff authorization to seize him without penalty. If he [the householder] does not do that, he should respond on behalf of the debtor or wrongdoer; and if he is defeated, he should pay as if he were the guilty party.

8. Those who steal lumber or other things from another person's house

Whoever steals lumber, stones, tiles, bricks, cement, or covering from any house should pay for them as a thief or should be cleared as in the case of theft, or else one can prove his guilt with witnesses.

9. Those who fear the collapse of something

Whoever fears the collapse of a wall, of a house, of a beam, or of the fire of a nearby house should warn the owner of the wall, house, or beam, accompanied by the *iudex* and the *alcaldi* or before the council, so that he should demolish the wall or the beam, or he should bolster it or watch over it. And if after the warning, the wall, or those things which he was warned about, cause any damage, he should pay it double. If after the warning he causes the death of a person, he should pay double the penalty and depart as an enemy in perpetuity. And we say "after the warning" for this reason; because no one, unless he has been warned beforehand, has to pay any penalty for a person or animal that a wall, a timber, or a house in ruins injures or kills, or because he falls down a well or into a gutter, or any other accident happens to him from these things. All other harm that a house does to another by reason of the waters or by any other thing, if immediately after receiving the warning it is not corrected, the owner of the house should pay for it double, as has been said.

10. Those who climb onto another person's house

Whoever climbs onto another person's house should pay ten *aurei* and double the damage caused.

11. The house from which weapons are thrown

If illegal weapons are thrown from any house causing any damage, and the plaintiff ignores who causes this, let the owner of the house swear for himself and for all those who eat his bread, as is established in the code.

12. Those who throw water through a window or spit on a person

Whoever throws water through a window or spits on a person should pay ten *aurei*, if it can be proved; otherwise, he should be cleared as in the case of the dishonor of the body.

13. Those who defecate in front of the door of another

Whoever defecates in front of the door of another should pay two *aurei* and the same person should sweep up the material deposited if it can be proved; otherwise, he should swear with a citizen and should be believed.

14. Those who stone another person's door

Whoever stones another person's door should pay three hundred *solidi* if it can be proved; otherwise, he should be cleared with twelve citizens and he should be believed.

15. Those who throw bones onto another person's house

Whoever throws horns or bones onto another person's house or leaves them before the doors should pay five *aurei* if the plaintiff can prove it; otherwise, he should be cleared with a citizen and should be believed. This precept is established for those who do not dare to dishonor a person openly, except by this manner.

16. Those who throw stones onto another person's house

Whoever throws stones onto another person's house or through a window should pay ten *aurei* and double the damage caused if it can be proved; otherwise, he should be cleared with two citizens and should be believed.

17. Those who enter the house of another following something of their own

Whoever enters the house of another person following something of his own does not have to pay any penalty if he enters through a door that is open. Whereas he who enters another's place [where the door is closed] should pay the penalty of five hundred *solidi*, as in the case of housebreaking.

18. Those who enter the house of another person because of livestock which has been taken as security

No one should enter a house because of livestock taken as security. If someone, then, takes himself into the house against the will or without the knowledge of the one who has it as security, he should pay the penalty for housebreaking and should restore double the livestock.

19. The height of houses

Whoever constructs a house should raise it to the height that pleases him.

20. The shared wall

Whoever wants to place his house against another person's wall first should pay half the cost of building the wall and later should build onto it, but in any case the shared wall will be on common land. Because if the land is not common, no one can build onto a wall against its owner's will.

CHAPTER VII
Public Land of the Council

1. Those who work on the public land of the council

Whoever works on the public land or on a street of the council, both in the city and in a village, should pay the same council sixty *menkales* and should leave the property free and open. If someone occupies it and this person is injured or dies, there should be no penalty for this reason. If someone sells real estate of the council, he should pay double for it, in amount and quality, to that same council. And the one who has purchased it should lose the amount he has given for it and also should leave the property, as has already been said. No one can give, or sell, or pledge [as security], or validate, or occupy a property of the council against litigation.

2. Quarries and gypsum beds

All the quarries, gypsum beds, millstone quarries, tile works, and also the perennial springs should be common property of the council. Whoever has a millstone quarry or any of these things mentioned previously on a property of his should sell it to the council for a double-sized property, and it becomes communal. If someone occupies it against another of the council, he should pay a hundred *aurei*.

3. Those who occupy a quarry for a certain time

Whoever occupies a millstone quarry, a gypsum bed, a tile works, or a quarry for more than thirty days should lose his work and it will belong to the person who first appropriates it. If someone occupies it, he should pay ten *aurei*.

4. The springs of the council

All springs of the council possess thirty *stadia* [approximately 1470 square feet] of space around their surroundings.

5. The *podium* on the street

Whoever makes a *podium*[1] on the street, it should be theirs and the council's and should be in the service of both, and it should never be for rent to anyone. If someone rents it to another, they should pay sixty *menkales* to the *almutazaf* and to the plaintiff.

6. Those who make a pasture in a village

Whoever makes a pasture in a village should make it with the approval of this village; otherwise, it should not be legal.

7. Those who possess a pasture next to a road

Whoever makes a pasture bordering on the public land or on a road should place a fence around it; if he does not do it, he should receive no payment from those who cause him damage. If he seizes payment, he should pay an *aureus* to the plaintiff and return double the sureties.

8. The penalty on animals that enter into pasture

The pasture of the council of the city should be guarded at all times from all classes of livestock and animals, except the horse, the mule, and the ass. For the damage done because of a mare, its owner should pay a half *menkal*; because of an ox, a fourth part of a *menkal*; because of a pig, a fourth part of a *menkal*; because of fifty sheep, five *solidi*; because of five geese, an eighth part of a *menkal*. He who reaps grass in there should pay five *solidi*. [Those responsible for] damage done at night should pay double penalty. Nevertheless, no one should pay any penalty for the livestock that graze in the pasture when passing by the road.

9. That no one has a pasture for animals of the hunt

No one should have a pasture for rabbits in the district of Cuenca, or for deer or fish.[2]

10. When no one responds for real estate after a year and a day

Whoever holds a designated [piece of] real estate, a term of a year and a day having passed, should not respond for it, unless it is property of the council or of the Church, which no one can give nor sell, and excepted also the property belonging to one who has gone on pilgrimage, or to a captive, or to an orphan who has not reached the age of discernment. However, for any other real estate one has to respond at all times, giving guarantees as to how he acquired it. Nevertheless, if someone commits a crime, such that he would suffer the capital penalty for it if one can catch him, he should not be entitled to his property if after a year and a day he returns and finds it occupied by another.

11. All holdings are equalized at any time

All other holdings should be equalized, whenever the plaintiff wants to measure them.

12. Those who, after paying their price, do not want to validate real estate

Whoever sells a property, after he has collected his price, validates it [by signing a validation document] when it pleases the buyer in his parish, on Saturday at the hour of vespers or on Sunday at the hour of mass. If the seller does not want to validate it, he should pay the buyer five *aurei* for each Sunday that has lapsed since the announcement of it until he [the seller] validates it.

13. The writing of a validation

After the property is ratified, the buyer of the real estate should make a document and write the names of five citizens or more on it, or [the names of the] children of citizens of the same parish. And when it is necessary, he should affirm, with five of those persons listed, that by now one year and a day has passed since it was acceptably validated; [if] he fails, then the parish should be believed. If the witnesses who were written down have died, the buyer should swear with two citizens that those witnesses were present to see and hear the ratification, and that the document is authentic.

14. The [claim] that is demanded before a year and a day, starting from the ratification

The one who holds ratified real estate that someone demands from him before a year and a day should give bondsmen, as is established in the code; [if] he gives the bondsmen, he should retain his real estate free and immune. If he does not give bondsmen, he should abandon the real estate with the penalty of ten *aurei*. If he gives bondsmen who are defeated in judgment, he should pay double the real estate in quantity and quality, and also ten *aurei*.

15. The seller who does not leave bondsmen

If the seller of real estate does not produce bondsmen and the buyer [of the real estate] is defeated in judgment with the witnesses, the seller's bondsman should pay double the real estate in quantity and quality to the buyer, with a fine of twenty *aurei*.

16. The seller who cannot substantiate the real estate

If the seller cannot substantiate real estate, he should pay double with the penalty of ten *aurei*.

17. The seller or buyer who backs out on the deal

If someone sells real estate and later backs out on it, he should pay double the amount he has received. If the buyer is the one who backs out on it, he should lose the money that he has given for it.

18. The one who is to give bondsmen for real estate

If someone is to give bondsmen for a property, he should give them concerning the property, identifying the bondsman who himself sold it, pledged it [as security], or gave it, and so should complete the judgment. Likewise, if he gives as bondsman a citizen who holds a valuable house in security, in this he fulfills the code of Cuenca; he [the bondsman] is also the one who should restore double the property, if he [the giver of the bondsmen] is defeated in judgment.

CHAPTER VIII
Concerning Mills

1. Mills, channels, and dams

The mill that someone builds on his property should have an access path three paces wide and also a space of nine paces surrounding it; otherwise, it should not be legal.

2. Those who build a mill by the bed of the river

If someone wants to build a mill in the midst of a riverbed, he should build it without any penalty and it should be legal in perpetuity, provided it has its own entrance and exit, as has been indicated above; otherwise, it should not be legal.

3. Those who build a new mill

Whoever builds a new mill should take care not to harm another mill constructed previously; no part of it should be higher, lower, well to the right, or well to the left; because if by chance the new mill impedes or obstructs the mills that are already built, it should not be legal and it should be dismantled.

4. Those who make a new dam

New dams should likewise be dismantled if they cause any impediment to the old [ones] that are above or below them, to the right or to the left.

5. Those who make a new millrace

If someone makes a new millrace, no one should build a mill in it that harms it or hinders the mills for which he has made the millrace.

6. That the builder of the millrace is to select the best locations

He who makes a millrace also may build as many mills as he can make in the most suitable location that he himself selects. And just as the [owners of] old mills can destroy the new that hinder them, and for the same reason the [owners of] old dams can destroy the new, thus, by the same right, the [owners of] old millraces may destroy the new.

7. That the builder of a millrace is to build a bridge if it is necessary

Whoever makes a millrace himself likewise should build a bridge if the council deems it necessary.

8. That the mills which are lower should not harm those which are higher; place a marker between one and the other

Since it often happens that mills that are lower do harm to those that are higher because of excess water, we command for this reason that, when the waters diminish from [normal] level in the month of August, a post should be driven between the two mills, at a distance of nine paces from the hollow in which the waterwheel of the higher mill turns, and on that [post] a marker should be placed. This being done, [if] the water later covers the marker due to the mill that is lower, the owner of the mill should pay the plaintiff ten *aurei* and also should lower the water level immediately. If it is not done, he should pay ten *aurei*, starting from the warning for as many days as the water remains above the marker through his fault; nevertheless, if the place is such that he cannot drive the stake in there, he should set the mark in any other position that pleases them [the parties involved].

9. Those who build false mills

Because of those who build false mills in order to anticipate properties [connected to] their rights, we command that whoever wants to construct a mill should build it in such a way that it is truly a mill, to which the people should be accustomed to go and give material for grinding; otherwise, it should not be legal.

10. The water that is leaked from a dam

If water is leaked from a dam, a mill, or a millrace and causes damage to another's property, the one who owns the dam, the mill, or the millrace should pay all the damage the water causes. If later it obstructs again and if he cannot avoid it, he should buy the property at the price that two *alcaldi* determine, or give in exchange for it one property of equal extension and quality and in similar but double [sized] site. However, this should be the choice of the plaintiff.

11. The joint owners of mills

If there are two or more joint owners of a mill or of other real estate, when one of them wants to work, all should work. But the one that does not want to work should pay twelve *denarii* for every day he misses work, or double the costs of renting workers for the tasks of the mill, according to the calculation the other joint owners make. If the joint owners cannot force him in this way, his rent should be in bond until he pays double the amount.

12. Those who do not clean the borders of their canals

Those who do not clean the borders of their canals should pay two *aurei* for every week that they avoid doing it.

13. Those who set a mill on fire

Whoever knowingly sets another's mill on fire should pay three hundred *solidi* and double the damage caused if it can be proved; but if not, he should be cleared as in the case of theft.

14. Those who break into a mill

If someone breaks into a mill, he should pay as in the case of breaking into a dwelling. If the miller sets the mill on fire by accident, he should pay the damage caused and nothing more; but if no one believes him, the damage occasioned being restored, he should clear himself with twelve citizens and should be believed.

15. Those who break a wheel or other things of a mill

Whoever knowingly breaks a wheel of a mill, a grindstone, a canal, a drill, or an iron part of the grinding machinery should pay ten *aurei*; otherwise, he should clear himself as in the case of theft. If someone steals these things, he should pay as a thief if it can be proved; but if not, he should clear himself as in the case of theft.

16. Those who break a wheel of a watermill, of an orchard, or of a bathhouse

He who knowingly breaks a wheel of a watermill, of an orchard, of a bathhouse, or of a well should pay ten *aurei* and double the damage caused if he is declared guilty; but if not, he should clear himself as in the case of theft.

17. Those who wrongly break another's dam

Whoever wrongly breaks another's dam should pay ten *aurei* and double the damage caused if he is declared guilty; but if not, he should swear with two citizens and should be believed.

18. Mills, dams and millraces that harm the old ones

[Concerning] all the dams, mills, and millraces that harm the old [ones], those who made them should dismantle them immediately in the term of three days, starting from the date of the finding of the judgment. And if the party does not want to do it, he should pay daily ten *aurei*, half to the plaintiff and half to the *alcaldi*, and also double the damage occasioned, until he destroys what he has to destroy. For this fine the *alcaldi* should take sureties until he pays.

19. The water of the mills that is necessary for orchards

If the water of a mill by which they grind is necessary in order to irrigate the orchards, they [the orchard owners] have it these two days in the week; that is, on Tuesday and on Friday, whether water from the millrace or from the river; the water is led off at that point and received by that place where the *alcaldi* see that less damage is occasioned to each one.

20. According to what law the mills are supposed to grind

From the feast of Saint John until that of Saint Michael, the mills should grind to the fifteenth; in the remaining time they should grind to the twentieth.[1] If someone breaks this precept, he should pay an *aureus* to the *alcaldi* and to the plaintiff.

21. The salary of millers

The miller should receive a fourth part of the fees for use [of his mill].

22. Those who penetrate a house or a mill of another

Whoever penetrates through a house or mill of another should pay the fine of housebreaking, even though nothing is carried away from there; but if he causes damage in there, he should pay for it as a thief.

CHAPTER IX
Marriages and Wills

1. Marriages and wills

I command that whoever espouses himself to an unmarried woman of the city should give twenty *aurei* as dower, items of a given value, or sureties valued at twenty *aurei*.

2. The dower to a widow of the city, to an unmarried villager, and to a widow villager

He should give ten *aurei* as dower to a widow of the city; he who contracts with a single village woman should present ten *aurei* as dower; to a village widow, five *aurei*.

3. That after the death of the male no one pays dower

It is understood that after the death of the male, no one has to pay a dower; and even though the woman has sureties, they should not be valid, because the dower was not claimed before the death of the male; but the items of value given should remain valid for good.

4. The person who rejects his or her partner after the betrothal

If the husband rejects the wife after the betrothal, or the wife the husband, the bondsmen of the one who rejects should pay one hundred *aurei* and double the damage caused.

5. The husband who rejects the wife with whom he had carnal relations

If the husband has had carnal relations with the wife and later rejects her, he should pay one hundred *aurei* and should depart an enemy.

6. What the husband should receive if the wife dies before the wedding, or the other way around

If the wife dies before the wedding or before contracting marriage, the husband should receive the clothing and as much as he has given her. If it is the husband who dies, the wife should take all her trousseau.

7. After defloration or cohabitation, the clothing belongs to the wife

After the marriage is contracted and the woman is deflowered, the clothing will belong to the wife whenever the male should die.

8. No one pays a fee to the palace due to lacking heirs

Whoever dies before or after the marriage without making a will should not pay to the Palace any fee for lacking heirs. Furthermore, if someone does not have a near relative, all his goods should be distributed, both movable goods and real estate, according to his wishes, if he dies after having made a will.

9. Those who die without making a will

If someone dies without making a will and has a near relative, his parish should receive a fifth part of the livestock but not of other things, that is, sheep, oxen, cows, and all the other animals, except a saddle horse. The nearest relatives should receive the remainder, and they should do what they want with the body of the dead.

10. One who dies without making a will and without close relatives

If someone dies without close relatives and without making a will, a fifth part of his livestock should be given to the parish of his host or *señor*. The rest should belong to his *señor* or his host.

11. No one can leave something to his wife in his will against the wishes of his heirs

He who makes a will cannot leave anything to his wife if his heirs are absent or opposed; nor can the wife to her husband.

12. Those who make a Christian of one of their Moors

Whoever of you makes his Moors Christians and these do not have children, their [the Moor's] *señor* should inherit their [the Moor's] goods. If the *señor* of the converts or proselytes does not survive them, the children of the *señor* should inherit their goods.

13. All those who settled down on another's property are vassals of the real estate's owner

We command of your servants and proselytes, and of their children and of all the people who reside in your houses in general, that the *señor* of the house where they live should receive the payment of all the pecuniary penalties that occur there, and no other.

14. The Palace does not receive the pecuniary penalty for homicide, except for the death of the *señor* of the house

The Palace should not receive the pecuniary penalty for homicide, except for the death of the *señor* of the house. All those who reside in another's houses or properties should be vassals of the *señor* of the property or houses, and they should respond for tributes and maintenance of bridges, roads, and public works.

CHAPTER X
The Right of Succession of Children and Parents

1. The right of succession of children and parents

Any child should inherit the goods of his father and mother, movable goods as well as real estate. The father and mother [should inherit] the movable goods of the children. The father, however, should not have to inherit the real estate of his child which comes to the latter through inheritance. Regarding the other real estate which the parents acquire jointly, the one who survives, father or mother, should inherit this for lifetime use only, by right of inheritance through their child, if he lives at least nine days. After the death of the father or mother, the real estate returns to the estate.

For this reason I command that, although the surviving parent has to inherit this real estate for lifetime use, and the real estate has to revert to the estate, the survivor should provide bondsmen who will guard the real estate from harm. The real estate that belongs to the child through his estate should revert to that estate the day the survivor dies.

2. The nearest relatives of a dead person are his heirs

The relatives who are nearest [in blood] and also citizens should inherit the goods of their deceased relative. If someone comes forward as a closer relative than these others, this person should inherit the goods of the deceased but first should provide bondsmen who establish that this person should have been an inhabitant of Cuenca for at least ten years. Those who do not do this should not inherit.

3. Those who enter a monastic order

Whoever enters a monastic order should take with him only a fifth portion of his movable property, and the rest, joined with the entirety of his real estate, should remain for his heirs. It will be seen as unjust and inequitable that someone should disinherit his children by donating their movable property and real estate to the monks, because it is established in the code that nobody should disinherit their children.

4. Children are under the power of their parents

Children should be under the power of their parents and are family members until they should contract marriage. And until that moment, everything the children acquire or obtain should belong entirely to their parents; the children holding nothing against their parents' will.

5. Parents respond for the crimes of their children

Parents should respond for the crimes of their children, whether or not the latter should be sound in judgment. If someone enters the home of another and commits any crime, whether or not they should be a hireling of the house, the owner of the house should not respond with a surety for them unless he defends them. If he defends them, he should respond for them or bring them to give juridical satisfaction. But if they do not return to the house of their *señor*, or the *señor* does not go forth in their defense, no one should respond for them but their parents. Nevertheless, if a child commits a homicide, even though he should be in the pay of another, no one should respond for him except his parents, because they should pay the pecuniary penalties; however, the parents should not depart as enemies unless they are blamed for the homicide. Then, if they are accused and convicted of homicide, they are obligated also to depart from our city as enemies. If the child is bereft of one of his parents, the one who acts as his guardian should respond for him until the child is given the portion of goods that belongs to him. After the partition of goods, the guardian does not have to respond.

6. Parents do not respond for the debts of their children

Parents should not respond for the loans or debts of their children.

7. The disturbed child

If a father or mother has a disturbed child and is concerned for paying the pecuniary penalties of the crimes that he might commit, he should hold the child captive or bound until he calms down or is treated, while he remains deranged, so that the child does not cause damage. The parents have to respond for any damage that he causes, even if they have renounced him in front of the council or have disinherited him. This precept is established so that none may say that their child is insane or disturbed and renounce him before the council and then, with concealment and deception, cause him to kill someone or start a fire or do any other harm.

8. Separation of the wife and the husband

When husband and wife, for any reason and by common agreement, want to separate, only those things they have acquired together should be distributed equally and nothing else; they should also distribute equally the works that both have completed on their property. And after one of those who has been separated in life dies, the survivor should receive nothing from the other's goods, but rather the heirs of the dead person should be those to receive all his or her goods, and these should be divided among themselves.

9. The partition of goods of parents and children

All partitions of goods that are done in the presence of three citizens and recorded should hold as firm, so that the partition or the names of the witnesses are written in the public record, because, if some or all of the witnesses have died, he who holds the document should swear with two citizens that this is authentic, and he should be believed, in case some of the heirs deny the partition. Likewise, the division and the partition are firm and sound that the parents, whether healthy or sick, had made for their heirs, being all present without exception and in agreement; because the partition done in another way by the father or the mother is not legal. The donation should also be accepted and sound that the father and mother confirm only by oath.

10. The document of partition

The document of partition should have this formulation: "All should know absolutely, those present as well as those to come, that I, N., desiring the end of all flesh, which one is born for, so that before a man should die he should pay the debts of nature, allot and concede to my heirs and successors that, by right of patrimony after my death, according to hereditary right, they should possess my things, all that I have acquired with my sweat and my service up to the present day, as much in movable property as in real estate, and in this manner: to G., my firstborn son, the vineyard that is within the district of Cuenca, near the river, with the orchard that lies within it; I leave you also all the houses that I built or bought in the locale N.; to R., my younger son, the field N. or the vineyard with the portion [of land] that belongs to it. Witnessed by those whose names appear below: *F.P.D.J.* Era one thousand two hundred.[1] *N.*, being king. *N.*, being *iudex*. *N.*, being *merino*. *N.*, being *sagio*."

11. Also regarding the partition

If the spouses have children and are not separated in life, and neither of the two has other children, when one of them dies, having settled all the common debts that they have contracted jointly, and having paid also the share of the dead for alms for their soul and their shroud, their children or heirs should distribute all the goods of the dead among each other, both goods and real estate. If a child dies, the surviving parent should inherit his goods, as has already been said. But if the child has a descendant, the latter should succeed him [the child] and not the father or the mother.

12. Also regarding the partition

When the surviving parent dies, the children or heirs, having paid the debts, the alms for his soul, and the shroud, as has been said, should allot all his goods, both movable goods and real estate.

13. Also regarding the partition

Whoever dies without descendants, the closest relatives should inherit the goods, both movable goods and real estate. The son should not distribute that real estate belonging to the surviving parent, which was obtained before their wedding or possessed from their estate. Likewise, neither the heirs nor the children should give to their surviving parent a share of the real estate of the deceased parent, which was possessed before the wedding or from their own estate.

14. The things that the couple has acquired together

On the day of the wedding, absolutely everything promised to the married couple or given jointly or separately to them should be held in common, both in life and in death.

15. The debt that remains after the partition

If after the partition any debt remains, the survivor should pay it together with the heirs, in proportion to the amount that each one has received of the deceased's goods. And although the deceased does not have anything that the children can inherit, nonetheless the [children] have to respond for the [parent's] debt; but if the surviving spouse does not have children, the survivor should pay the entire debt that they contracted jointly, and nothing else.

16. The widower who before the partition wants to get married again, or the other way around

The widower who has children and wants to get married again, first should give his children the portion that belongs to them by right of their mother, and subsequently should marry. By the same manner, if he has children of the second wife and she dies, and he wants to get married for a third time, he first should distribute to the children of the second wife, giving as much to them as belongs to them by right of their mother, and subsequently he should marry; and thus he proceeds with the marriages to [any] others. The widow who wants to get married does the same.

17. How the children have to distribute with their father and their stepmother, or the other way around

If a widower does not want to share with the children of the first wife before getting married again, because of ignorance or greed, at any time that the children of the first wife want to share, he should take half of all the goods, both movable goods and real estate, which have been acquired before or after the death of their mother, once they separate the real estate of the stepmother's estate and those things that are acknowledged as her property. This done, he should share in the same manner with the children of the second wife, and later with those of the third, if he has them and their mother had died. And thus he should share successively with all the children, once their respective mothers have died.

18. The partition of the heirs and the stepmother

If it is the father who dies, while the second, third, or fourth wife still lives, although he has children of her, nonetheless before the stepmother or their children receive something, the son of the first wife should take half of all the goods that the father acquired together with the mother or later on. Next, the son of the second wife should take half of all the remaining goods. And thus, the children of the mothers who have died being paid, the wife who still lives should receive half of all the goods that remain. Later all the children of the deceased, both of the mothers who are dead and of those still alive, should divide what has remained with each other in equal portions. This also we say about the widower who has children of several mothers and who, the last having died, had still not made the partition.

19. The partition of the heirs with the stepmother and the stepfather

If the husband has children by several mothers, and the wife has them equally by different husbands, and the children of each one of them want to share with their parents, the children of the first wife and those of the first husband should take half of all the goods, both movable goods and real estate, and should share them with each other. Later the children of the second wife and those of the second husband should take half of the other remaining half, both movable property and real estate, and so on, in each one of the cases. Nevertheless, if one of the children mentioned knows of something that was his deceased mother's or father's, he should take it for himself alone and should not share it.

20. The partition of a single stepchild with several [children]

If the husband has children by another wife and the wife has a single son by another husband, or the other way around, when they want to share with their parents, he who is the only son together with the others should take half of all the goods of their parents, both movable goods and real estate. Later he who is the only son should take half of the share taken with his stepbrothers, and should distribute the other half among the other siblings in equal shares; since he is the only son, by right of his father or mother, half of the half should belong to him, and the others should have the other half of the half by right of their father or mother and nothing else. But the entire other half should stay with the children whom they have in common for the lifetime of the parents. After [the parents'] death, all the children, both those that they have in common and those who had [already] received shares, should distribute equally all the goods that remain.

21. The sterile who jointly exchange or purchase anything

If the husband and the wife are sterile and they jointly purchase or exchange anything, or build houses or mills, do any work or planting on some real estate of one or the other, when it is necessary they should distribute these in equal shares, both in life and in death. When one of them dies, the survivor should be entitled to half this work, and the closest relatives of the deceased, to the other half; the other real estate should return to their estate.

22. The gifts that the father and mother give their children the day of the wedding

When the parents get their sons or daughters married, all that they give them should be held as fixed always, provided that the other children can be reimbursed in the same manner. Because, when the partition is undertaken, the latter should be entitled equally to the goods that belonged to their parents now deceased. If by the day of the partition the siblings who have not received anything yet do not have that which can reimburse them, their siblings should bring as much of the goods of their father or mother that they received in excess of the others, so that they all should thus remain equal, all the debts having been paid first, as has been said.

23. Suspicion regarding the parents

If the children suspect that their mother or father conceals something from them in the allotment of the things they are supposed to share with each other, the father or mother should swear to them that they are not concealing any of the things they are supposed to distribute. Nevertheless, if after the oath the heirs find out that some things that should have been given to them were not given them, they should take them without any penalty and should share them with each other; but the father or mother, by having refused it, should not have any share of them.

24. The suspicious stepmother or stepfather

If the heirs suspect that their stepmother or stepfather conceals from them some things which they should be given equally to share, [the stepparent] should swear alone up to a value of five *menkales*, and should be believed; from five to ten [*menkales*], [the stepparent] should swear with one citizen; for ten [*menkales*] or more, with two [citizens], and should be believed.

25. Also concerning the suspicious stepmother or stepfather

Equally, if the children or heirs suspect that their father or mother or their stepfather or stepmother lies about saying that they owe something, the children should prove it as is established in the code, but the witnesses should respond to the challenge [by combat or judicial duel].

26. The heirs distribute when it pleases one of them

The partition is to be made after the death of the father or mother when it pleases one of the heirs. If someone does not want to do it, he should pay ten *aurei* to the *alcaldi* every day and to the complainant until the partition is made, if the complainant can prove it with witnesses.

27. The parents cannot give some of their heirs more than others

We command for the above reasons that neither the father nor the mother, whether healthy or sick, should be able to give something to any of their children, either healthy or ill, but rather all should receive equally, both of movable property and of real estate.

28. Condition of the will

Whatever someone orders given in his will for the intention of his soul is held as firm; except that neither the wife can give anything to the husband nor the husband to the wife if the heirs are absent or opposed.

29. The will that the heirs reject

If the heirs reject the will, the executors should affirm it and they should be believed; a master [of law] and any citizen are sufficient in order to attest executors.

30. The pregnant wife after the death of her husband

If the husband dies without having children and leaves his wife or his concubine pregnant, she should retain, under written document, all the possessions of the deceased and she should also provide bondsmen who guard them undamaged. If she gives birth within nine months, she should guard them for her child and meanwhile she should live on these same goods.

31. The parents do not inherit the goods of the son who does not live nine days

If the child does not live nine days, all the things should be given to the heirs of the deceased for their allotment. If he lives nine days, the mother should keep the movable goods by hereditary right. The real estate should revert to the deceased's estate the same day in which the child dies.

32. The will of the child who is still under the power of his parents

One should consider any will a child makes before contracting marriage as frivolous and invalid and judge it broken. The child being under patrimonial power, he cannot grant nor leave anything in a will, since his goods already belong to his father or mother; absolutely everything will belong to his father or mother, the one that survives, except the real estate that is considered part of his estate, as has already been said; the other real estate the child has acquired should belong to the father or mother, the one that survives, as well as the movable property.

33. The wife who pretends by deceit that she is pregnant

If the wife or the concubine pretends by deceit that she is pregnant, she should restore double all that the heirs of the deceased have spent in their verification.

34. The upbringing of the orphan

If the child is still young after the death of his father or mother, the surviving parent should have [custody of the child], with all the goods that belong to it from the deceased, by written document, until [he is] twelve years old, and the [parent] should annually submit accounts of the child's *peculium* to his nearest relative. And if his relative sees that his *peculium* should increase in good faith, then [the parent] should continue having [custody] until the [end of the] fixed term. But if the close relatives of the orphan see that [the parent] wastes it or does not increase it [the *peculium*], one of the relatives who is closer should be made guardian, receiving the child and his goods under his care; and this [guardian] likewise should submit accounts annually of the orphan's goods to the other relatives. If they see in the accounts that his *peculium* is decreasing more than increasing, they should remove the child and his goods and surrender them to him in whose care by good faith the orphan's *peculium* increases. All the damage that someone causes to the goods should be paid double. After the child completes his twelve years, he should have free power to go or stay with whom he pleases.

35. The unweaned orphan

If the orphan is still unweaned, his nurse should receive annually for three years twelve *menkales* from the child's goods and a bed for sleeping. The three years having lapsed, the child should be separated from the nurse. The child should have food and clothing from his own goods.

36. The unity of goods of the husband and of the wife

Although it has been said above that, after the death of the husband or wife, the heirs should share with the one who survives, nonetheless, if while both are alive the husband and the wife make a unity of goods, as is established in the code, no heir or child should share with the survivor while living. The law of the unity of goods establishes that the indivisibility should be sound and firm, but it agrees that it must be made before the council or before the parish and that all the heirs should concede this without exception. I say "all the heirs," so that none of them should be absent, because if any heir is missing or one of them present opposes, it should be held as illegal and invalid.

37. The child who has compassion for his needy father or mother

If a child, moved by pity, receives in his house his needy father or mother, who dies there, no other claim to partition with the pious son for reason of the parent [can be made], except for the things that [the parent] bore with him to the son's home. But if the son has spent the things the parent brought to his house, for his own necessities or those of his father or mother, he should not respond for them. Nevertheless, if the other coinheritors suspect him, he should swear alone that he has not kept anything of the goods of their father or mother.

We give this same judgment concerning the child who stays to live with his father or mother and who has sold some things for his necessities, for which the others suspect him.

38. The child who does not have compassion for its needy father or mother

If a child who is wealthy does not have pity for his needy father or mother, and the needful one complains to the *iudex* or to the *alcaldi*, these [officers] should seize him with all his goods and should put him under patrimonial power; nevertheless, the father or mother should live on the goods of their child with moderation, during every day of their life, so that they should not have a right to waste, donate, sell, or bequeath those goods in a will, but only to live on them with moderation. After the death of the father or mother, the child should have full control and power over the things that have remained, so that they should not be given in any manner in order to share them with the remaining heirs.

39. The father who sends his son as hostage in his place

If someone sends his son in his place as hostage, which is commonly called *refeno*, to the land of the Muslims and has not redeemed him within a term of three years, the *iudex* and the *alcaldi* should apprehend him [the father] with all his goods and should send him in the place of his son to the land of the Muslims, and they should liberate the son from captivity. For this reason we command that whoever gives his son as security without the order of the council, or sends him as hostage, if it is not under the above terms, should die a traitor's death. In like manner it is not permissible to give a daughter as security, either as *refena* or as pledgling; and if someone does it, he should be burned alive. If the *iudex* and the *alcaldi* do not do justice thus, the council should take them as sureties for the redemption of the hostage or of the person who has been pledged. What we say about a daughter is valid for any woman who has been given as security or sent as hostage; this precept is established so that the Muslims should not ravish Christians; because, as the wise assert, the Saracens never seize the Christians, save for the audacity of the Christians who are with them and of the children of the Christian women whom they should have as wives.

40. The salary that a child acquires as servant

All that a child earns as salary or by any other manner should belong to his parents, as has already been said. Just as the parents are accustomed to suffer for the excesses and wicked deeds of their children, so it is also just that they should be pleased to obtain something of their earnings and revenue. Therefore, a child should give over absolutely everything he earns outside his parents' house to share with his siblings provided he or she is not married, because after contracting marriage [children] are not obliged to give anything of what they earn for partition.

41. The child who strikes his father or his mother

Although it is forbidden that either the father or the mother should disinherit a child of theirs, nonetheless, we command that they disinherit the one who injures his father or mother and, also, that [that child] should be the enemy of his siblings forever.

42. The prerogative of the widowers

A widower or a widow who wants to remain in the state of widowhood should leave these things outside the partition: to the widower, his horse and his weapons, both those of wood and those of iron; neither the bed in which he was lying with his wife before nor the hunting hawks should enter in the draw. For the widow the bed that she was accustomed to share with her husband should remain outside partition; she should also be given a field [that produces] a *kaficius* from seeded land, a yoke of oxen and an *arançada* [approximately 447 square meters] of vineyard, but not of the grape arbor. This is what should belong to the widowers by right of widowhood and nothing else. These rights of widowhood should be conceded to them from what they have acquired jointly and not of other things. And if by chance, when the day of the partition arrives, there are none of these above-mentioned items, they should be given only what is there and nothing else, and in such state as they are.

43. The widower who does not want to remain in the state of widowhood

Nevertheless, the widower or widow who does not want to remain in the state of chaste widowhood should give everything he had received during widowhood for the partition, when it pleases the heirs.

All that the siblings acquire jointly, after the partition of their estate, should be [held in] common, both in life and in death, and the acquired goods should be distributed when it pleases any of the siblings.

CHAPTER XI

No One Should Pay the Pecuniary Penalty of Homicide for a Man Killed During Sports

1. No one should pay the pecuniary penalty of homicide for a man who was killed during sports

We also command that no one should pay any penalty or homicide fine for a person who was wounded or even killed, outside the walls of the city, in the short lance game of the council or in the games of a wedding, by being pushed by a horse, or with a lance, with a shield or in any other way whatever; since if someone does lance riding within the walls of the city and injures or kills someone, he should pay the pecuniary penalty and the damage that he has caused. Anyone who hurls a stone, a light throwing lance, a lance, or other thing of this nature and injures, kills, or causes any damage to someone should pay the pecuniary penalty and the damage that he has done.

2. Those who hurl tournament lances outside the walls

He who throws tournament lances outside the walls of the city and in this sport hurls a stone, an arrow, a lance or other thing of this nature, and injures, kills, or causes any other injury to someone, should not pay any pecuniary penalty. But if it is suspected that he caused the damage deliberately, he clears himself according to the Code of Cuenca.

3. The animal that injures or kills another

If an animal injures or kills another, its owner should pay the damage that has been done according to the oath of the plaintiff and of a single resident, or he should place the harmdoer in the hands of the plaintiff, if he [the plaintiff] can prove it; otherwise, he [the accused owner] should clear himself with any resident and should be believed.

4. The animal that injures a person

The owner of the animal that injures or wounds someone should pay the doctor all the costs of his healing. This same should hold true in the case of a fracture of an arm or a leg.

5. The animal that kills a person

If an animal kills someone, the owner of the animal should pay three hundred *solidi* or surrender the harmdoer. Be it known that the owner of the animal has to choose between paying the fine or surrendering the harmdoer, both for the fatality and for other injury.

6. Nine days having lapsed, no one should respond for the damage caused by an animal

No one should respond for the damage caused by a dog or another animal that has not been reported within the term of nine days, starting from the date of the damage.

7. A frightened animal

If an animal frightened by someone, or some oxen because of a fly, cause any damage, its owner should not pay anything or surrender the harmdoer; he then who has frightened it has to pay the fine or the damage that occurs because of this. Equally, if a horse running loose or wild kills someone or causes any other harm, neither the rider nor the owner should pay any pecuniary penalty for this or depart as an enemy; but if one of them is suspect, he should swear with twelve citizens and should be believed.

This same judgment is valid for the one who in the lance hurling, in the wedding sports, or in the hurling of lances, stones, or small throwing lances, kills someone or causes any damage. The same judgment applies to the one who frightens an animal, if he says that he has done it unknowingly; that is to say, that he is cleared, as prescribed in the code and the pecuniary penalty is sought.

8. Those who injure someone with illegal weapons

Whoever causes wounds to someone with illegal weapons should pay thirty *aurei*; if he breaks a bone, sixty; if he injures him with illegal weapons, but if he does not cause him wounds, he should pay twenty *aurei*. If he takes up weapons, although he does not succeed in injuring with them, he should pay ten *aurei*.

9. What are illegal weapons

The illegal weapons that in no way are legal to take up with anger within the confines of the city, or to injure with them, unless one should be punished in the manner that has been said, are these: all iron implements, all clubs, any stone, and in general whatever things can injure or kill someone.

10. Those who come in a gang

Whoever comes in a gang and takes out weapons, injures, or causes wounds to someone should pay double the pecuniary penalty for the crime he has committed if he is convicted; but if not, he should be cleared by two of four named from his parish.

11. For dishonoring a body in a village

For all dishonoring of a body that is done against the villagers in a village, there should be named those witnesses who swear to it, except [in the case of] homicide. And those named witnesses should take an oath in front of the tribunal of the *alcaldi* on Friday; he who is not present, and who is judged as such, should lose the case.

12. Those who present a complaint to the *alcaldi*

Whoever presents a complaint to the *alcaldi* and subsequently makes an arrangement without them or is not present for the judgment should pay the entire claim, and if it is suspected that he has made arrangements for the pecuniary penalty judgment, he should clear himself with any resident and should be believed.

13. Those who form a gang in the city

Whoever forms a gang in the city against the council should pay double the pecuniary penalties of the crimes that it [the gang] commits, both he and all his collaborators; and equally, if someone takes up illegal weapons, he should pay twenty *aurei*; if he injures someone, forty; if he causes him wounds, sixty; if he kills him, four hundred. He who denies it and cannot be declared convicted by witnesses should swear with twelve citizens or respond by judicial combat. He who strikes someone with fists, pulls out hair, or insults him should likewise pay double. If he denies it, he should swear with two of four named from his parish. If the *iudex* or an *alcaldus* encounters him in that gang, he should also pay double, and moreover he should lose the charge that stands.

14. Those who kill a guest

Anyone who invites someone to his house to eat or to drink or calls him to consult and kills him should be buried alive below the dead person. This same penalty should apply to the one who kills his master whose bread he eats and whose orders he obeys, or who puts him [the master] in the hands of his enemies so that they do with him what they please.

15. He who kills a companion

Anyone who on the road kills a companion who relies on him should be buried alive under the dead. If [the accused] denies it and cannot be convicted with witnesses, he should be cleared with twelve citizens and he should be believed. But if he cannot be cleared, he should pay as has been said; however, it remains in the election of the plaintiff to accept the justification or [demand] that the suspect should respond by judicial combat. Anyone who injures or kills the *Señor* of the city or surrenders the castle through betrayal should be torn apart limb from limb.

16. He who assaults someone

Anyone who, in isolated territory or in populated land, by day or at night, assaults a person not discredited, or [who is] accepted [in the community], or a bondsman of sureties, should pay sixty *menkales*. If he injures him or removes anything from him, he should pay double the pecuniary penalty of the crime which he has committed and restore double the damage caused, with the fine of sixty *menkales*, if it can be proved; otherwise, he should be cleared with two of four named from his parish and he should be believed. But if he causes him to die, let him [the assaulter] be hurled from the city cliffs if he is captured. If he flees, he should lose everything he possesses for a fine of four hundred *aurei*, and his house should be demolished, and he should not be received in the city in the future, but rather should suffer permanent exile, if it can be proved; otherwise, he should clear himself with twelve citizens and should be believed, or he should respond with judicial combat; the plaintiff elects the one that pleases him more.

17. Larceny and robbery

Anyone who is declared convicted of burglary or robbery, let him be hurled from the city cliffs; otherwise, if he is not convicted and he denies it, he should swear [by himself] only and should be believed, if the value of the lost goods is up to five *menkales*; from five up to ten *menkales*, he should swear with any resident; from ten to twenty, with two citizens; from twenty up, the plaintiff should elect between the suspect swearing with twelve citizens and being believed, or swearing by himself and responding to the challenge [by combat]. If he fights in judicial combat and is beaten, he should pay double the demand and a ninth to the Palace.

18. He who catches a thief outside the city

Anyone who captures a thief outside the city should lead him in front of the council of the same city, and there he should be punished; anyone who does not do this and instead punishes him outside the city should pay one hundred *aurei* to the *iudex* and to the *alcaldi*.

19. He who injures another's Moor

If someone injures another's Moor, he should pay five *solidi* for doing it; he who kills him, fifteen *aurei*; but if he is a Moor set aside for prisoner exchange, and his *señor* already has bondsmen for the redemption and can confirm it, as is established in the code, he who killed the Moor should pay the promised redemption; for another Moor, whether or not a servant, he should not pay more than fifteen *aurei*, as has been said.

20. He who injures or kills a free Moor

Anyone who injures or kills a free Moor should pay for him, as for a Christian.

21. The free Moor who injures or kills a Christian

If a free Moor injures or kills a Christian, for injuring him he should pay the pecuniary penalty according to the Code of Cuenca; for killing him, he [the Moor] should be put in the hands of the plaintiff, so that the plaintiff should take the money from the pecuniary penalties, and finally he should do with his [the Moor's] body what he wants.

22. He who violates another's Moorish woman

Whoever violates another's Moorish woman should pay her dowry, as if she were a married woman of the city.

23. He who has a child with another's Moorish woman

If someone has a child with another's Moorish woman, this child should be the servant of the *señor* of the Moorish woman, until his father redeems him. Also, we say that such a child should not divide with his siblings that which corresponds to the patrimony of their father, while he remains in servitude. Later should he become free, he should take a share of the goods of his father.

24. He who violates an unmarried woman

Whoever violates an unmarried woman or abducts her against the will of her parents should pay three hundred *solidi* and depart as an enemy; his collaborators should pay three hundred *solidi* each and also depart as enemies. And if she subsequently surrenders to the will of her abductor, she should be disinherited and as an enemy should join her abductor.

25. He who violates a married woman

Whoever violates a married woman or abducts her should be burned alive if he can be captured; if he cannot be captured, all his goods should belong to the husband, and the violator should be his enemy in perpetuity. If she goes with him voluntarily, and he is captured in her company, in the city or in its confines, both should be burned alive.

26. What woman should be believed concerning violation

The woman who is a complainant through violation should complain to the *iudex* and to the *alcaldi* in a term of three days starting from the date of the violation, having clawed her cheeks. If the violator denies it, he should swear it with twelve citizens or respond with judicial combat, the one which is more pleasing to the complainant. And if he loses, he should depart as an enemy in perpetuity, and his collaborators [should depart] for one year, each one of them [the collaborators] also paying a fine of three hundred *solidi*.

27. He who violates a religious woman

Whoever violates a religious woman let him be hurled from the city cliffs if he can be captured; but if not, he should pay five hundred *solidi* from the goods that he possesses.

28. He who surprises his wife in adultery

Anyone who finds his wife with another in adultery and kills her should not pay any fine or depart as an enemy; similarly, if he kills the adulterer or the adulterer escapes wounded. But if the husband kills her in other circumstances, he should pay the corresponding pecuniary penalties and should depart as an enemy. Also, if he kills or injures the adulterer and not his wife, he should also pay the corresponding pecuniary penalties.

29. He who insults another's woman

Whoever insults another's woman, calling her prostitute, worn-out horse, or leprous, should pay two *aurei*, and also he should swear that he does not know whether she has that defect; or else, if he does not want to swear it, he should depart as an enemy. But if someone violates a public prostitute or insults her, he should pay nothing.

30. He who grabs a woman by the hair

Whoever grabs a woman by the hair should pay ten *aurei* if she can prove it; otherwise, he should swear with two of four named from his parish that he did not do it, and he should be believed.

31. He who pushes a woman violently

Whoever pushes a woman violently should pay five *aurei*. If she falls to the ground from the force of the push, although it does not cause her wounds, he should pay ten *aurei*; but if it causes her wounds, he should pay thirty *aurei*.

32. He who carries off the clothing of a naked woman

Whoever carries off the clothing of a woman who was bathing, or robs her, should pay three hundred *solidi*; if he denies it and the plaintiff cannot prove it, he should swear it with twelve citizens and should be believed; the public prostitute remains excepted, for she does not have a right to any pecuniary penalty, as has been said.

33. He who cuts the bosom of a woman

Whoever cuts the bosom of a woman should pay two hundred *aurei* and depart as an enemy; if he denies it, the plaintiff should select between the oath of twelve citizens or the challenge [to combat], the one which pleases her more.

34. He who cuts the skirts [or clothing] off a woman

Whoever cuts the skirts off a woman without command of the *iudex* or of the *alcaldi* should pay two hundred *aurei* and depart as an enemy; if he denies it, he should clear himself with twelve citizens and should be believed, or he should respond by judicial combat.

35. The woman who abandons her child

Any woman who abandons her child in any place should be whipped and, also, she should be obliged to take care of it.

36. The bigamist who has two women simultaneously

Anyone who has a legitimate wife in another place and gets married to another in Cuenca while the first woman still lives, let him be hurled from the city cliffs. If a woman has a husband in another place and gets married to another in Cuenca, she should be burned alive; if she is taken by a man as a concubine, she should be whipped in the square and in all the streets of the city and expelled from this place.

37. The married man who has a concubine openly

If a man who has a legitimate wife, already in Cuenca, yet in another place has a concubine, both [man and concubine] should be tied up together openly and whipped.

38. The woman who puts her child in the care of the father

Any woman who places her child in the care of the father, in spite of him giving her eight *menkales* a year, should be whipped. For which, we command by the code that the woman who has a child with someone should care for her child, and that the father should give her annually eight *menkales* for other nurses until it is three years old, as it is in the code. But if the father does not want to give this payment, the mother should return their child to him without fine.

39. The woman who miscarries knowingly

The woman who aborts knowingly should be burned alive if she admits it; otherwise, she should clear herself by means of the ordeal of hot iron.

40. The woman who says she is pregnant by someone

The woman who says that she is pregnant by some man, and he does not believe her, should take the hot iron, and if it burns her, she should not be believed; but if she survives without burns, the father should receive his child and raise it, as is established in the code.

41. Those who cast spells

The woman who casts spells on men, animals, or other things, should be burned alive; but if it cannot be proved, she should be cleared by means of the ordeal of [hot] iron. If a man was the spell caster, he should be exiled from the city after being shorn and whipped; if he denies it, he should be cleared by means of judicial combat.

42. The herbalists and the witches

The woman who is an herbalist or witch should be burned alive, or cleared by means of the ordeal of [hot] iron.

43. The woman who kills her husband

The woman who kills her husband should be burned alive or cleared by means of the ordeal of [hot] iron. In this case, all [accused] women have to take up the iron; in the other case [of an herbalist-witch], no one has to take up the iron other than the prostitute who has fornicated with five men or the procuress.[1]

44. Procuresses

Women who are shown to be procuresses or panders should be burned alive; if a woman is only suspected and she denies it, she should be cleared by means of the ordeal of [hot] iron.

45. The shape of the iron

The iron in order to do justice is placed four feet high approximately, so that the one who has to prove her innocence should place her hand under it; she should hold [an iron] of a palm's length and of two fingers' width. She who grasps the iron should carry it a distance of nine paces and deposit it smoothly on the ground; but first, it should be blessed by a priest.

46. The heating of the iron

The *iudex* and the priest heat the iron, and meanwhile no one should approach the fire, so that no one by chance should cast any spells. She who must grasp the iron should first be examined carefully, so that she should not have any charms; later, she should wash her hands in the presence of all and grasp the iron with dry hands. After she has seized it, the *iudex* should immediately cover her hand with wax and onto the wax put flax or linen; then, he should bind the hand with a cloth. Once this is done, the *iudex* should lead her to his house and after three days should examine the hand; if the hand is burned, she should be burned alive or suffer the penalty to which she is sentenced. Only that woman bears the iron who has demonstrated that she is a procuress or one who had fornicated with five men; any other woman who is suspected of larceny, of homicide or of arson should swear or provide a judicial combatant, as is established in the code.[2]

47. Who sells a Christian

If a man or a woman sells a Christian, he or she should be burned alive if it can be proved; otherwise, the man should accept judicial combat and the woman should take the iron. If someone sells a Christian and flees, he should never be reconciled with the council.

48. The woman who is surprised with an infidel

If a woman is surprised with a Moor or with a Jew, both should be burned alive.

49. Who injures or kills a pregnant woman

Whoever kills a pregnant woman should pay the fine for double homicide if the plaintiff can prove it; but if not, he should clear himself as in the case of double homicide. If he only injures her, and because of this she miscarries, he should pay the fine for wounds and for homicide if she proves it; but if not, he should clear himself as it is in the code on homicide and likewise on wounds.

50. The wife whom the husband suspects

If any husband has suspicion that his wife is unfaithful, but he cannot prove the truth of the deed, the woman should give him juridical satisfaction, swearing with twelve female residents, and she should be believed; and if she cannot give satisfaction, the husband can abandon her with impunity.

51. The nurse who gives bad milk to the child whom she nurtures

If the nurse gives bad milk to the child whom she nurtures, and because of this the child dies, the corresponding pecuniary penalties being paid, she should depart as an enemy.

CHAPTER XII
Insults to Men and Many Other Violent Acts

1. Insults to men and many other violent acts

Whoever calls a man treacherous or traitor to his face should pay ten *aurei* if he cannot prove [the truth of] what was said with proper witnesses.

2. He who is accused of [being a] traitor

If someone is accused of being a traitor, he should clear himself by means of judicial combat; if he wins, he should be reinstated in the field and collect the pecuniary penalty cited above; if he loses, he should be expelled from the city and his house should be demolished to the very foundations. But if the accusation is betrayal of the castle or the death of or wounding of the *Señor*, one should abide by the penalty cited above.

3. He who calls someone a leper

He who calls someone a leper, horn-bearer [cuckold], fornicator, or son of a fornicator should pay two *aurei* if he [the victim] can prove it; and likewise, he [the perpetrator] should swear with two citizens that they are not aware that he dishonored him; otherwise if he does not want to swear it, he should depart as our enemy; if he denies it and [the victim] cannot prove it, he should swear with two citizens that he has not said this, and he should be believed.

4. He who puts his hands in anger in another's hair

Whoever puts his hands angrily in the hair of another should pay five *aurei*; and if he throws him to the ground, he should pay ten *aurei* if the plaintiff can prove it; but if not, he should be cleared by two of four named from his parish.

5. He who pushes another violently

Whoever pushes another out of indignation should pay two *aurei*; if from the force of the push [the victim] falls to the ground, he [the pusher] should pay ten *aurei*; if he leaves welts because of this, he should pay thirty *aurei*, if he is declared guilty with witnesses; but if not, he should be cleared with two of four named from his parish, as it is in the code, and he should be believed.

6. He who hits another with his fist

Whoever hits another, with his fist or with the palm of his hand, from the shoulders upward should pay ten *aurei* for each blow; if he causes welts, he should pay twenty *aurei* if he admits it; but if not, he should clear himself with two of four named from his parish. Whoever hits another, with the fist or with the palm of the hand, from the shoulders downward should pay two *aurei* for each blow, provided that he injured him in a spirit of anger; if he denies it, he should clear himself with two of four named from his parish and he should be believed.

7. He who causes welts on the neck or on the face of another

Anyone who claws another on the neck or on the face should pay two *aurei*; if he denies it, he should clear himself with two of four named from his parish and he should be believed.

8. He who ruptures one eye of another

Whoever ruptures the eye of another should pay one hundred *aurei*; if he denies it, he should clear himself with twelve citizens or he should respond by judicial combat.

9. He who breaks another's tooth

Whoever breaks another's tooth should pay twenty *aurei*; if he denies it, he should be cleared with twelve citizens or he should respond by judicial combat.

10. He who cuts off someone's finger

Whoever cuts off someone's finger should pay twenty *aurei*; if he denies it, he should clear himself with twelve citizens or he should respond by judicial combat.

11. He who cuts off someone's thumb

Anybody who cuts off someone's thumb should pay fifty *aurei*; if he denies it, he should clear himself with twelve citizens or he should respond by judicial combat.

12. He who cuts off someone's arm

Anybody who breaks someone's arm should pay fifty *aurei*. He who cuts it off, should pay one hundred *aurei*. If he denies it, he should clear himself with twelve citizens or respond by judicial combat.

13. He who breaks someone's leg

Anyone who breaks someone's leg[1] should pay fifty *aurei*. He who cuts off another's foot, should pay one hundred *aurei*. If he denies it, he should clear himself with twelve citizens or respond by judicial combat.

14. He who cuts off someone's ear

Anyone who cuts off someone's ear should pay ten *aurei*. If he cuts off both [ears], he should pay twenty *aurei*; if he denies it, he should clear himself with twelve citizens or respond by judicial combat.

15. He who cuts off someone's nose

Anyone who cuts off someone's nose should pay fifty *aurei*; if he cuts off his nose together with the lip, he should pay one hundred *aurei*; if he denies it, he should clear himself with twelve citizens or respond by judicial combat.

16. He who castrates a man

Whoever castrates a man, should pay two hundred *aurei* and should depart as our enemy; if he denies it, he should be cleared with twelve citizens or he should fight in judicial combat. However, if he surprises him with his wife or with his daughter and he castrates him, he should pay nothing.

17. He who shaves a man

Whoever shaves a man should pay ten *aurei* and, moreover, look after him in his house, treating him as if it had been himself, until the hair or the beard should have grown back; if he denies it, he should clear himself with two of four named from his parish and he should be believed.

18. He who scalps someone's beard

Whoever scalps someone's beard should pay two hundred *aurei* and he should depart as our enemy if the plaintiff can prove it; but if not, he should clear himself with twelve citizens and should be believed, or he should respond by judicial combat.

19. He who injures someone in the tribunal

Whoever in the sessions of the tribunal, in front of the door of the *iudex*, in the tribunal of the *alcaldi*, in the council, or in the market does something such that he has to pay a pecuniary penalty because of it, should pay it double; as, for example, if someone takes up illegal weapons, he should pay twenty *aurei*; if he injures someone, he should pay forty *aurei*; if he causes wounds, sixty *aurei*; if he causes a bone-fracturing injury, one hundred *aurei*; if he kills, four hundred *aurei*; he who denies it, should swear with twelve citizens and should be believed. Whoever injures someone with his fist, pulls hair, or insults another should pay the same double fine; if he denies it, he should clear himself with four named from his parish. Likewise, the *iudex* or the *alcaldus* should pay when he injures or abuses his companions in the tribunal.

20. The malefactor [as] prisoner

Anyone who injures a prisoner being held for the of commission of a crime before [the prisoner] is condemned by sentence of the council should pay hundred *aurei* to the *iudex* and to the *alcaldi*. If he cannot pay, he should lose his right hand.

21. He who challenges someone

Whoever challenges someone in the council, in the market, in front of the door of the *iudex*, in the tribunal of the *alcaldi*, or in the fairs, without order of the *alcaldi*, should pay one hundred *aurei*; and those who took part with the insulter should each pay fifty *aurei*; and, also, the insulter should reinstate him [the victim] before he goes from the council, from the door of the *iudex*, from the tribunal, or from the market or the fairs. If he doesn't want to do it, the *iudex* should put him in prison, from which he should not leave until he reinstates him [the victim] and he pays the fine. Moreover there are insulting words which are equal to a challenge, such as these: "you swore falsely," or "you swore a lie" or calling one "false" or "traitor," or saying "I will make you [say] the truth," or "I will engage you in judicial combat over this," and other similar things.

22. The grabbing of reins

Anyone who pulls his hands violently on the reins which the *miles* holds, or stops his horse so that he [the rider] is thrown, should pay three hundred *solidi* if the *miles* can prove it; otherwise, he should clear himself with twelve citizens and should be believed.

23. The stopping of a *miles*

Whoever makes a *miles* descend from his horse by force should pay five hundred *solidi* if the *miles* can prove it; but if not, he should clear himself with twelve citizens and should be believed. Anyone who mistreats another with spurs or goads should pay three hundred *solidi* if the plaintiff can prove it; but if not, he should clear himself with twelve citizens and should be believed.

24. He who hurts a man by kicking [him]

Whoever hurts another by kicking [him] should pay ten *aurei*; if [the kicker] causes him wounds, he should pay twenty *aurei*, if the plaintiff can prove it; but if not, [the kicker] should clear himself with two of four named from his parish. If he kicks while [the victim] is standing, [the kicker] should pay one *aureus* for each kick if [the victim] can prove it; but if not, [the accused] should clear himself with two of four named from his parish and he should be believed.

25. He who hits another on the buttocks

Whoever hits another on the buttocks should pay five *solidi* for each hit if the plaintiff can prove it; but if not, he should clear himself with two of four named from his parish and should be believed.

26. He who seizes by one of the ears

Whoever seizes another by the ear should pay the same fine that we have cited above for the hair.

27. He who hurts another in a game with a kick or in another manner

If someone hurts another in a game with a kick or in another manner, he should pay nothing, unless the injured one can prove that he was outside of the game; then if someone hurts him after being outside of the game, [the one who hurts him] has to pay the pecuniary penalty of the crime that he has committed, according to the Code of Cuenca.

28. He who is surprised in sodomy

Whoever is surprised in sodomy should be burned alive. He who says to another: "I will fornicate with you through the anus," if [the witness] can prove that this is true, both [speaker and person spoken to] should be burned alive; but if not, the one who told such a dishonor should be burned alive.

29. He who puts his backside in the face of another

Whoever puts his backside in the face of another or farts in his face should pay three hundred *solidi* and depart as our enemy, if he [the victim] can prove it; but if not, he [the accused] should swear with twelve citizens and should be believed.

30. He who injures someone with an egg

Whoever injures someone with an egg, with a *butello*, or with a *cucumere* [two kinds of cucumber], or with any other thing that can dirty him should pay ten *aurei* if the plaintiff can prove it; but if not, he should clear himself with two of four named from his parish and he should be believed.

31. He who compels another to swallow some filthy [thing]

If someone compels another to eat up some filthy [thing] by force or deceit, or he puts it in his mouth or in his face, he should pay three hundred *solidi* and depart as our enemy, if he [the victim] proves it with witnesses; but if not, he should clear himself as in the case of homicide.

32. He who makes a ballad

Whoever invents an abusive ballad about another, should pay ten *aurei*, if [the accuser] can prove it; but if not, [the accused] should swear with two of four named from his parish and should be believed.

33. The weakened limb

Whoever injures another in any limb, causing the loss of its strength, should pay the fine that has been noted above on the subject of the amputation of a limb.

34. The stick

Whoever thrusts a stick into the anus of another outside his house should pay two hundred *aurei* and depart as an enemy, if it can be proved; but if not, he should be cleared with twelve citizens and he should be believed, or he should swear alone and respond to the challenge by judicial combat, whichever pleases the plaintiff more.

CHAPTER XIII
No One Should Respond for Counseling

1. No one should respond for giving advice

I command that no one should respond or pay any fine for giving advice. However, he should respond if he advises the selling of a Christian. I also command that each one should pay the same fine, even if he should go in assistance of another and the fight should be another's fight.

2. Whoever takes part in a gang should pay, except their wives

Whoever takes part in a gang in order to lend aid to someone should pay double the pecuniary fine for the crime that they have committed, even though he should be that one's son or his blood kin, except for his wife; if the wife takes part in the gang of her husband, or if the latter is in the gang of his wife, the couple do not have to pay double [fines] for this, since it is a single fine for both.

3. He who holds another's wife

If someone holds another's wife, he should pay three hundred *solidi* and should be considered an enemy.

4. He who sells food to the Muslims

Whoever sells or gives weapons or food to the Muslims let him be hurled from the city cliffs, if it can be proved; but if not, he should clear himself with twelve citizens and should be believed; or he should swear alone and respond to the challenge by judicial combat, the one which pleases the council more. We call food bread, cheese, and everything which one can eat, except for living livestock.

5. The servant who kills or injures a Christian

If someone's servant or Moor hurts or kills a Christian, his master should pay the fine for the crime that he has committed or he should put the injurer in the hands of the plaintiff, the servant's master choosing that which pleases him more.

6. The portion of the pecuniary penalties which the *alcaldi* should not have

Moreover, I command that neither the Palace nor the *alcaldi* should have a part of the pecuniary penalties for the crimes of dishonoring, of pushing, of pulling hair, or in the challenging to combat, if not done in the council, in the market, in the tribunal, or in front of the door of the *iudex*. The above fines should belong to those who suffer the offense. However, the *alcaldi* should demand the fourth part of the fines, allotting their amount for the work on the walls, and rendering an account for the money from these fines.

7. The profanation of graves

Whoever digs up a cadaver should pay five hundred *solidi*, since he has thrown it violently from its resting place. If someone steals the tombstones of a sepulcher or otherwise seizes them, he is obliged to respond by reason of theft.

Whoever robs the clothing of the dead should pay five hundred *solidi*, because he has violated a grave; but if not [proven], for each one of these things he should clear himself with twelve citizens and should be believed.

8. He who boasts of another's woman

Whoever boasts of another's woman, should pay three hundred *solidi*, and he should depart as an enemy, if it can be proved; but if not, he should clear himself with twelve citizens or he should respond by judicial combat.

9. She who gets married against the will of her parents

The woman who gets married against the will of her parents should be disinherited and [become] the enemy of her parents.

10. No one should respond without the plaintiff

No one should respond for a fine without the plaintiff, not even for debt, both as much for the fine as for the debt, if the plaintiff does not give bondsmen, so that if anyone later reclaims the fine or the debt, the bondsmen should pay double to the defendant.

11. The brother who complains to the *alcaldi*

Whoever takes sureties to the one who complains to the *alcaldi* or to the *iudex* for a pact of confraternity should return double the sureties and, also, he should pay ten *aurei to* the *iudex* and the *alcaldi*.

12. The outsider artisan

Whoever meets an artisan from another region working in the district of Cuenca should take him prisoner without any penalty until he is redeemed. We make it this way, so that the artisan citizens of Cuenca should earn more, and also so that all the villagers should come to the city market.

13. The murdered person who does not have relatives

If someone kills a person who has no relatives, the *señor* on whose property [the victim] is found should challenge him and charge the pecuniary penalties. If he is not located on someone's property, the one whom the deceased had designated as a relative and who [the deceased] had ordered to receive the pecuniary penalties should challenge [the killer] on behalf of [the deceased]. If the deceased dies without making a will and he is not found on the property of someone, the one who should bury him should challenge on the victim's behalf and collect the pecuniary penalties, and procure himself greater honor.

14. He who gives his animal to a mediator

Whoever gives his animal to a mediator, if he who received it loses it, he [the mediator] should pay [the owner] half the value of the animal and nothing more; but if the animal died, he should not pay anything for that which he received, swearing that it did not die because of his fault.

15. He who having an item of his own reclaims it

If someone has an item belonging to someone else who reclaims it, he should pay double as a thief to him who reclaims it, and to the Palace the ninth [of its value], if the possessor has not purchased it from the other.

16. He who denies borrowing it

If someone has borrowed [an object], such as a plow, a shovel, a pitchfork, or other things of this type, and fails to return it to him, [the borrower] should pay the damage that ensues up to a value of five *menkales*, by the oath of the plaintiff; from five to ten, by oath of the plaintiff and of a citizen; from ten up, by oath of the plaintiff and of two citizens.

17. Latrines

Everyone who has an uncovered latrine in view of any street should pay five *aurei* daily until he covers it. If the latrine causes a bad smell by a street or in the vicinity, and the owner of the latrine does not repair it in the three days following the warning, [the owner] should pay one *aureus* daily until he repairs it. For these pecuniary penalties the *almutazaf* should take sureties and divide them with the plaintiff, in conformance with that established in the code.

18. The prohibition of windows

Whoever has a wall of his house in another's corral and wants to open a window in that [wall] should open it to a height above the chest. The window has to be one hand wide only and not more. If someone makes it lower or wider, he should pay an *aureus* to the owner of the corral, to the *iudex*, and to the *alcaldi* daily until he should close it.

19. The drains of houses

Each house should receive the drainage of another, according to how it seems to the *iudex* and to the *alcaldi*, until the water goes out to the street or to the location of a fall.

No one should make a trash heap on another's property, except on the public land. Whoever wants to build a house should receive land on the common land of the council. If someone breaks the precept of this law, he should pay five *aurei* daily until he rectifies it, by agreement with what is established.

20. The departure of a citizen from his parish

No parish should respond for the citizen who has not been given to it and is not registered in the census. The citizen should never leave his parish until he pays all the money for which he remained obligated to the parish as its citizen. After his departure, he is not required to respond for obligation or debt of the parish contracted subsequently. The departure should take place on Saturday at the time of vespers, or on Sunday at the time of mass.

CHAPTER XIV

The Penalties for Murderers:
The Challenged

1. All murderers should pay two hundred *aurei* and the eighth part of three hundred *aurei*, and should depart as enemies

Whoever commits a homicide should pay the fine of two hundred *aurei* and to me, the eighth part of three hundred *aurei*. The remainder of this three hundred *aurei* remains for you [citizens of Cuenca], for love of God and for your disposal. Then these three hundred *aurei* return to me by right, in order to do with them what seems to me [best]. The murderer, after paying the pecuniary penalties and the eighth part of the fine of homicide, should depart as an enemy. Nevertheless, before he should pay the pecuniary penalties and depart as an enemy, he should be challenged on Sunday before the council in this manner.

2. The nearest relatives of the dead should challenge the murderers only and not another; this should remain the choice of the *alcaldi*

The nearest relatives of the dead should challenge before the council on Sunday all those who have injured or killed, and also those who have ordered it, up to five and not more. If there are four, three, or two principals in the homicide, only these should be challenged and not others. If there is only one murderer, he only should be challenged and no other. Therefore, I command that no one should challenge those who are free of blame for homicide because of hate or for money.

If someone is challenged and he denies the homicide, the *alcaldi* should see and investigate diligently if the accused has blame in the homicide or not; if he has blame, he should pay and depart as an enemy, as it has been said; but if he does not have [blame], he neither pays nor departs as an enemy. However, if the challenged [person] promises that he is going to prove with witnesses that he does not have blame in the homicide, he should do it before the third Friday following and he should respond by judicial combat; but if not, it should not be legal.[1]

3. The stranger who wants to challenge

There are many who are not the kin of the dead and, nevertheless, out of greed for the fines, pass themselves off as relatives and can be included in the same homicide, in order to better themselves intentionally. Thus, should any unknown relative challenge, we command, in order to avoid all these tricks, that any stranger that should challenge a citizen first should give valid bondsmen before the council that he will pay all the kin for the right which obtains in the judgment, so that no one demand it for this reason. If he does not do that, either to validate one or to challenge the other, he should give juridical satisfaction. The bondsmen being given, he should swear with two citizens that there is not another closer relative of the deceased in the nearby territory; this done, the suspect should respond to him.

4. He who wants to greet his enemy

Everybody who wants to greet his enemy should greet him before the council on Sunday and not in another place.

5. No one should challenge for a homicide more than once

No one should challenge for a homicide more than once.

6. The challenger should give a truce to his enemy until the first Friday

After the plaintiff has challenged his enemies on Sunday, as has been said, he should give him a truce until the first Friday following. If the challenged does not present himself that Friday to give judicial satisfaction, the challenger should strike him down without any penalty. However, he should not lose the case until three Fridays have lapsed from the day on which he challenged him, as it will be noted later on.

7. A single challenged [person] who confesses in the presence of the *alcaldi*

If there is only one challenged person and on Friday he confesses before the *alcaldi*, he should pay the pecuniary penalties and he should be an enemy in perpetuity. If he denies [the charge], he should clear himself with twelve citizens and be greeted,[2] or he should swear alone and should be challenged [to combat]; this remains the choice of the plaintiff. If he is challenged and he loses on the field, he should pay the pecuniary penalties and should depart as an enemy for good. If he remains victorious, he should be reinstated on the field and greeted in the council.

8. Two challenged persons confess

If there are two challenged persons and both confess on Friday, they should pay jointly all the fines; later, the plaintiff should choose which of the challenged should depart as an enemy in perpetuity and which for one year.

9. Two challenged persons, of whom one confesses and the other does not

If one of the challenged persons confesses and the other does not, the confessed should pay half of the fine and should be an enemy in perpetuity; the other should swear with twelve citizens and should be greeted, or he should swear alone and respond to challenge by combat, whichever the plaintiff prefers. If he fights in judicial combat and wins, he should be reinstated on the field and greeted in the council. If he is beaten, he should pay half of the fine and depart as an enemy in perpetuity.

If they both deny it, the plaintiff should choose which of the two should fight in judicial combat. If he is victorious, he should be reinstated on the field and greeted in the council. If he is vanquished, he should pay half of the pecuniary penalties and depart as an enemy in perpetuity; the other should clear himself with twelve citizens and should be greeted; if he cannot complete it [clear himself], he should pay half of the pecuniary penalties and depart as an enemy for one year.

10. Three challenged persons confess

If there are three challenged persons and all confess on Friday, they should pay jointly the pecuniary penalties. Later, the plaintiff should choose which of them ought to depart as an enemy for a year and which in perpetuity; the third should be greeted. If one of the three challenged confesses and the other two do not, the confessed [one] should pay half of the fine and depart as an enemy in perpetuity. Later, the plaintiff should choose which of the remainder ought to fight in judicial combat. If he who fights is beaten, he should pay half of the fine and should be an enemy for one year. If he wins, he should be reinstated on the field and greeted in the council. The third should clear himself with twelve citizens and should be greeted. If he cannot clear himself, he should depart as an enemy for one year.

11. Three challenged persons, of whom two confess and the other does not

If there are two confessed persons and a third who is not, the confessed [ones] should pay all the pecuniary penalties. Later, the plaintiff should choose which of the confessed ought to depart as an enemy for a year and which in perpetuity. The third should clear himself with twelve citizens and should be greeted. If he cannot clear himself, he should depart as an enemy for one year.

12. Four challenged persons confess

If there are four challenged persons and all confess on the Friday, they should pay jointly all the pecuniary penalties. Later, the plaintiff should choose which of the challenged ought to depart as an enemy for a year and which in perpetuity; the two reinstated should be greeted.

13. Only one confesses and the other three do not

If only one person confesses and the other three do not, the confessed should pay half the fine and depart as an enemy in perpetuity. Later, the plaintiff should choose which of the three reinstated ought to fight in judicial combat; if he wins, he should be reinstated on the field and greeted in the council; if he is beaten, he should pay half the fine and depart as an enemy for a year. Each one of the other two should clear himself with twelve citizens and should be greeted. He who cannot clear himself should depart as an enemy for one year.

14. Four challenged persons, of whom two confess and the other two do not

If there are two confessed persons and two not, the confessed should pay all the pecuniary penalties. Later, the plaintiff should choose which of the confessed ought to depart as an enemy for a year and which in perpetuity; then each one of the other two should clear himself with twelve citizens and should be greeted. He who cannot clear himself should depart as an enemy for one year.

15. Four challenged persons, of whom three confess and one does not

If there are three confessed persons and one not, the confessed should pay all the pecuniary penalties. Later, the plaintiff should choose which of those three ought to depart as an enemy for a year and which in perpetuity. The third confessed person should be greeted; the fourth, who denies [the charge], should clear himself with twelve citizens and should be greeted. If he cannot clear himself, he should depart as an enemy for one year.

16. Five challenged persons confess

If there are five challenged persons and all confess on the Friday, they should pay jointly all the pecuniary penalties. Later, the plaintiff should choose which of the challenged ought to depart as an enemy for a year and which in perpetuity; the reinstated three should be greeted.

17. Five challenged persons, of whom one confesses and four do not

If one person confesses and four do not, the confessed should pay half of the fine and depart as an enemy in perpetuity. Later, the plaintiff should choose which of the others ought to fight in judicial combat; if he wins, he should be reinstated on the field and greeted in the council; if he is beaten, he should pay half of the fine and depart as an enemy for a year. Each one of the others should clear himself with twelve citizens and should be greeted. He who cannot clear himself should depart as an enemy for one year. If there are two confessed persons and the other three are not, the confessed should pay all the pecuniary penalties. Later, the plaintiff should choose which of the confessed ought to depart as an enemy for a year and which in perpetuity. Each one of the other two should clear himself with twelve citizens and should be greeted. He who cannot clear himself should depart as an enemy for one year.

18. Five challenged persons, of whom three confess and two do not

If there are three confessed persons and two are not, the confessed should pay all the pecuniary penalties. Later, the plaintiff should choose which of the confessed ought to depart as an enemy for a year and which in perpetuity; the third confessed should be greeted. Each one of the others who denies [the charge] should clear himself with twelve citizens and should be greeted. He who cannot clear himself should depart as an enemy for one year.

19. Five challenged persons, of whom four confess and one does not

If there are four confessed persons and one is not, the confessed should pay all the pecuniary penalties. Later, the plaintiff should choose which of the confessed ought to depart as an enemy for a year and which in perpetuity. The two confessed and reinstated persons should be greeted; the fifth, who denies [the charge], should clear himself with twelve citizens and should be greeted. If he cannot clear himself, he should depart as an enemy for one year.

20. Only one person challenged who does not present himself before the tribunal

If there is only one person challenged and he is not present to give juridical satisfaction on the Friday, that one alone should pay all the pecuniary penalties and depart as an enemy in perpetuity.

21. Two challenged persons who do not present themselves before the tribunal

If there are two challenged persons and neither of them presents himself before the tribunal, the plaintiff should choose which of the confessed ought to depart as an enemy for a year and which in perpetuity; and they also should pay all the pecuniary penalties, in conformance with the code.

22. Two challenged persons, of whom one presents himself before the tribunal and the other does not

If one person presents himself and the other does not, and he who presents himself confesses, he should pay half of the pecuniary penalties and depart as an enemy for a year; but if this one denies it, he who has not presented himself should pay half of the pecuniary penalties and depart as an enemy in perpetuity; the non-confessed should clear himself with twelve citizens or he should swear alone and respond by judicial combat, that which most pleases the plaintiff. If he fights in judicial combat and wins, he should be reinstated on the field and greeted in the council; if he is beaten, he should pay half of the fine and depart as an enemy for a year.

23. Three challenged persons, of whom one presents himself before the tribunal and two do not

If there are three challenged persons and one presents himself before the tribunal and two do not, those who have not presented themselves should pay all the pecuniary penalties and depart as enemies, one in perpetuity and the other for a year. The one who has presented himself should clear himself with twelve citizens and should be greeted. If he cannot clear himself, he should depart as an enemy for one year.

24. Three challenged persons, of whom two present themselves before the tribunal and the other does not

If two persons present themselves and the third does not, he who has not presented himself should pay half the fine and depart as an enemy in perpetuity. Of the two who have presented themselves, the plaintiff should choose which of them ought to fight in judicial combat; if he wins, he should be reinstated on the field and greeted in the council; if he is beaten, he should pay half of the fine and depart as an enemy in perpetuity. The third should clear himself with twelve citizens and should be greeted. If he cannot clear himself, he should depart as an enemy for one year.

25. Three challenged persons, none of whom present themselves before the tribunal

If none of the three challenged persons present themselves before the tribunal, they should pay conjointly all the pecuniary penalties. Later, the plaintiff should choose which of them ought to depart as an enemy for a year and which in perpetuity; when the third presents himself,[3] if the pecuniary penalties have been paid, he should be greeted.

26. Four challenged persons, of whom one presents himself before the tribunal and three do not

If there are four challenged persons and one presents himself before the tribunal and the other three do not, those who have not presented themselves should pay all the pecuniary penalties; one of them should depart as an enemy for one year and the other in perpetuity; when the third presents himself, if the pecuniary penalties have been paid, he should be greeted; the fourth, who has presented himself, should clear himself with twelve citizens and should be greeted. If he cannot clear himself, he should depart as an enemy for one year.

27. Four challenged persons, of whom two present themselves before the tribunal and two do not

If two persons present themselves and the other two do not, the ones who have not presented themselves should depart as enemies, one for one year and the other in perpetuity, and they should pay all the pecuniary penalties. Of the two who have presented themselves, each one of them should clear himself with twelve citizens and should be greeted. He who cannot clear himself, should depart as an enemy for one year.

28. Four challenged persons, of whom three present themselves before the tribunal and one does not

If three persons present themselves and one does not, he who has not presented himself should pay half the fine and should be an enemy in perpetuity. One of the three who has presented himself should pay half the pecuniary penalties and should be an enemy for a year, if he fights in a judicial combat and is beaten. But if he wins, he should be reinstated on the field and greeted in the council; in addition it should remain the choice of the plaintiff as to which of those ought to fight in judicial combat. Each one of the others should clear himself with twelve citizens and should be greeted. And he who cannot clear himself should depart as an enemy for one year.

29. Four challenged persons, none of whom present themselves before the tribunal

If none of the four challenged persons present themselves before the tribunal, all should pay conjointly the pecuniary penalties cited above. One of them should depart as an enemy for a year and another in perpetuity. The two who have not departed as enemies, the pecuniary penalties paid when they present themselves, should be greeted.

30. Five challenged persons, of whom one presents himself and four do not

If there are five challenged persons and one presents himself and four do not, those who have not presented themselves should pay all the pecuniary penalties. One of them should depart as an enemy for one year and another in perpetuity. When the other two present themselves, with the pecuniary penalties paid, they should be greeted; the fifth, who has presented himself, should clear himself with twelve citizens and should be greeted. If he cannot clear himself, he should depart as an enemy for one year.

31. Five challenged persons, of whom four present themselves before the tribunal and one does not

If four persons present themselves and one does not, he who has not presented himself should pay half the fine and should be an enemy in perpetuity. Later, the plaintiff should choose which one of those who have presented themselves ought to fight in judicial combat. If he wins, he should be reinstated on the field and greeted in the council. If he loses, he should pay half the fine and should be an enemy for a year. Each one of the other three should clear himself with twelve citizens and should be greeted. And he who cannot clear himself should depart as an enemy for one year.

32. Five challenged persons, of whom three present themselves before the tribunal and two do not

If three persons present themselves and two do not, the ones who have not presented themselves should pay all the pecuniary penalties and depart as enemies, one for one year and the other in perpetuity. Each one of the other three who have presented themselves should clear himself with twelve citizens and should be greeted. He who cannot clear himself should depart as an enemy for one year.

33. Five challenged persons, of whom two present themselves before the tribunal and three do not

If two persons present themselves and three do not, the ones who have not presented themselves should pay all the pecuniary penalties and depart as enemies, one for one year and another in perpetuity. The third of those who have not presented themselves, paying all the pecuniary penalties when he presents himself [if the first two did not], should be greeted. Each one of the two who have presented themselves should clear himself with twelve citizens and should be greeted. He who cannot clear himself should depart as an enemy for one year.

34. Five challenged persons, none of whom present themselves before the tribunal

If none of the five challenged persons present themselves before the tribunal, all should pay conjointly the pecuniary penalties; one of them departs as an enemy for a year and another in perpetuity. The other three, when they present themselves, paying the fines, should be greeted.

35. The day the plaintiff ought to designate in the council who should be his enemy for one year and who in perpetuity

On the third Friday, the session of the tribunal of the plaza closes for those who have not presented themselves; the first Sunday following the day of the session of the tribunal, the plaintiff should designate in the council whom he wants to depart as an enemy for a year and whom in perpetuity.

36. What the challenged person who does not present himself before the tribunal has to lose

Any challenged person who does not present himself before the tribunal should lose all the property that he has, both movable goods and real estate, for the aforementioned pecuniary penalties, until he pays all the fines.

37. He who protects the property of a murderer

Whoever protects some of the goods of a murderer who has fled should pay all the pecuniary penalties of that person.

38. He who has some of the goods of a fled murderer

If someone has some of the goods of a fled murderer, he should surrender them to the *iudex* and the *alcaldi*, and they should have the power to sell them, pledge them, or corroborate whatever of the goods they hold until they are able to guarantee the value of the pecuniary penalties.

39. How the suspect has to give judicial satisfaction for concealing the goods of a murderer

Whoever the *iudex* and the *alcaldi* believe hides something of the goods of a murderer should give them judicial satisfaction by swearing with two citizens, and they should be believed.

40. He who buys some of the goods of a murderer

If someone buys some of the goods of a murderer before he pays the pecuniary penalties, the sale should not be legal.

41. How the murderer has to pay the pecuniary penalties

The murderer should pay the fine for homicide after he has been declared at fault in the plaza within twenty-seven days in this way: in the first nine days he should pay a third part of the aforementioned fine in clothing; in the nine days following, another third in livestock; the other third part in gold, in the last nine days. But if he has not paid all the fine in the plaza within the twenty-seven days, as has been said, for that which remains the relatives of the deceased should cut off his right hand and, moreover, he should depart as an enemy.

42. How many *aurei* the fine ought to be worth

Whoever has to pay *aurei* for the fine should pay them at a rate of three and a half *menkales* per *aureus*.

43. The *iudex* holds the murderer prisoner

The *iudex* should hold the murderer in prison if he does not give bondsmen for the aforementioned fine.

44. The bondsmen who cannot hold the murderer

If the bondsmen are not able to hold the murderer on the day assigned for the litigation, as the code states, they should pay all the pecuniary penalties that they pledged. If they are not able to pay them, they should enter the prison of the *iudex* until they should pay them.

45. The challengers and not their relatives collect the money of the fine

The challengers, be they one or several, should collect the part of the money of the pecuniary penalties that belongs to them, and to no other, if they have challenged legitimately.

46. He who committed some crime and is made prisoner upon fleeing

If someone injures or kills a man, and upon fleeing is made a prisoner by the *iudex* or by the *alcaldi*, and in the prison a relative of the one killed or hurt or any other who is not a relative injures or kills him [the prisoner] before he is declared guilty according to law, [he who injured or killed the prisoner] should pay double the fine of the crime that has been committed and should depart as an enemy. If others beside the *alcaldi* arrest [someone who injured or killed the prisoner], and they do not defend him until he gives bondsmen in accordance with the Code of Cuenca, and he is injured or killed while in their power, those who have killed or wounded him should pay double the fine for the crime that they have committed.

47. Those who stop him from fleeing

If those who have arrested him do not retain and guard him until they surrender him to the *iudex* and to the *alcaldi*, and by chance he escapes them, they should pay all the pecuniary penalties. But those who have arrested him should not pay anything for the death of the prisoner if he has been injured or killed against their will.

48. He who kills a prisoner

He who kills a prisoner, should he be in the town or outside of it, should pay double the fine for the crime that he has committed.

CHAPTER XV
Surety Bondsmen

1. He who kills a man over surety bond, security, or guarantee

I command that whoever kills a man regarding a surety bond, security, or guarantee, if he flees, should pay four hundred *aurei*, as has been said. If he is made a prisoner, let him be hurled from the city cliffs.

2. The *fuero* of the surety bondsmen

If the *alcaldi* do not discover where to collect the payment of the pecuniary penalties, the surety bondsmen should pay them all in the term of twenty-seven days; namely, a third part in clothing, another third part in livestock, and the other third part in gold. If they do not pay this fine in the term of twenty-seven days as has been said, the term being lapsed, they should be deprived of food and drink until they perish of hunger and thirst in prison.

3. The surety bondsmen who can hold the accused

If the surety bondsmen can hold the accused and put him in the hands of the *iudex*, they should remain safe and free of that bond.

4. The murderer who denies the bond

If the murderer denies the surety bond, the secretary of the council should confirm it with the *iudex* or with an *alcaldus*, and he should pay as has been said. If the secretary or the *iudex* does not discover the bond, two *alcaldi* confirm it, and he should pay, as it is in the code. If they are not able to prove the surety bond, as has been said, and the murderer alone admits the death, he should pay two hundred *aurei*. For the surety bond the plaintiff should choose, or the murderer should swear with twelve residents and should be believed, or he should swear alone and respond by judicial combat; if he loses, he should suffer the capital penalty, as has been said before many times; if he wins, he should pay two hundred *aurei* and depart as an enemy, as it is in the code; but he remains safe from [the charge] of betrayal. If he denies the death and the surety bond and cannot prove it with witnesses, he should be cleared with twelve residents or respond to judicial combat; if he loses, let him be hurled from the city cliffs; if he wins, he should be reinstated on the field and greeted in the council. If the traitor succeeds in fleeing and the surety bondsmen deny the bond, the *iudex* or those *alcaldi* should prove that [the bondsmen] received them, and [the bondsmen] should pay four hundred *aurei*. If [the *iudex* or the *alcaldi*] are not able to prove it, [the bondsmen] should be left in peace and no one should disturb them hereafter for that cause. If the *iudex* or the *alcaldi* who received the bondsmen are no longer living, each one of the bondsmen should clear himself with twelve residents and should be believed; if they are not able to clear themselves, they should pay four hundred *aurei* for the above pecuniary penalties.

5. In what time period the bondsmen should be renewed

For the above reasons, so that such bonds should not be cast into forgetfulness, we have considered it just to establish in the code that all the surety bondsmen should be renewed every year in the council and that the secretary should register them for the term of thirty days, starting from the feast of Saint Michael.

6. In what manner should surety bondsmen be given

Whoever should give surety bondsmen in accordance with the Code of Cuenca, should give them for himself and for all his kin who reside within the district of Cuenca.

7. He who does not want to give surety bondsmen

He who is suspect and does not want to give surety bondsmen in accordance with the Code of Cuenca, should give them, although it is against his will, within a term of three days. But if he still persists in not wanting to give them in any way, the *iudex* and the *alcaldi* should arrest him and he should remain in the stocks three days. The three days having passed, he should be expelled from the city. After he has been expelled from the city, if he is again found in the town or in its district, the *iudex* should detain him for a fine of one hundred *aurei*, and the *señor* of the house in which his presence is attested should pay as much again.

8. The confessed enemy who returns to the city before being greeted, and his presence is attested in some house

If, after having departed from the city, the opponents of a confessed enemy attest that he is found again in the city or in its villages, the *señor* of the house in which his presence is attested should pay one hundred *aurei*. Even if [his opponents] cannot attest his presence in any house, however, if they suspect that someone has received him in his house, he [the suspected householder] should agree himself to swear with twelve residents that, after having been expelled from the city [the confessed enemy] has not entered again into [the householder's] house and he should be believed. But if he does not want to swear it or he cannot complete the oath, he should pay one hundred *aurei*, as it has been said above.

9. The [person] injured with illegal weapons who injures or kills the one who hurt him

Although earlier the code ordered that everyone who injures or kills someone should pay for the crime, nonetheless if someone injures another earlier with illegal weapons or he thrusts his hand into the beard, and he who has suffered the insult then hurts or kills that one, he [who endured the earlier injury] should not pay for the crime or depart as an enemy.

10. All the goods, as much of the murderer as of his wife, should be seized for the husband's crime

Since there are places and peoples that have the custom and the code concerning when the husband commits a homicide, a robbery, or a similar crime for which he has to lose all property, that his wife should withdraw half first, identifying all the goods that belong to her, and the other half should be seized for the fine; in order to eradicate this custom, we command that anyone who kills or betrays a man or commits any other crime of this nature and succeeds in fleeing, the *iudex* should seize all the goods, as much of the husband as of the wife, for the fine of the crime that has been committed, even though the real estate or furnishings are the wife's and not the husband's; because it should not surprise [one] that, if the wife is accustomed frequently to enjoy the gains that her husband brings her, she ought to endure sometimes the loss of the goods because of her husband. It is just that those accustomed to sharing the same happiness should also participate in sadness when it arrives. Once the fine is paid, that which remains of furnishings or immovable goods or of the money should be returned to the wife, or to those who should inherit her goods.

11. The relatives of those punished with the capital penalty have a right to their goods

But if a person suffers the capital penalty because of the commission of a crime, the nearest relatives should inherit his goods, as much the furnishings as the real estate.

12. He who finds an old treasure

All who find an old treasure should keep it and should not respond for it to the king or to another *señor*. But if someone finds a treasure on another's holding, the owner of the holding should have a right to half of the treasure.

13. Another statute concerning the *telonearius*

We also grant, that the one who is the *telonearius* in Cuenca should not demand the *pedaticus* of someone, either in the town, or outside of it, except of whom he can demand it by right. And although the merchant has not paid the *pedaticus* in the town and the *telonearius* overtakes him on the road, he should take from him only the toll that he should charge him by right and no other fine, not even if he makes him return to the town.

CHAPTER XVI

The Election of the *Iudex* and the *Alcaldi*

1. Election of the *iudex, alcaldi, notarius,* and *almutazaf;* the designation of *andadores* and their payment

Each year on the Sunday following the feast of Saint Michael, the council should name the *iudex, alcaldi, notarius, andadores, sagio,* and *almutazaf,* according to the code.

2. The statute regulating the appointment of these charges each year

We say "each year" because no one ought to hold a charge or an office of the council for more than a year, unless the council in full session requests it by acclamation. And the same Sunday, the parish from which the *iudex* ought to receive the charge for that year should designate a wise *iudex,* who is sensible and who knows how to discern between what is true and what is false, between what is just and unjust, and who, furthermore, should possess a house and a horse in the city.

3. The statute regulating those who do not reside in the city

In this way, anyone who does not possess a horse and a house in the town that is occupied by family members at the time, or during the previous year, should not be the *iudex.* In the same way, anyone should not be either the *iudex* or an *alcaldus* who wants to gain such offices by force. Also, each parish should designate its *alcaldus* on the above-mentioned day, with the same [stipulations] as have been indicated for the *iudex;* that is to say, that he should have a horse and a house in the town that has been occupied by family members during the previous year.

4. The dissenting parish in the *iudex*'s election

But if some parish on the cited date does not agree to designate its *iudex,* the *iudex* and the *alcaldi* of the previous year should elect him, drawing lots among five men from the parish over which the *iudex* will be in charge, honorable and prudent men, as we have said above. He on whom the draw falls should be the *iudex,* and no other.

5. The dissenting parish in the election of the *alcaldus*

Equally, the *alcaldi* of the previous year should choose the *alcaldus* of the parish that is not in accord [on the election date]. The one who wants to

gain the tribunal or the office by influence of his family, the king or the *Señor*
from the town, or sells the charge or assumes the office before swearing in,
should not ever be *iudex* in his lifetime nor occupy a charge or office of the
council.

6. The oath of the *iudex* and of the others given office

The election of the *iudex* being completed and confirmed by all the
people, the *iudex* should swear on the Holy Gospels that neither for love of his
parents, nor for fondness of his children, neither by desire for money, nor by
shame of anyone, neither by requests nor bribes from friends, citizens, or
strangers, should he break the code nor should he be diverted from the road of
justice. Afterward the *alcaldi* should swear this same thing, and after the
notarius, [so do] the *almutazaf* and the *sagio*.

7. All those who have been elected swear in the council

All these should take their oath in the council, and they should also swear
loyalty to the council in its entirety, saving the honor of the king. Whether the
andadores should swear in the council or in the court of the *alcaldi* ought not
to be important, only that they should swear.

8. The *iudex* or *alcaldus* who will not be honest

If the *iudex* or an *alcaldus*, after the swearing in, is declared guilty of a lie
or falseness, he should lose his charge or council office; furthermore, he
should be prohibited from being accepted as a witness; and for all the damage
that occurred because of this, he should pay double. The *iudex* has this same
penalty, as also the *alcaldus* who conceals the truth or asks the witnesses
something other than that which he should be judging, or asserts a lie, or is
not honest with the council, or makes a case neglectful of the judgment of the
Code, or prevents it [the Code] being read, threatening the *notarius* or abus-
ing him verbally.

9. The *iudex* and the *alcaldi* pay one hundred *aurei* to the king

I command that the *iudex* and the *alcaldi* should be impartial to the poor
and to the rich, to the noble and to the non-noble. And if through their fault
anyone does not find justice, and for this reason brings his complaint to me,
and I should prove that it has not been judged according to the code, the *iudex*
and the *alcaldi* should pay to the king one hundred *aurei* and to the plaintiff,
double the claim.

10. The *iudex* who does not want to send an *andador*

Whoever presents a complaint to the *iudex*, to the *alcaldi*, or in the council, for which the *iudex* has to send an *andador*, and he does not send him until the following day, the plaintiff should report him to the *alcaldi*, and the *iudex* should pay ten *aurei* to the *alcaldi*, and to the plaintiff double the claim. And if the *alcaldi* do not want to compel the *iudex*, they should pay ten *aurei* to the council, and to the plaintiff double the claim.

11. He who presents a complaint in the council before [presenting it] to the *iudex* and to the *alcaldi*

Whoever presents his complaint in the council before communicating it to the *iudex* and to the *alcaldi*, should pay ten *aurei* to the *iudex* and to the *alcaldi*; and he against whom the complaint was lodged should have a part, as one of the *alcaldi*.

12. The pay of the *iudex*

The *iudex* should receive forty *menkales* as remuneration for the service that he gives to the council, and the council should pay them to him; he should receive also the seventh part of the fifth [of booty] and of those things that the council delivers voluntarily to the king or to the *Señor* of the town. It is said "voluntarily," because the Council of Cuenca does not ever have the obligation to give anything by the code or by right to the king, to the *Señor* of the town, or to any other, since I have made it free of all submission to the king and to the *Señor* of the town, of all tax, rent, and *fazendera*. However, where it is the king or the *Señor* of the town, the *iudex* does not have a right to the seventh part of the fifth [booty tax]. Furthermore, the *iudex* has right to five *solidi* by the judgments at his door, and also to the seventh part of the pecuniary penalties that correspond to the Palace which he collects.

13. The things that remain [in the possession of] the outgoing *iudex*

If on the cited Sunday of his departure, the outgoing *iudex* retains something of what was given, which the council has to deliver to the *Señor* of the town, or of the fifth, or of the accounts of the council that may not have been paid, the new *iudex* should pay it and should take from him [the former *iudex*] what corresponds to him in right. Thus, if the *iudex* or the outgoing *alcaldi* on that date have a prisoner for penalty still not judged or [who has] not confessed, the *iudex* with the new *alcaldi* should judge him and collect, as is fair. If on the above-mentioned Sunday, the *iudex* and the outgoing *alcaldi* have a prisoner for judgment or for a confessed crime, they should collect those [penalties] or do what they please. The *iudex* should divide all the other pecuniary penalties with the *alcaldi*, and the *alcaldi* with the *iudex*, except those which have been said.

14. Neither the *iudex* nor the *alcaldi* judge anyone against their will

It should be known that neither the *iudex* nor the *alcaldi* are to judge anyone but those who are presented for their judgment; this precept is for those who are accustomed to coerce those who are presented for judgment.

15. What the *iudex* should do

The *iudex* has to receive surety bondsmen for the pecuniary penalties of the council. He should collect the fifth and the pecuniary penalties and the things that the council gives for service to the king, or to another. He should receive bondsmen for the penalties and complaints that arrive before him. He should receive bondsmen from the *andadores* and houses with sureties from those whom the council holds by its rights. He should do justice to all those who bring complaint to him. He should take sureties from those who refuse to give them or take them away. He should judge before his door those who are presented before the court.

16. The proclamation of the meetings of the court

The hour proclaimed, the meeting of the court should be from the third hour to the sixth. The beginning of the meeting should be proclaimed in the court in both plazas. The *iudex* should judge before his door with a judging *alcaldus* and not with any other.

17. If the *iudex* is absent from the city

If the *iudex* is absent from the city for some obligation, he should put one of the judging *alcaldi* in his place to judge in his absence and [the substitute] should fulfill the task at all times. If he does not do it thus, this acting *iudex* should pay all the damage that occurs by his fault in the city. These are the things that the substituting *iudex* ought to do personally. All we give corresponds to the *iudex* and to the *alcaldi*, to do justice to the malefactors, to give judgments all over the city, and to perform jointly the judgments on Friday.

18. The plaintiff who cannot obtain justice by fault of the *iudex* and of the *alcaldi*

If someone who has been injured complains to the *iudex* or to the *alcaldi*, and they do not give him legal satisfaction immediately, [the *iudex* or to the *alcaldi*] should pay double the claim or double the damage that happens through this. The council should divide this pecuniary penalty with the plaintiff.

19. The substituting *iudex* whom the annual *iudex* sends to take sureties outside the city, and he has the sureties taken from him

If the annual *iudex* sends one in his place to the villages to take sureties and they are taken from him,[1] the annual *iudex* should pay ten *solidi* as a fine, if the substitute *iudex* can prove it with a citizen.

20. The one who takes the sureties from the annual *iudex* outside the city

If someone takes the sureties from the annual *iudex*, he should pay five *aurei* and the *alcaldi* should take sureties for both fines.

21. The one who takes the sureties from the *alcaldi* outside the city

Likewise, if that treacherous one does this same thing to the *alcaldi*, he should pay ten *aurei*, and the council should take sureties for all the pecuniary penalties, as is said below.

22. What the substituting *iudex* receives from his pecuniary penalties

The substituting *iudex* receives half of his pecuniary penalties [that portion of fines that is paid to the iudex as a part of his income], and the annual *iudex* the other half.

23. What the *andador* receives from his pecuniary penalties

The *andador* or *sagio* [both judicial functionaries] should receive a fourth part of his pecuniary penalties.

24. The *iudex* shares in the pecuniary penalties of the *alcaldi*, and vice versa

The *iudex* and the *alcaldi* should divide their pecuniary penalties, except for the penalty of the ten *solidi*, as has been said.

25. The sales agent of commodities of the council

The *iudex* and the *alcaldi* should designate a public seller of commodities, who is commonly called *venditor*, who should be Christian, Jewish, or Muslim. Everyone who finds another [unauthorized person] selling these commodities should take them away without any penalty.

26. The *iudex* who accept gifts for judgment

If the *iudex* or an *alcaldus* secretly accepts gifts for judgment from some of the litigators, his judgment should stand voided, and, furthermore, he should pay double the claim for that which the judgment had been given.

27. The office of *notarius*

The *notarius* should be honest in the reading of the Book,[2] in the accounts of the council and in the polling list of the council, in such a manner as to preserve it always as he had written it with the sworn witnesses. He should also guard against erasing or writing something in the Book without order of the king or of all the council. He should keep the accounts of the *iudex* and of the *alcaldi* faithfully, so that he should commit nothing fraudulent with them.

28. The pay of the *notarius*

The council should give to the *notarius*, if he keeps these things that have been said faithfully, forty *menkales* and a Moorish captive of war, when the council makes a military campaign and gains something. The request that he makes to the council should be submitted at the end of year.

29. The penalty for the dishonest *notarius*

If the *notarius* is declared guilty of falsity or of fraud up to a value of one hundred *menkales*, he should pay double, as a thief; of one hundred or higher, if he is seized in [the act of] fraud or if he has erased or added something in the book of the judgments, his right thumb should be cut off and he should pay double the damage that he has caused.

30. The pay of the *alcaldi*

The council should pay to each one of the *alcaldi* ten *menkales* for the service rendered to the same. Should anyone complain of some *alcaldus* on the court, the *iudex* and the other *alcaldi* should immediately require him to give legal satisfaction to the plaintiff; and until he does this, no other case should be treated.

31. The office of *almutazaf*

The *almutazaf* should be the superintendent [in the market] of the measures of cereals, wine, oil, and salt, and of weights and pounds;[3] of the butchers, shopkeepers, tavern keepers, bakers, fish sellers, hunters, pot sellers, tile makers, brick makers, water sellers, woodcutters or wood sellers, retailers, and apothecaries and herbalists. And the *almutazaf* should swear in the council that he will keep faithfully the things that the code commands or that the council orders.

32. He who complains to the *almutazaf*

If anyone complains to the *almutazaf* for some of these above-mentioned things, he should immediately take sureties for the fine of the obligation that will be stated below.

33. How the fine of the *almutazaf* should be divided

This fine should be divided into three parts: the *almutazaf* should divide a third part with the plaintiff; the remaining two-thirds should belong to the council to close the gaps in the city [wall].

34. The negligent *almutazaf*

If the *almutazaf* is negligent in these things that have been said, or he does not do justice to the plaintiff, or he makes an arrangement secretly with anyone, he should pay ten *aurei* to the *iudex*, to the *alcaldi*, and to the plaintiff.

35. The account that the *almutazaf* should give

If the *almutazaf* is not found in the plaza, so that there is no one to do justice for the plaintiffs regarding the things that we have indicated above, he should pay ten *aurei* to the *iudex*, to the *alcaldi*, and to the plaintiff. Furthermore, the *almutazaf* should give account to the council of his stewardship of office; if he is declared guilty of the commission of fraud in some things, his ears should be cut off and [his head and beard] should be shaved, he should be flogged over all the streets, or he should redeem himself for one hundred *aurei*, whichever more pleases the council.

36. The *almutazaf* inspects the measures each week

Each week he should prove all the measures and above-mentioned weights, namely those of the bakers, tavern keepers, shopkeepers, butchers, etc. And from those he finds shortening their measure, he should take sureties for the fine of ten *aurei* and, furthermore, he should destroy [the weights] in the presence of all without any penalty. He should also see that no one throws manure or garbage in the streets; and if anyone dirties them, he should take sureties for a fine of five *solidi*.

37. Any citizen can possess measures

Any citizen of Cuenca can possess weights and measures in his house without any penalty, as long as he has them legally. But anyone who has illegal measures or weights should pay the pecuniary penalties, according to the Code of Cuenca.

38. The office of *andador*

The *andadores* ought to carry the messages of the council and the notices that the *iudex* and the *alcaldi* order, because the *iudex* and the *alcaldi* are to be held above all. Also, by the code, one of the *andadores* should be present before the *iudex* from morning until night. The *andadores* should punish the malefactors and should guard the prisoners that the *iudex* holds for some penalty or fault. Also all the *andadores* should be always present in the court of the *alcaldi* on Friday. If all the *andadores* are not present on Friday, while the *alcaldi* are in the court, and by [the *andadores*] fault something happens there, [the *alcaldi*] should take sureties from [the *andadores*] in the amount of an *aureus*. If one of the *andadores* is not present before the *iudex* each day, as has been said, all should pay jointly an *aureus*.

39. The *andador* who does not fulfill the order of the *iudex*

If one of the *andadores* does not fulfill the orders of the *iudex* or of the *alcaldi*, he [*iudex* or the *alcaldi*] should hire another with money of this one and should send him to the place where this one refused to go.

40. The *andador* who badly fulfills the message of the council

If one of the *andadores* badly fulfills the message of the council, of the *iudex*, or of the *alcaldi* within the district of Cuenca, he should pay five *aurei* to the *alcaldi* and to the plaintiff; if it is outside the district, he should pay ten *aurei*.

41. The dishonest *andador*

If one of the *andadores* is sent to the king as honest and changes the judgment that has been given in the court of the king, his tongue should be cut out.

42. The *andador* who takes sureties without orders

The *andador* who takes sureties without orders of the *iudex* or of the *alcaldi* should return them double and should pay an *aureus* to the *alcaldi*.

43. The *andador* who takes sureties by order of the *iudex*

When the *andador* takes sureties by order of the *iudex* or of the *alcaldi*, they should be delivered to that place at whose order he took the sureties. The one who receives them should be the watcher of the *andador* who takes the sureties, if it is necessary. If the *andador* does not do this and deposits the sureties in another place, pawns them, or undersells them, he should pay double the sureties to the plaintiff, and to the *iudex* and to the *alcaldi* he should pay an *aureus*.

44. If the *andador* has been sent to take sureties from the court

If the *iudex* and the *alcaldi*, while they are in the court, send an *andador* to take sureties, anyone who removes [the sureties] should pay five *solidi* if the deed takes place in the city; if they are taken from him in the villages, the one who takes them should pay ten *solidi*, if the *andador* can prove it with a citizen, the same in the town as outside.

45. The pay of the *andadores*

The council should give to the *andadores*, as pay for their services, an eighth part [of the tax] of each owner of a property and of each craftsman who possess twenty *menkales* or more, except the *milites* and the officeholders.

46. The *andador* who guards a prisoner

If one of the *andadores* has a prisoner in his custody and he escapes from the prison, the *andador* should take the place of the fugitive and should pay what that one had to pay, or he should bear the penalty that was destined for the fugitive.

47. The *venditor* whom the *alcaldi* designate

The *venditor* whom the *alcaldi* designate first should swear loyalty in the court of the *alcaldi*.

48. The penalty for the dishonest *venditor*

Once having given the oath, if the *venditor* is declared guilty of falseness or theft up to a value of five *menkales*, his ears should be cut off; up to ten, his right eye should be removed; up to twenty, both [eyes] should be removed; and for twenty or higher, let him be hurled from the city cliffs.

49. What the sales agent ought to receive from the things that he sells

The sales agent should receive a *denarius* for each *aureus* from the things that he sells, and in addition to that he should have a share of the things that he sells.

50. The sales agent does not buy anything of the things that have been delivered to him to sell

It should be forbidden for the sales agent to retain or buy something of the things that have been delivered to him to sell.

51. What the sales agent ought to receive from the animals that he sells

When the sales agent sells a Moor or some property, he should receive a half *menkal*; if he sells a horse, he should receive eight *denarii*; if he sells an ass or an ox, he should receive four *denarii*.

52. The sales agent leaves a watcher

The sales agent should leave a watcher over the things that he has sold. If he does not want to leave a watcher and the other can prove it, the sales agent should pay double the entire claim.

53. The office of *sagio*

The *sagio* or town crier should proclaim the council by order of the *iudex*, and not by any other, three times in both plazas. He should announce the meetings of the court at the door of the *iudex*. He should announce anything that the *alcaldi* order him to, except to the council and the meetings of the court at the door of the *iudex*. He should announce all the things lost that the plaintiff brings to him. He should announce also what things have been found. He should announce the auctions of the military campaigns [*almofallas*], both in the town and outside it. He should guard the door of the court of the *alcaldi* on Friday and not any other day.

54. What the *sagio* ought to receive from the auctions of the animals and for his proclamation

If the *sagio* sells a riding animal, he should receive four *denarii*; for an ox or for an ass, he should have two *denarii*; for a Moor, an *obolus* and no more. If he demands more for some proclamation, he should pay an *aureus*. If a lost animal appears, thanks to his proclamation both in the town and outside it, he should have two *denarii*; for a Moor, he should receive four *denarii* if he [the owner] is a citizen or from within the district of Cuenca; for a Moor who is not from within the district, he should receive a *menkal*. For the other things, he should receive proportionally one *obolus* for each *aureus*.

55. The pay of the *sagio*

The *sagio* should receive from the council twenty *menkales* as payment at the end of the year.

56. The *sagio* who does not comply with his obligations

In the things that pertain to the office of *sagio*, if there occurs some prejudice through his fault, he should pay an *aureus* to the *iudex*, to the *alcaldi*, and to the plaintiff.

CHAPTER XVII

Concerning the Manner in Which Each One Obtains His Rights

1. Concerning the manner by which each one obtains his rights over his debtor who resides in the city, or concerning that against whom he has some case, taking sureties in his house in this way

Whoever has a complaint against another who possesses an inhabited house in the city, on the first day he should take a straw [from the house or property] as a sign, with a citizen of his opponent's parish or with a citizen who dwells in one of the three or four nearby houses. We order the taking of the sign on the first day for this reason: because, if the pledger wants to accept the code by that sign, more sureties should not be taken from him. But if the pledgee [creditor], contrary to what is said, takes sureties from him and does not want to accept the legal satisfaction by the sign, he should return the sureties with five *solidi*. What we said regarding the sign, we say of other sureties. If someone does not want to depart from the code regarding the sign, his opponent should take sureties each day without any penalty until he departs from the code. However, he should not take bread dough wrapped in cloth from [the debtor] as sureties, or the bedclothing from one who lies sick, nor living chattel [animals] if he finds inanimate chattel. If he does not find inanimate sureties, he should take living chattel. If he finds nothing but bread dough, he should place this on a clean cloth and should take it as security. If he does not find other sureties than those which are in the bed of the sick, he should inform the citizen in whose company he is taking sureties, and then he should take the doors of his choice from all the rooms or the corral. The doors being seized, next he should cite [the debtor] judicially before the door of the *iudex*, as is established in the code. If he cannot carry the doors, he should inform the aforementioned citizen and immediately should cite his opponent judicially, as has been said.

2. The injured pledgee

If the pledgee [creditor] is injured or insulted in his opponent's house, the debtor should pay double the fine of the offense that has been committed, according to testimony of the citizen who had gone with him to take the sureties in place of the *sagio*.

3. In the taking of sureties the testimony of the *sagio* will be believed

The testimony of this citizen or of the *sagio* will always be believed regarding all the things that happen in the taking of sureties, both for those sureties as well as for the pecuniary penalties.

4. The pledgee who does not possess a house

If the pledgee does not have a house in the city or it is unknown, the above-mentioned citizen should guard the sureties. And if he does not want to do it and the pledger loses his sureties, the *sagio* should pay for them.

5. The pledger who leaves it to the code

When the pledger leaves it to the code, the pledgee should designate *alcaldi* with him for judging [the sureties]. If both accept the judgment, the sureties should become free immediately and they should be returned before sunset. If the judgment is not satisfying to any of them, he should appeal to the Friday court. But if the pledgee is the one who appeals, the sureties should be returned, as has been said. If the pledger is the one who appeals, the sureties should not be returned.

6. The free sureties by judgment of the *alcaldi*

The sureties that remain free by judgment of the substitute *alcaldi* should be returned that same day before sunset. If the pledgee does not return them that same day, he should pay to the pledger five *solidi* for each night that the sureties remain in his house.

7. He who does not want to accompany his fellow citizen to take sureties

If a citizen does not want to go with another fellow citizen to take sureties, he should pay five *solidi*.

8. The pledgee who does not want to depart from the code regarding the sureties

If the pledgee does not want to depart from the code regarding the sureties from the pledger, the pledger should obtain witnesses and, if on that same day he does not depart from the code, on the following day he should return the sureties with five *solidi*. If the pledgee does not return the sureties that day and they remain a single night in his house, the pledger should take sureties each day from him and should not depart from the code, nor give legal satisfaction to him nor answer for anything, until he should recover his sureties together with five *solidi*. Once the sureties are recovered, he should give legal satisfaction, if it is again demanded.

9. He who takes sureties to spite

Whoever takes sureties to his pledgee or cites him judicially to spite him should pay five *solidi* and that same day return the sureties; if he does not do it, he should pay the same five *solidi* anew, for as many nights as the sureties have passed in [the pledger's] house. [If the pledger] takes sureties to spite the other before giving legal satisfaction or requesting from the pledgee, according to the code, [then the pledgee] should take sureties to him, or vice versa.

10. He who prevents a citizen from taking sureties in the city

Whoever prevents a citizen from taking sureties in the city or removes [sureties from the surety taker] should pay a half *menkal*, and the *iudex* should take sureties sufficient for the fine and for the claim and should divide the amount of the fine with the plaintiff. If anyone prevents the *iudex* from taking sureties in the city, he should pay an *aureus*, and the *alcaldi* should take sureties sufficient for him who prevents it for the claim and for the fine.

11. He who prevents the *alcaldi* from taking sureties in the city

Whoever prevents the *alcaldi* from taking sureties in the city should pay ten *aurei*, and the council should take sureties for the fine and for the claim and, furthermore, for a fine of sixty *menkales*.

12. The pecuniary penalty of the council when it takes sureties

Whoever incites the council to take sureties for those who have had them removed, be it known that they should pay sixty *menkales*. The fine of these sixty *menkales* for which the council has taken sureties belongs to the council and not another to do with them what pleases the people involved.

13. The plaintiff does not receive anything from the pecuniary penalties of the *iudex* or from those of the *alcaldi*

The plaintiff should not receive anything from the pecuniary penalty of the *iudex* or from that of the *alcaldi* which proceeds from the taking of sureties; on the contrary, the *iudex* and the *alcaldi* should divide them mutually beforehand.

14. When the *iudex*, the *alcaldi*, or the council do not find sufficient sureties

When the *iudex*, the *alcaldi*, or the council go to take sureties for the previously cited pecuniary penalties, in the city as well as in the villages, and they do not find sufficient sureties for the claim and for the fine, they should take the guilty party prisoner and he should not leave the prison of the *iudex*, until he pays the above-mentioned pecuniary penalties and makes satisfaction by law to the plaintiff or pays the claim to him.

15. He who prevents the council from taking sureties

If anyone by revolt out of arrogance or of a faction attempts to prevent the council from taking sureties, he should pay one hundred *aurei*, and each one of his collaborators the same; furthermore, the council should seize from the rebels their houses and goods until they pay all the pecuniary penalties and the claim. Furthermore, if in that revolt anyone of the council kills one of them, he should not be an enemy or pay any fines because of this. But if any of the rebels injures anyone of the council, he should pay double the fine of the offense that has been assigned, in accordance with the Code and the Ordinances of Cuenca. If he kills him, let him be hurled from the city cliffs immediately.

16. The pledgee who finds the door closed three times in a day

If the plaintiff wants to take sureties in a house and finds the door closed three times in a day, be it known, on the next day at the noon hour, he should inform the citizen with whom he has come to take sureties and next he should call on the *iudex*; the *iudex* should open the door with impunity and deliver to the plaintiff sufficient sureties appropriate to the claim and, furthermore, he should take sureties at the same time for the fine of a half *menkal*, already cited above.

17. He who attests that there are people in a closed house

If the plaintiff, during some of the above-mentioned hours, attests with any citizen that there are people within the house, he should call at the door and, if they do not want to open to him, he should make his claim to the *iudex* immediately and the *iudex* should open the door and take sureties for the claim and for the fine, as in the case of theft of sureties.

18. He who removes sureties and denies it

When the pledger says to his pledgee that he has not removed the sureties from him or prevented him from taking them, and that he [the pledgee] has brought a case wrongfully to the *iudex* against him, then the pledgee should prove with the testimony of the citizen with whom he sought to take sureties, that the pledger took the sureties from him, and this should redeem the sureties by the power of the *iudex*. If the pledgee cannot prove it, it should be he, the same one [the pledger], who redeems the sureties by the power of the *iudex*.

19. When the annually [elected] *iudex* is healthy in the city, a substitute is not legal

When the annual *iudex* is healthy in the city and sends another to take sureties in his place, the one who deprives him [the replacement] of the sureties should not pay any fine. If the *iudex* is sick in the city or he has departed it, the one who remains in his place should have the all-embracing power of the *iudex* until the annual *iudex* should be returned to the city.

20. If the *iudex* dies prematurely

If the annual *iudex* dies before his term of office is complete, it should be the *iudex* in his place who ought to inherit his goods, and all that the heir acquires by the office of the *iudex* should be divided with the other heirs, as with the remaining goods. If he has no heir, the council should designate a *iudex* who will be pleasing to those of the parish where the charge of the *iudex* derived.

CHAPTER XVIII

The Citations

1. The citations: how each one ought to be applied judicially to its adversary, either from the city or from the villages

If the plaintiff finds his adversary in the city, one who does not possess a house there, he should summon him in the presence of three citizens on the following day before the door of the *iudex*; if the one summoned presents himself on the following day, he should bring with him sureties in the amount of five *aurei* and, before responding, he should place them as guarantee in the power of the *iudex*; afterward [the parties involved] should have the judgment and, if any one of them is not pleased with the judgment, he should appeal to the Friday court. If it is the pledged who appeals, the *iudex* should deliver the sureties to the plaintiff. If it is the plaintiff who appeals, the sureties should remain free.

2. He who is not present on the indicated day

If any of the litigants is not present on the indicated day, as has been said, he should pay five *solidi*, of which the *iudex* should receive half, and the other half goes to him who was present.

3. He who does not bring sureties on the indicated day

If the one summoned does not bring the sureties, as has been said, he should pay five *solidi*, of which the *iudex* should receive half and the plaintiff the other half.

4. He who says: "I have a lord"

It is not legal for the one summoned to say, "I have a lord," unless he is a hired servant, plowman, gardener, or shepherd. If he is not one of these and is not present on the indicated day, he should pay five *solidi*. If he is a gardener, shepherd, plowman, or hired servant, sureties should be taken in the house of his lord until justice or legal satisfaction is obtained.

5. He who shows another's house with sureties

It is not legal for anyone to show the plaintiff someone else's house with sureties; on the contrary, he should present himself on the indicated day or he should pay, as has been said.

6. He who surrenders a house with another's sureties

Whoever surrenders a house with another's sureties should pay ten *aurei*, except if it is given by the king or by the *Señor* of the city.

7. He who finds his debtor outside the town

If the plaintiff finds, outside the town or in a village, either his debtor or one against whom he has some legal case, who does not possess a house in the city, he should cite him within three days before the door of the *iudex*. When the one summoned presents himself within the three days before the *iudex*, he should bring with himself sureties in the amount of five *solidi* and should place them in the power of the *iudex*. Afterward, the *iudex* should hear the reasons of the one part and the other, and finally render judgment regarding what will be just. But the litigant who does not like the judgment of the *iudex* should appeal to the Friday court; if it is the plaintiff who appeals, he should return the sureties to the one summoned immediately; if it is the one summoned who appeals, the *iudex* should deliver the sureties to the plaintiff immediately. Furthermore, it should be known that the summoner, either from the town or from the villages, when the sureties are delivered to him, ought to keep them so that they will not be neglected, until they should be freed by judgment of the *iudex* and of the *alcaldi*.

8. The plaintiff who neglects the sureties

If some plaintiff neglects the sureties, causes them some damage, or pawns them in some place, he should return them double.

9. The sureties freed by the judgment of the *alcaldi*

All sureties that remain freed by judgment of the *iudex* or of the *alcaldi*, if on that same day they are not returned, their possessor should pay five *solidi* daily, as has been indicated above.

CHAPTER XIX
Bondsmen

1. Bondsmen who ought to be accepted from those who do not possess houses

If the plaintiff meets his debtor or one against whom he has any legal case, he should demand a bondsman from him; if he does not want to or cannot provide one, [the plaintiff] should tell him directly that he will accompany him to enter prison; if he does not want to [go to prison], he should pay ten *aurei* to the *alcaldi* and to the plaintiff; he also should pay as much to whomever defends him. The *iudex* should take sureties for these pecuniary penalties and, also, he should make the debtor a prisoner if he does not give a bondsman for the fine and for the claim. Whoever provides a bondsman should not be made a prisoner, but rather the plaintiff should cite him for the judgment on Friday and he should pay the fine there to the *iudex* and also give judicial satisfaction to the plaintiff; otherwise, he should not leave from the tribunal; furthermore, he should be made prisoner.

2. He who stops one who wants to provide a bondsman

Whoever stops one who wants to provide a bondsman, according to the Code of Cuenca, should pay three hundred *solidi*, except if he is a thief or malefactor; since in such instances a bondsman should not be legal. Equally, [the defendant] should not be detained who says to his opponent: "Come with me and I will give you a bondsman"; but on the spot [the defendant] should give him the names of three citizens who are legal within the walls [of the town]; these being designated, [the defendant] should go with him to look for them. If they do not find any of those named at his house, [the defendant] should be arrested without any penalty [to the plaintiff]. He should also be arrested if, even though they find them, they do not want to be bondsmen for him. But if they find another who is willing to be a bondsman for him on the road, he should not be arrested. The bondsman being accepted, the plaintiff should have sureties at the house of his opponent, if he has one, and he should obtain his right, as has been said. If he has no house, he should be summoned before the door of the *iudex*; if he does not present himself, the *iudex* together with the plaintiff should take sureties from the bondsman daily for the claim and for five *solidi*, until he brings the debtor to give judicial satisfaction. When [the defendant] presents himself, each one should obtain his right, as has been indicated.

3. He who becomes a prisoner by lacking a bondsman

Whoever is arrested for lacking a bondsman should leave the prison as soon as he is able to provide a bondsman. He who does not want to accept this should pay three hundred *solidi*, unless he has been made a prisoner and declared guilty because of acknowledged debt.

4. Who should be accepted as a bondsman

No one should be accepted as bondsman unless he possesses a house with sureties in the city. Therefore, a married woman cannot be the guarantor of anyone, because she is under the control of her husband; nor [can] the son, while he is under his father's power; for the same reason, neither a servant, nor the *iudex*, nor a sworn *alcaldus* of the council, nor the clerk, since all of these are prohibited to him; nor the clergyman, unless by order of his bishop, of the archdeacon, or even including an archpresbyter, since the secular *iudex* does not have jurisdiction over a clergyman. However, all these, namely, the *iudex*, the *alcaldus*, the clerk, and including the clergyman, can be bondsmen of those who eat their bread, provided they swear previously that they do eat their bread and obey their orders; but prior to swearing the oath, they should not be accepted.

5. Bonds are not legal after a half year has lapsed

The bond made by someone should be invalid after a half year has lapsed, except the bond by wage earners or by servants.

6. He who is the bondsman of a professed debtor

He who is the bondsman of a professed debtor should have a term of twenty-seven days in order to seek the debtor for whom he is bondsman.

7. The bondsman should come to swear every nine days

Whoever is the bondsman of a professed debtor and has accepted the term of twenty-seven days in order to find him should swear each nine days that he has looked for him at every opportunity and has not been able to find him; if he has not presented himself to swear it every nine days, he should lose the case and should pay the bond immediately.

8. The bondsman who cannot hold the debtor

The bondsman who presents himself to swear and cannot hold the debtor by the third period of nine days should pay all the bond instead of the debtor and he should not have more time either to pay or to bring in the debtor.

9. The bondsman who cannot raise the amount of the debt

If the bondsman cannot raise the amount of the debt, the *iudex* should detain him and put him in the power of the plaintiff.

10. The bondsman presents the debtor within twenty-seven days

If the bondsman can get hold of the professed debtor, [the debtor] should be received in place of the bondsman and the bondsman should remain free of prison; the debtor should remain in prison until he pays all the debt. If the bondsman can get hold of the professed debtor before he is arrested and present him to the plaintiff, the *iudex*, and the *alcaldi*, he [the bondsman] should remain free of the bond.

11. When the bondsman remains free of the bond

When the bondsman remains free of the bond, the debtor should be arrested immediately and should not leave the prison until he pays, and, even if he wants to give another bondsman, he should not be heard.

12. The one for whom the bondsman pays something

If the bondsman pays something for the debtor, the same one who placed him as bondsman should pay double for all which has been delivered.

13. The bondsman who can hold the debtor's wife or children

If the bondsman enters within the term to present the debtor on the appointed day and [if] he [the debtor] does not want to present himself with [the bondsman], and places witnesses and all that for which the bondsman pays for the bond [the sureties], the debtor should pay double. And when he pays for the bond, the children or the wife of the debtor, if he has them, should pay it double if the debtor flees. If, before the bondsman pays, he cannot find or bring the debtor, as has been said, but he can make the wife or the children of the debtor acknowledge the debt, the plaintiff should accept them instead of his debtor. If the children or the wife of the debtor deny the bond, the bondsman should prove it according to the code, as if he were dealing with the debtor himself. If the debtor does not have children or a wife, the one who has a right to his goods should respond for him.

14. He who is the bondsman of a debtor who has not confessed his debt

He who is the bondsman of someone who has not confessed his debt and cannot present him within the term of twenty-seven days should respond to the plaintiff instead of to the one whose bondsman he is, and the plaintiff should prove to the bondsman what he would prove to his opponent, as the code prescribes. If he cannot prove it, he [the bondsman] should swear on behalf of the other and should be believed.

15. He who wants to quit being a bondsman before the *alcaldi*

Whoever wants to be free of being a bondsman should present the debtor before the plaintiff and two *alcaldi* or three citizens and say "I depart from this bond," and then be free; [if he does this] in any other fashion, [he should] not [be free].

16. He who denies the bond

If the bondsman denies the bond, the plaintiff should prove it, as it is in the code, and the bondsman should pay double the claim. If the plaintiff cannot prove it, he should lose the case.

17. He who is a bondsman of a malefactor

Whoever goes before the *iudex* and the *alcaldi* as the bondsman of a thief, a homicidal person, a criminal, or a malefactor, whom he will present to the council or to the king, and cannot present him on the appointed day should himself suffer the penalty that the accused ought to suffer.

18. The debtor or bondsman of nine days

If someone pledges money or is a bondsman or debtor of money or says before the sworn *alcaldi* or their substitutes "I will pay this money," those *alcaldi* should give him as sentence that he should pay that money within the term of nine days. If he does not do it, he should pay it double and an *aureus* as fine to the *alcaldi* who gave him the sentence.[1]

19. The debtor of the nine days who does not present himself on the appointed day

Each time as the plaintiff summons his debtor and [the plaintiff] promises that he is going to prove [the debt], immediately [the *alcaldi*] should give him a term in order to prove it, and it should not be legal to appeal to the king or to the Friday [tribunal] or the code. If [the debtor] does not present himself on the appointed day, he should lose the case, and the *alcaldi* should take sureties for double the demand and, also, an *aureus* of fine. In the same manner, they should take sureties daily, as many times as the one who is summoned is not present on the appointed day, for the fine of an *aureus*, half of which the *alcaldi* should receive, until he presents himself before the tribunal. After the debtor acknowledges his debt in the tribunal before the *alcaldi*, he should be made prisoner until he pays.

20. He who fears that his debtor is going to flee

If the plaintiff is afraid that his debtor is going to flee or escape, including [the debtor] who does not present himself before the tribunal, he [the plaintiff] should demand a bondsman from him so that, if the debtor does not pay the debt within the appointed term, the bondsman should pay [the debt] in his place in the term of nine days and also the fine of the *alcaldi* and of the termination [of the extension] of the term.

21. Do not give a term of nine days to the bondsman, except for the same debtor

The summoned bondsman of a debtor should not be given another term for nine days except for the same debtor. If the bondsman does not pay on the appointed day, he should pay double the claim and the fine, as would the debtor himself.

22. He who does not want or cannot provide a bondsman

If the plaintiff making claim to a debtor summons a bondsman, and the debtor does not want or cannot provide one, he [the debtor] should be arrested without any penalty.

23. The debtor summoned for nine days who does not present himself on the appointed day and neither pays nor possesses a house

If the debtor does not pay in the appointed term, nor presents himself before the tribunal, nor possesses a house or sureties, and the plaintiff does not have a bondsman from the debtor, the *iudex* should detain [the debtor] where he wants so that he can be found and delivered to the plaintiff for double the claim and for the fine for the termination of the [extension of] the term.

24. The debtor summoned for nine days who is outside of the district

If the summoned debtor does not pay in the fixed term or is outside of the district of Cuenca, no one should present himself before the tribunal in his place, not even his wife or his children, but, that being so, they should pay double the money and the *aurei* of the fine, as has been said repeatedly.

CHAPTER XX
Witnesses and Accusers

1. Witnesses; how the plaintiff should prove the debt of a summoned debtor who denies it

If the summoned debtor denies the debt or the fine, the plaintiff should prove it with the *alcaldi* who judged them, and if he proves it, the debtor should pay double the claim, and to the *alcaldi* an *aureus* of fine and also five *solidi*.

2. He who should prove by means of money

Before the plaintiff seeks to prove [his case] by means of some money or by means of [nonmonetary] debt, he who denies [the debt] should give sureties which are worth double the claim or the same [amount of] money, or he should submit to imprisonment in the power of the *iudex* or of the *alcaldi*; after this the plaintiff should prove it.

3. He who does not want to give sureties

Whoever, having sureties, wants to submit to imprisonment in the power of the *iudex* or of the *alcaldi* he should not be accepted, but rather, the *iudex* and the *alcaldi* should compel him to give sureties. If he has no sureties, he should swear that he does not have them and submit to imprisonment.

4. He who does not want to receive witnesses

Whoever ought to receive witnesses and does not want to give sureties or accept witnesses should lose the case and the *iudex* should arrest him immediately, and until he pays he should not leave the prison.

5. He who does not present himself on the day of the testimony

If someone ought to receive witnesses and does not present himself on the indicated day, if he is encountered in the city, the *iudex* should put him in prison, whence he should not depart until he pays all the debt.

6. He who ought to testify and, after promising to do so, fails

If the plaintiff promises to present witnesses and he cannot testify with them, he should lose his claim.

7. The same concerning the bondsman of the debtor summoned within nine days

If the debtor provides a bondsman and does not pay in the indicated term nor is he found in the town, the bondsman should pay the debt and the fine, as has been said.

8. He who denies the bond nine days

If the bondsman denies the bond, the plaintiff should prove it as he would to his debtor. If the bondsman of the summoned debtor does not want to accept the witnesses or give sureties for double the debt or present himself on the indicated day, he should lose the case; also, the *iudex* should arrest him immediately and put him in the power of the plaintiff.

9. The debtor or the bondsman of the nine days who flees from the prison

If the summoned debtor or his bondsman flees from the prison outside the city, the plaintiff should capture him without penalty anywhere he wants, wherever he can find him.

10. He who should receive witnesses for money within the nine days

Whoever should receive *alcaldi* or witnesses, should first provide the money that the claim costs or sureties that are worth double the entire claim, or offer his [own] imprisonment, swearing that he does not have sureties; if he does not do this, he should lose the case, be arrested immediately, and should not leave the prison until he pays all the debt.

11. He who refuses legal witnesses

He should lose the case who ought to receive witnesses and refuses them, they being legal. He who ought to testify and does not have competent witnesses the day of the term, as it is in the code, should lose the case.

12. Which witnesses are competent

The code and also the statutes of law [passed in addition to the code] establish that the citizens of the city and the children of citizens of the city may swear and testify against a citizen of the city or against the son of a citizen of the city, and not any other. All those are designated citizens of the city, as much of the city as of the villages, who are inscribed in the census list: *attemplantes* [a resident class lacking full citizenship], tenant farmers, *milites*, and prebendal clergymen. All these should testify against a citizen and against any other man; but only a resident should testify against a resident.

13. That the witnesses are legal in the city or outside it

Whoever testifies for debt or for claim should testify in the city with three citizens; outside the city, with two. All who deny any demand or debt which the plaintiff can prove should pay double the claim, as it is in the code.

14. He who ought to testify with the *alcaldi*

Whoever denies a debt or a claim, and the plaintiff, on the contrary, can prove it with the sworn *alcaldi* or with the substitutes, should pay the plaintiff double and the *alcaldi* five *solidi*. Then if all the *alcaldi*, both the sworn and the substitutes, are victorious over someone who ought to testify, they should receive five *solidi* for their rights from those who had denied such.

15. He who testifies about sureties

If the plaintiff testifies about sureties for double the debt, the *iudex* should give the sureties to him who testifies immediately. And if those sureties are not released within the term of nine days, they should be lost, as if they have been bought by one and sold by the other.

16. Two *alcaldi*, sometimes sworn, sometimes substitutes, can testify

Although under a prior heading this [chapter] ordered that in the city three citizens should testify and outside of it two, two *alcaldi*, sometimes sworn, sometimes substitutes, can testify inside and outside of the city.

17. The debtor who says that he has already paid

If a debtor says to the plaintiff that he has already paid him or another by his order, or that, by his command, he has given the amount of the debt in any portion, and the plaintiff denies it, the debtor should prove it and should be believed. If he cannot prove it, the plaintiff should swear [that the debt is still owed] and the debtor should pay double the claim. In order to avoid such disputes, it is established that everybody who ought to pay a debt should pay it in the presence of the *alcaldi* or of citizens, who can prove it with him when it is necessary.

18. When twelve-year-old boys should be accepted as witnesses

A twelve-year-old son of any citizen may testify [in cases involving] up to twenty *menkales*; [in cases involving more than] twenty *menkales*, he may testify if he is willing to respond to the challenge by combat; and if he does not want to respond, he is not eligible to testify.

CHAPTER XXI

Testimony of Responsible Intermediaries or of Substitute *Alcaldi*

1. Testimony of responsible intermediaries or of substitute *alcaldi*

Whenever witnesses, responsible intermediaries, or substitute *alcaldi* attest [in cases involving] up to twenty *menkales*, they should be believed; [in cases involving more] than twenty *menkales*, if they are not believed, they should be challenged [usually to a trial by combat].

2. The testimony of the sworn *alcaldi* or that of the *iudex*

If the sworn *alcaldi*, the *iudex*, and the *notarius* attest together, they should not be challenged and should be believed.

3. The testimony of the sworn [*alcaldi*] and of those not sworn

If the *iudex*, some of the sworn *alcaldi*, or the *notarius* attest together [in cases involving] up to twenty *menkales* with others not sworn, if they are not believed, they should be challenged.

4. He who challenges for a claim of less than twenty *menkales*

He who challenges the witness, the substitute *alcaldi*, or the responsible intermediaries for twenty *menkales* or less should pay sixty *menkales*.

5. The clergyman who testifies with a layperson

If a clergyman testifies with a layperson for more than twenty *menkales*, if he is not believed, he should be challenged together with the layperson. If he challenges luck[1] against the layperson, he should fight in judicial combat, as the code prescribes; if the layperson challenges against the clergyman, he [the clergyman] should defend his innocence by presenting seven clergymen as witnesses who hold equal or higher rank. Also, if he testifies with one who subsequently dies, he should similarly defend his innocence with seven witnesses.

6. The clergyman who challenges a layperson

If a clergyman challenges a layperson, the latter should justify himself with twelve citizens and after having been justified, he should be believed and reinstated.

7. The layperson who testifies with one who dies

If a layperson testifies for more than twenty *menkales* with someone who subsequently dies, if he is not believed, he should be challenged.

8. The *iudex* who renders judgment at his door

When the *iudex* renders judgment at his door, he should be believed and should not be challenged.

9. How those challenged should throw for luck

Witnesses who are challenged throw for luck by the hand of the *alcaldi*, and the one against whom the luck falls should fight in judicial combat. If he is victorious, he should be believed and reinstated; if he is defeated, he should pay double the claim to the one who was challenged.

10. One's companions help him in the expenses and in the fine

The companions of the one against whom the luck has fallen should help in all the expenses and in the fine, so that, although he is defeated, he should not pay any more than any other of the companions [who were also] challenged. If a clergyman and a layperson are challenged, and the clergyman ought to prove his innocence as has been said, the layperson should help him by paying half the expenses. If it is the layperson who ought to justify by luck, the clergyman should help him in all the expenses by paying half. If the clergy-man or the layperson ought to testify for one now dead and he is challenged, he should not throw for luck with anyone. But if it is the clergyman and he cannot justify himself, he should pay double the claim, as the code prescribes, without anyone helping him. If it is the layperson, he should have this same sentence.

CHAPTER XXII
Fighters of Judicial Combat

1. What day the fighters should be matched
Whoever should fight in judicial combat should be matched [with an opponent] on Saturday and not on Friday, as it has been said.

2. He who says that he is sick
If he who is challenged is sick at the same time at which he is challenged, he should indicate the illness to the *alcaldi*, if it is external; but if the illness is internal or is in a location that gives him shame to show it, he should swear that he cannot fight because of that illness and not for another reason, and he should be believed. If in that same moment he does not show the illness or say that he is ill, later it should not be legal for him to indicate that cause, but instead he should be matched and should fight.

3. The term of the sick person
To the person who quits fighting for reason of illness, the *alcaldi* should give a term of nine days to present another equal combatant in his place, as we say below.

4. The challenged who has the luck go against him
Whoever is challenged, after the luck has gone against him, immediately says right there if he wants to fight in judicial combat on foot or on horse.

5. He who says that he wants to fight on horse
If he says that [he wants to fight] on horse, the *alcaldi* should give him a term of twenty-seven days so that the plaintiff may bring in each nine-day period five gentlemen who should not be professionals on salary, nor special-ists, nor left-handed, but rather are the equal of the challenged.

6. The equality of the fighters on horse

When the horsemen are presented, the *iudex* together with the *alcaldi* should examine faithfully which of the combatants introduced is similar to the challenged in everything. If none of the fifteen horsemen introduced in the three nine-day periods are the equal of the challenged, he [the challenged] should swear immediately and should be believed and reinstated. If someone is the equal of the challenged, the challenged should keep a vigil that night, and the following day attend the mass, dressing himself in arms. Later the challenged should swear that he defends the truth; immediately the challenger should challenge him. Next the challenger should swear that the challenged has sworn falsely. And these oaths should be made next to the altar, touching the Holy Gospels. Having done this, they should depart for the field of judicial combat. When they are at the field, the *iudex* and the *alcaldi* should point out the markers on the field to them, allowing for the movement of the sun. Once they begin to fight, if either of them should pass over the marker, he should be judged defeated. He who challenged should always pursue and the challenged should defend.

7. The challenged who remains unbeaten until the third day

If the challenger cannot defeat the challenged before the setting of the sun on the third day, the challenged should be believed and be immediately reinstated on the field. Also, if he defeats the challenger, he should be reinstated immediately on the field.

8. The challenged who is defeated

If the challenged party is defeated and the judicial combat concerns false testimony, he should pay double the claim and the plaintiff should hold him [to it] until he pays.

9. A defeated defendant over whom the Palace has right

If the challenged is defeated in judicial combat regarding a pecuniary penalty of which the Palace should have a portion, the *iudex* should retain him until he pays, except when he provides bondsmen sufficient for all of the claim on the same field. The Palace should never put him in jail.

10. The challenged who defeats the challenger

If the challenged defeats the challenger and the fight lasts three days, on the third day at the ninth hour he should descend from the horse and the other should pursue him until sunset. If the fight is left without decision until that hour, or won, the litigants should be treated as has been said above.

11. The challenged who says that he wants to fight in judicial combat on foot

If the challenged says that he wants to fight on foot, the *alcaldi* should grant the challenger a term of twenty-seven days to present five combatants on foot in each nine-day period; they should not be professionals, nor left-handed, nor blacksmiths, but equal to the challenged; nor a man who had already fought in judicial combat in Cuenca.

12. The same concerning the equality of the fighters on foot

When those five combatants on foot are introduced in each nine-day period, the *iudex* together with the *alcaldi* should examine faithfully which of the introduced fighters is similar to the challenged in everything; and if they find one similar to him, [the equal] should fight. That is, first, each one should swear that he will exhibit all his strength in that fight. And if the challenger throws the challenged to the ground two times, he who makes claim should bring another five combatants on foot in the second nine-day period, and he does the same. And if they cannot be matched in the third nine-day period, the challenged should swear alone and should be believed and reinstated. If they are matched by the third nine-day period, as has been said, they should keep a vigil, swear, and go to the field as has been indicated above.

13. The weapons of the fighters

The weapons of the horseman established in the code should be the following: mail jacket, helmet, upper arm and thigh armor, lance, shield, and two swords. For those on foot they should be the same, minus one sword.

14. The fighter who carries hidden weapons onto the field

If any of the combatants carries other weapons onto the field or does any bad deed, for this alone he should lose the case.

15. He who gives other weapons to a combatant in the field

Whoever knowingly gives other weapons to any of the fighters should pay one hundred *aurei*. Also, anyone who says any word to the fighters after they have begun to fight should pay sixty *menkales*.

16. He who passes over a marker on the field

Whoever crosses the markers on the field should pay sixty *menkales*. These pecuniary penalties should be for the *alcaldi* and for the plaintiff; but responsible intermediaries[1] enter and position themselves where they please.

17. The markers on the field are not drawn in

The markers that the *alcaldi* have placed the first day, both for horse as for foot [combat], should not be drawn in until the fight has finished. The horses and the testicles of the gentlemen should always be respected. The combatants should eat and sleep together at the house of the *iudex* until the fight is completed.

18. The guarding of the combatants

The same *iudex* should guard the litigants from all conversation with other men, and the following day the *iudex* and the *alcaldi* should place the litigants on the field in the same way that they removed them; also, they should place their weapons on the field in the same way that they found them.

19. The agreement of the litigants

The combatants should arrange themselves when they please, both before the fight and during it, except when the challenge is for larceny or for homicide. But if it is for larceny or for homicide, they should not arrange themselves without the Palace [taking part] once the fight has begun.

20. The wage of the hired fighter

The pay of a hired combatant should be twenty *menkales*. If he is defeated, he should only receive ten; if he winds up dead, those ten *menkales* should be granted to his wife or to his heirs. Once [the combatants] are on the field and have begun the fight, he should receive ten *menkales*, even if the fight is stopped by agreement. But if any arrangement is made before he is armed, he should not collect anything. Once he is armed, until the combat begins, he should receive five *menkales* if an agreement is reached.

21. The dead combatant

He who ends up dead on the field should be considered defeated. He who has killed him should pay no fines for it nor depart as an enemy.

22. The lances of the fighters

By the code, the points of the combatants' lances should be blunted.

23. The *andadores* guard the weapons of the fighters

After the fighters are positioned on the field, the *andadores* should guard their weapons and receive a *menkal* as pay for their work; and if any weapon is lost or stolen, they should pay for it.

24. Proclamations on the field

The *sagio* should proclaim that which is necessary on the field, as has been said above. The combatant who does not want to reinstate his opponent by order of the *iudex* and of the *alcaldi* should pay one hundred *aurei* to the *alcaldi* and to the plaintiff.

CHAPTER XXIII
Debtors Who Flee from the City

1. The debtor who flees from the city before giving a bondsman

If a debtor departs from the city before providing a bondsman, the plaintiff should take sureties at the home of his debtor, as it has been said above.

2. The wife who says that her husband is not within the district

If a wife says that her husband is not to be found within the district of Cuenca, she should swear before the *alcaldi* that she tells the truth and also include in the oath that he did not leave because of fear of that debt; and then the *alcaldi* should grant her a term of twenty-seven days to bring in her husband to give juridical satisfaction.

3. The wife swears each nine-day period

If the wife does not bring in her husband during any of these three nine-day periods, she should come each nine-day period to swear that her husband is still not within the district of Cuenca.

4. The wife who does not want to swear

If the wife does not come to swear within these terms, the plaintiff should take sureties daily at the home of his debtor or should take what is owed him until he recovers his money, if the debtor's wife acknowledges the debt.

5. The wife who does not acknowledge the debt

If the wife of the debtor does not acknowledge the debt, she should respond judicially on behalf of her husband, and all that the plaintiff litigates with her should be firm and legal.

6. The child of the debtor

If the debtor does not have a wife but does have children, the plaintiff should bring the case that we have said against the children that he would have brought against the wife.

7. The debtor who does not have a wife or children

If the debtor does not have a wife or children, the one who is entitled to his goods should respond in his name, as the wife and the children of the debtor would do.

8. One who comes before the tribunal once on behalf of the debtor

Whoever comes before the tribunal once on behalf of the debtor for any case should not be accepted again in front of the tribunal for the same case.

9. The husband who comes before the tribunal

If the husband comes in person before the tribunal under the above terms, or his wife presents him, and he does not pay the debt immediately or does not give juridical satisfaction to the plaintiff and leaves the city, no one should come before the tribunal for him thereafter; but rather, the plaintiff should take sureties daily from him until his wife pays the debt or gives juridical satisfaction on behalf of her husband.

10. The debtor whom someone meets in the district

No one should come before the tribunal for the debtor who is found within the district of Cuenca, but the plaintiff should take sureties from him daily until he obtains his rights or recovers the amount of the debt.

11. The debtor who has gone to the king

If the wife or the children who possess the goods of the debtor say that he is not within the district of Cuenca because he has gone to the king, or on pilgrimage, or to hunt, the plaintiff should await his return.

12. He who has gone on a military expedition

He should likewise await the return of the debtor if [the debtor's] wife says that [the debtor] has gone on a military expedition or in the *requa*.[1]

13. He who has gone to hunt

If [the debtor's] wife says that he has gone to hunt, [the plaintiff] should await him, as has been said, but the wife should swear that she will not send him bread or provisions where he might be.

14. He who has gone for business

If [the debtor's] wife says that he has gone in the *requa*, [the plaintiff] should await the return of the *exea*;[2] if she says [he has gone] on the military expedition, he should await the return of the military commander or that of his other companions.

15. When the military commander or the *exea* returns

When the *exea*, the military commander, or his companions return from the military expedition or from the commercial expedition and the debtor does not return, the plaintiff should take sureties at the home of his debtor until he obtains his right or recovers the value of the debt.

16. The captive debtor

If the wife of the debtor says that her husband is captive, or ill, or dead, she immediately should respond in his name.

17. The sick debtor

Nevertheless, if she says that her husband is sick, she should have a term of thirty days and, if this lapses and if the debtor has not come, she should respond for him. And when she expounds any of these reasons, she should swear that she tells the truth and should be believed.

18. Just as the wife should respond judicially for the debtor, so also his concubine should respond

All that has been established and judged concerning the wife of the debtor should be established and judged for his children and his concubine, or for any other, if they possess his goods.

19. The term of the sick debtors who are within the district or outside it

All sick persons who are within the district or outside it, in the city or outside it, should have a term of thirty days.

20. The warned debtor

If the debtor wants to go to the king, or in the *requa* or on other business and, before he leaves, the plaintiff can prove the debt with three citizens or with two *alcaldi*, warning him that he should pay it, and he does not pay the debt before departing, from that moment the plaintiff should take sureties daily at the home of the debtor, and he should not respond judicially to his wife or to any other, until he recovers his money.

21. The wife declared guilty of her debt or of that of her husband, and the imprisonment of husbands and of wives

If the wife is declared guilty of her own debt or of that of her husband and she does not pay immediately, she should be seized without any penalty. Nevertheless, the confinement, except in chains, of women or children under the age of twelve should be avoided. Whoever puts them in another kind of confinement should pay ten *aurei* to the *iudex*, to the *alcaldi*, and to the plaintiff. The kinds of confinement for other persons should be these: jail, stocks, chains, foot chains, hand chains, and the tying of hands and feet, both in front and behind.

22. He who takes a prisoner out from the city

Whoever removes from the city someone who is imprisoned because of debt should pay ten *aurei* as a fine, half for the *iudex* and the *alcaldi*, and the other half for the plaintiff.

23. He who arrests someone outside the city

Whoever arrests a man outside the city for lacking a bondsman should take him to the city within the term of three days and, once there, should present him before the *iudex* so that [the *iudex*] can judge if he should be in prison or not. If he is guilty, he should be imprisoned; if he is not guilty, he should remain free.

24. No one should impede the prisoner from eating or relieving himself

Whoever holds a prisoner for any debt should not prevent him from eating or going out in order to relieve himself; the one who impedes him should pay ten *aurei*, if the prisoner can prove it with two citizens who possess houses contiguous to the one that holds the prisoner.

25. The prison of the declared debtor

If the wife or children of the prisoner acknowledging the debt want to enter prison in his place, being made to pass as debtors, they should be received before the *alcaldi*; and the one that does not want to accept them should pay three hundred *solidi*. However, the one who wants to enter instead of the prisoner, once inside, should not leave from there until he pays the whole debt.

26. The declared hostage who enters for another

Whoever, as a declared debtor, should it be his father, his child, or even his wife, enters the prison of the plaintiff should pay the whole debt within the term of twenty-seven days. After twenty-seven days lapse, he should pay double all that he owes, so that if he has been held for double the debt, and the term lapses, he should pay quadruple.

27. No one should be exempted from capture by indicating the sign of prison

It is not legal for anyone to say, "I will not enter into prison, because I am a prisoner," exhibiting a shackle on his hand or on his foot. Also, no one can defend a debtor outside his house from other creditors, saying: "The prisoner is mine," even though he exhibits the sign of prison.

28. No one should defend a prisoner outside his house

No one should defend a prisoner outside [the captor's] house for any other reason than for the captor going out to relieve himself.

29. The escaped prisoner

If the declared debtor or his bondsman, or a thief or a traitor or his bondsman escapes from the prison of the creditor and takes refuge in a church or in the Palace, he should be removed from there without any penalty; and if someone tries to defend [the escapee], [the defender] should respond in place of the person who fled.

30. Debtors [who are] servants or captives

If someone holds a captive who owes him something [and who is] a servant or a child of another, the *señor* or the father [of the captive] should pay the debt, if he [the captive] acknowledges the debt; if he denies it, he [the *señor* or the father] should respond and should give him [the plaintiff] judicial satisfaction, as he would do if he were captive. We say the same of the salaried laborer; that is, the one whose commands he carries out and whose bread he eats should respond in his place, if he has no other relatives. But if the laborer has relatives, the debtor should respond to them and not to another. However the *señor* or the relatives of the salaried laborer, whoever claims the debt, should first give bondsmen who will pay for the captive, regarding the payment of the debt or the juridical satisfaction that the debtor gives him.

CHAPTER XXIV
Those Who Appeal to the Court of the *Alcaldi* on Friday

1. Those who appeal to the court of the *alcaldi* on Friday

Those who appeal to judgment on Friday should be from the city or from the villages. Their appeal should not be impeded and they should have a decision that same Friday.

2. Those who are not pleased with the decision of the Friday [court]

If one of the litigants is not pleased with the decision, he should appeal to the code in the part in which the judgments of all legal cases should have [been recorded].

3. What day the charter should be read to those who appeal to it

The decisions of the code are always read on Monday to those who appeal to it.

4. No one impedes the judgment of the charter

Anyone, be it the *iudex*, the *alcaldi*, or any other, who wants to impede or fails to fulfill the judgment of the code should pay one hundred *aurei*, one half to the plaintiff and the other half to the king. He should pay equally one hundred *aurei* who, although he is the *iudex* or one of the *alcaldi*, judges some other thing that is not the one exclusively that the code prescribes, changing the substance of the case.

5. The judgment that the charter cannot clarify

If there occurs any case that the code does not define, it should remain in the arbitration of the *alcaldi* and of the *iudex*. And if one of the litigants does not like the decision of the *alcaldi*, he should appeal to the council, as has been stated at the beginning.

6. What ought to be tried on Friday at the court of the *alcaldi*

On Friday, at the tribunal of the *alcaldi*, no other thing is done other than giving judgments, receiving witnesses, and summoning before the tribunal those who ought to receive witnesses and testifiers on the following Friday.

7. He who appeals two times to the judgment on Friday for the same thing

Whoever appeals two times to the judgment on Friday or to the Charter for the same thing, should lose the case. He who reiterates a case, should pay ten *aurei* and likewise lose the case.

8. The *iudex* who prolongs the judgment of the charter

If the *iudex* or the *alcaldi* prolong for another the judgment of the tribunal or of the code by a day, they should pay that claim for which the case takes place, except for causes not included in this code. This is established so that all the plaintiffs can have their rights on Friday. Because of this we command that the matching of the fighters in judicial combat should be done on Saturday and not on Friday.

9. All the *alcaldi* should go to the tribunal on Friday

The *iudex* and all the *alcaldi* should go to the tribunal on Friday in order to judge the things that have been stated.

10. The penalty of the *alcaldus* who does not go to the tribunal

If any *alcaldus* is within the district of Cuenca and does not go to the tribunal on Friday, he should pay an *aureus* to the other *alcaldi*, or else he will be dismissed by his superiors.

11. The agreement of the *alcaldi*

After the *iudex* and the *alcaldi* stand in the tribunal, they should all place themselves in agreement in order to issue decisions as quickly as possible, and they should deliberate two by two or as it seems best to them.

12. The *alcaldus* who injures his companion

If any *alcaldus* says to his companion, "you lie," or another insulting word, he should pay ten *aurei*. If he incites him to fight, he should pay twenty *aurei*, and the *iudex* and the *alcaldi* should receive these pecuniary penalties; the offender should not receive any of this. That which we say concerning the *alcaldi*, we say concerning the *iudex*.

13. With respect to the *alcaldi* while they are present at the tribunal

While the *alcaldi* meet in the tribunal, no one should injure them or challenge them or contradict them concerning the judgment; he who does this should pay sixty *menkales*. This same precept should pertain to the *iudex* and the *notarius*.

14. He who harms the *iudex* or an *alcaldus* at the tribunal, or by the taking of sureties

Whoever injures an *alcaldus* or the *iudex* at the tribunal, or injures the *iudex*, an *alcaldus*, or an *andador* by the taking of sureties, should pay double the fine of the crime that has been committed, according to testimony of that citizen who has taken the sureties instead of the *sagio*.

15. No official of the council should take sureties in the absence of the citizen

Neither the *alcaldi* nor the *andadores* should take sureties in the absence of the citizen, as the code prescribes. However, the *iudex*, on whom is incumbent the greater responsibility, should take sureties from any citizen.

16. The official of the council who takes sureties in the absence of the citizen

If the *iudex*, an *alcaldus*, or an *andador* takes sureties in the absence of the citizen and he is seized or prevented, there should be no penalty [to the resisting party] for it.

17. The *notarius* should take sureties with the officials of the council

When the *iudex* or the *alcaldi* ought to take sureties for reasons of the council, the *notarius* should take these together with those [officials] and record the sureties of each one so that, if they are lost because of the failure of the *notarius*, he himself should pay them.

18. The collectors of the council

When the collectors of the council ought to levy the money of the council, and someone reviles or injures them because of the sureties, [the injurer] should pay double the fine of the crime that he has committed, according to testimony of that citizen who has taken the sureties with him in the place of the *sagio*.

19. The *Señor* should not enter the tribunal of the *alcaldi* on Friday

The *Señor* of Cuenca should not enter the tribunal of the *alcaldi* on Fridays; the remaining days in between he may enter when he pleases. However, while the *Señor* is present at the tribunal, no other should judge. If the *iudex* or an *alcaldus* judges while the *Señor* is present at the tribunal, he should pay the plaintiff the claim for that on which he has given the decision. This is established so that the *iudex* or the *alcaldus* will not judge wrongly for fear or respect of the *Señor*.

20. The *merino* should not enter the tribunal of the *alcaldi*

If the *merino* wants to enter the tribunal of the *alcaldi*, he should enter on Friday and he should remain there until the judgments have concluded. We prohibited the *merino* from entering into the tribunal on other days because, as the *iudex* should receive the pecuniary penalties for the profit of the council and of the Palace and for it he should be subjected to oath, it is not necessary that the *merino* should enter the tribunal the remaining days, as he may enter then more to pry than to judge. He should enter on Friday, because the *merino* ought to intervene in the agreements and in arrangements of the pecuniary penalties for the Palace.

21. The secret session of the tribunal

When the *iudex* and the *alcaldi* want to talk secretly, the *merino*, the *sagio*, and all the *andadores* should leave the tribunal, because that which is heard by any of these will never be secret.

22. The *andador* who gives an opinion before the *alcaldi*

Any *andador* who gives an opinion before the *alcaldi* or represents another should pay an *aureus*. Whoever reveals a secret of the tribunal should pay one hundred *aurei* and should register it so that he is not received as a witness in future.

23. The entrance of the litigants at the tribunal

All the litigants who present themselves to the judgment of the Friday [court] should enter the tribunal by order of the *iudex* or of the superior officers.

24. Those who enter the tribunal without the order of the *alcaldi*

If someone enters the tribunal without the permission of the *iudex* or of the superior officers, forcing his way past the doorkeeper, he should pay half a *menkal*. If the doorkeeper allows someone to pass without permission, he should pay as much.

25. The oath of the pecuniary penalty

When the litigants stand before the *iudex* and the *alcaldi*, he who claims [the plaintiff] takes the oath of *mancuadra*[1] first, if the claim amounts to more than a half *menkal*. For all cases to be judged, he who claims ought to first swear the *mancuadra* on the cross.

26. He who is not acquainted with his rights

If any of the litigants does not know how to defend his rights, an attorney should be appointed for him who is pleasing to him, provided that he is not the *iudex* nor an *alcaldus*. He takes the *mancuadra* oath; the opponent should respond by agreeing or denying; but before the denial or admission, the plaintiff should say what the claim is and how much and should also explain why he [the challenged person] responds to that claim. All the explanation concluded, the *alcaldi* should judge the one who denies or admits.

27. He who does not want to agree or deny or appeal to the code

If he who defends his cause does not want to deny or agree or appeal to the code, he should lose the case. This same we say of him who in the judgments in front of the door of the *iudex* does not want to deny or admit or appeal to the judgment of the Friday [court]. Also, if there is a case in front of the substitute *alcaldi* and he who defends does not want to deny or admit, he should lose the case, or else he should appeal to the judgment of the Friday [court]. If one of the two litigants accepts the decision at the door of the *iudex* or of the substitute *alcaldi* and the other does not, and he does not appeal to the judgment of the Friday [court], he should lose the case.

28. He who appeals after accepting the decision

Whoever after accepting the decision at the door of the *iudex* or of the substitute *alcaldi* appeals to the judgment of the Friday [court] or to another instance [level of appeal] should lose the case, except for the three situations cited above.

29. He who does not accept the decision of the Friday tribunal or appeal to the charter

If one of the two litigants accepts the decision of the judgment of the Friday [court] and the other does not, and he does not appeal to the code, he should lose the case.

CHAPTER XXV
The Manner of Pleading and the Witnesses

1. The manner of pleading, and that to which the code forbids one to respond juridically, and demonstrates [what is forbidden]

Although he who defends should deny or agree, nonetheless, if he knows how to plead something to which the code forbids him to respond juridically, he should state it and should not respond, as though he says: "You are demanding this and I am denying it, you in your turn deny or you admit if we had *alcaldi* for this, or not." And then the *alcaldi* should decide who demands, who denies or admits if they had *alcaldi* who judged them or not. If [that person] admits that [the disputants] had *alcaldi*, he should also say what judgment or what term [the *alcaldi*] conceded [the disputants]. If he admits this and it has not been presented in front of the tribunal, he should lose the case. If he denies something about the judgment or the term, and his adversary, on the contrary, can prove it with those *alcaldi*, similarly he should lose the case and, also, he should pay five *solidi* to the *alcaldi* who have attested it. But if he cannot prove it, he should pay double the claim, since he overcame his debtor unjustly. But if the defender of the debt denies that they had *alcaldi*, and his adversary, on the contrary, proves it with the *alcaldi*, the plaintiff should lose the case and should pay five *solidi*. If the defender cannot prove it, he should pay double the claim, since he overcame him unjustly. Nevertheless [the claim of] the debtor of nine days should not be legal, for this or any other reason, until he pays the debt. If the defender does not plead anything against his adversary, he denies or admits, as has been said. If he admits and he is the debtor, he should be summoned within nine days. If the claim is not for debt, he should be summoned at the pleasure of the *alcaldi* and he should pay the corresponding fine, or else he should give judicial satisfaction within the term of nine days. If he denies it, he [the plaintiff] should prove it as the code prescribes and present the witnesses, and receive double. If the plaintiff cannot prove it, he who denies it should swear alone and should be believed.

2. Which witnesses ought to be contested

Witnesses should not be accepted by the lawyer [of the defendant] if they are or were [involved] in that case, or by [the defendant's] enemy, or by one who has hope or a share in the claim, except the *alcaldi* and the council, and then the *alcaldi* should attest only for their judgment; and except also those associates who have constituted a society in order to earn money outside of the town, as, for example, in business, in raiding, in the *requa, etc.*

3. He who ought to testify with designated witnesses

If anyone should attest with designated witnesses or with the *alcaldi*, he should inform the witnesses regarding the day of the case, and if later some of the witnesses are not presented in front of the tribunal to testify, he should pay the claim for the one who should attest. And so that it is understood more clearly, we command that as many times as someone needs to testify, and the witnesses are not presented before the tribunal, he should pay as has been stated.

4. The witness who is sick

If some of the witnesses are sick, the plaintiff should make it known to his opponent one day before, and then none of the litigants should present themselves before the tribunal or should lose the case. If on going to the tribunal an illness or a pain overcomes the witness, as happens frequently, or he gets sick the night previous to the judgment, none should lose the case, even though the plaintiff has not warned his opponent a day in advance. If he does not believe that the witness has been overcome by illness or pain, for which he cannot be presented before the tribunal, the sick person, after having recovered, should swear, as it is in the code, that he could not present himself before the tribunal because of the illness or the pain he endured on the way or on the previous night; and then none of the litigants should lose the case.

5. The witness who is not found within the district

If some of the designated witnesses are not found within the district of Cuenca, the plaintiff should make it known to his opponent one day before so that he should not be present before the tribunal or lose the case. When the plaintiff has healthy witnesses or *alcaldi* in the district of Cuenca, he should set a new term with his opponent; and he who does not want to [set a new term] and is not present on the indicated day should lose the case. If the debtor says to his plaintiff that he now has paid him the debt and he promises that he will prove it, he should designate the witnesses and present them within three days before the door of the *iudex* if they are healthy and within the district of Cuenca.

6. The witnesses who are not found within the district

If the witnesses are not found within the district of Cuenca, [the defendant] should communicate with the plaintiff, as has been stated. If the plaintiff can testify that the witnesses can be found within the district of Cuenca and that they have not been presented before the tribunal, the one who should testify should lose the case. And if the truth of the matter is that they were not to be found within the district of Cuenca at the time that the plaintiff was able to see them, he should set a new term with his adversary. And he who does not want to set a term or present himself before the tribunal should lose the case.

7. He who ought to introduce witnesses for judgment at the Friday [court]

Whoever ought to present witnesses or testifiers for judgment at the Friday [court], should present them on the next available Friday.

8. He who ought to present witnesses for judgment at the door of the *iudex*

All the other witnesses and testifiers should plead at the door of the *iudex* by the third day following [the case being brought to the door of the *iudex*].

9. Examinations and the oaths of witnesses

When the witnesses are presented to testify, the responsible intermediaries, the *alcaldi*, the *iudex* or those who make the decision ought to question them and swear them in before they testify, saying: "If you say the truth about the things that we ask you, then Almighty God, who is King of Kings, *Dominus dominantium* and *Iudex iudicum*, should help you and save you in this world and in the next. And if you hide the truth of the things that we ask about because of shame, because of fear, because of money, or because of supplication, then Almighty God, who is King of Kings and *Dominus dominantium,* should destroy and confound you in the flesh and in the soul, with your children and wives and with those things that you love most deeply." And all the witnesses should respond, "Amen."

10. The witness who does not want to say "Amen"

If any witness does not want to say "Amen," he should not be received as a witness. If all say "Amen," the *alcaldi* should ask them if they were present to see and hear that [situation]. If they say yes to that, again the *alcaldi* should order them to say what they saw and heard about this, and then each one of the witnesses should say freely what he saw and heard, no one leading the witness. Whoever leads the witness should pay double the claim to the plaintiff, and the witness should not be legal. The testimonies being revealed, the *alcaldi* should examine if their testimonies are similar, because, if their testimonies are disparate, their testimony does not suffice. If one of the witnesses neglects to say through forgetfulness that he saw or heard it, or any other thing, he should be asked again whether he saw or heard it. If he says yes to that, it should be sufficient; but if not, it should not suffice. One includes [both] seeing and hearing in the testimony for this [reason], because no one ought to be admitted as a witness by only hearing or by only seeing. Since if he were admitted, then the deaf, the mute, and the blind would be admitted as witnesses.

11. No one should be admitted as a witness unless he saw and heard the thing

For this reason it is established that no one should attest except he who says, "I saw and I heard that about which I have been asked," and, also, who is in [possession of] his sound judgment, so that he should not be insane, or a lunatic, or possessed.

12. The testifiers who should be accepted

Whoever should swear, should swear on the cross, the plaintiff interrogating him in this manner: "Do you come to swear in accordance with what the *alcaldi* have judged?" And then the testifier should respond, "I [so] come."

13. Curses at sworn witnesses

Afterward the plaintiff should curse the sworn witness as he wishes, provided that he may not say of him that someone commits sodomy with him. He may say all the other curses that he pleases, and the sworn witness should remain quiet until the plaintiff orders him to say "Amen."

14. The sworn witness who replies

If the sworn witness does not want to say "Amen," when [the plaintiff] orders him, or upon saying the curses, the witness replies in some manner that curses [the defendant] or the plaintiff, he [the defendant] should lose the case.

15. He who says to the sworn witness "sodomite"

If the plaintiff says to the sworn witness that someone commits sodomy with him, he should lose the case and should pay double the claim to the sworn witness.

CHAPTER XXVI

The Festival Days on Which No One Should Be Allowed to Take Sureties or Cite to Judgment

1. The festival days on which no one may take sureties or cite judicially

Although it is given to the plaintiffs to take sureties from their debtors and cite them judicially, nonetheless there are days, hours, and times among those that no one may take sureties or summon anyone.

2. What the festival days are

The festival days are: Sunday for respect of the day; Tuesday by the statute of the market; the day of Christmas; the day of the Circumcision [1 January];

the day of the Apparition [Epiphany, 6 January]; the day of the Resurrection; the day of the Ascension; the day of Pentecost. No one may take sureties on these six festivals or within their octaves. Also, on the feast of Saint John [24 June], on that of the Assumption of the Virgin Mary [15 August], and on that of Saint Michael [29 September]. Similarly on these festival days no action should be brought against anyone.

3. What are the festival times

[The festival times are:] on a day of fasting after the dinner, and on the remaining days before the morning masses and after the vespers of the parish churches. Whoever takes sureties from another on these days and at these times should pay five *solidi*. And he who prevents one from taking sureties from the creditor should not pay any fine.

4. What are the festival periods

We also establish festival days by code, in the Lenten season, from the first Sunday of Lent until the Friday of the octave of the Resurrection; in such times no one should take sureties or have a case before the door of the *iudex* nor at the tribunal on Friday. Nevertheless, judgments may be held for cases of brotherhood with another village, for dishonoring of the body, for the salary of a hired person, and for a debt of bread and of wine. Also, there are festival days during the time of harvest, during which [times] the judgments and the taking of sureties should cease, except for damage to grain and to the remainder of the planting; excepted also are all cases of plowing, of irrigation, of dishonoring of the body, and of brotherhoods.

5. What day begins the festival periods

We establish these festival days: from the feast of Saint Peter [probably 1 August, marking his freedom from prison] until the last Friday of August. Festival days are also at the time of vintage, in which [periods] all the cases and taking of sureties should cease, except for things that pertain to the vintage, such as the panniers, barrels, and other things of this nature. We establish the festival days of the vintage from the feast of Saint Michael until the first day of the following November.

6. He who does not pay the debt because of the festival days

If [a debtor] ought to pay someone and does not want to pay him on the indicated day because of the festival days, the plaintiff should obtain witnesses to the fact that [the plaintiff] reclaims his money from [the debtor]; and if he does not pay him in the term of nine days, the festival days having lapsed, [the debtor] ought to render [the plaintiff] double the money or [whatever thing] he owes him.

7. The *alcaldus* who advises the litigants

After the litigants find themselves in the tribunal before the *alcaldi*, no *alcaldus* should presume to advise or defend the parties. He who does this should pay an *aureus* to his colleagues [the other *alcaldi*] who present themselves in the tribunal. The side of the one whom he defends or advises should lose the case. In this way, the *alcaldi* should not advise or counsel anyone in the cases, but only judge according to the testimony.

8. The casuistry of lawyers should not be legal at all

Among other things that ought to be strictly avoided [are] casuistries [of lawyers] which should not legal to anyone, except only the code and the just judgment.

9. How the lawyers should plead

The litigants and all the lawyers should plead standing. When the allegations [are] concluded, the tribunal should retire. Later the *alcaldi* should judge concerning those allegations, according to their consultation of the code.

10. The communication of the judgment

After the *alcaldi* have resolved the judgment, two of them should communicate the sentence in front of the door. And if one of the litigants does not like the judgment, he should appeal to the code, as has already been stated.

11. He who does not present himself before the tribunal on Friday or by the charter

He who is cited before the tribunal on Friday or by the code and does not present himself before the termination of the session of the tribunal should lose the case.

12. The litigants who name *alcaldi* outside the city

When the litigants of the villages name *alcaldi* outside the city, and one of [the litigants] does not agree with the judgment, he should appeal to the judgment of the Friday [tribunal] and present himself before the tribunal the first subsequent Friday; and he who does not present himself should lose the case. If the case does not take place on the first Friday, he should present himself before the tribunal on the next following Friday; he who does not present himself should lose the case.

13. When the *alcaldi* postpone the day of judgment

When on any occasion the council or the *alcaldi* must postpone the judgment, they should postpone it from the usual Friday and they should proclaim the Friday of the judgments.

14. Postponements of cases by reason of the emergency defensive muster

If the cases are suspended by reason of the emergency defensive muster [*apellitum*], starting from the third day in which the standard [of the city] entered Cuenca each one should present himself before the tribunal for his case, some at the door of the *iudex*, some at the Friday [tribunal].

15. Suspension of cases by reason of an offensive military expedition

If the cases are suspended by reason of an offensive military expedition [*expeditio*], each one should present himself for his case, whether at the door of the *iudex* or at the Friday [tribunal], nine days after the standard enters Cuenca.

CHAPTER XXVII

Those Who Appeal to the King

1. In what cases it is licit to appeal to the king

Whoever appeals to the king, if it is not in a claim or a case of ten *menkales* or more, should lose the case and the appeal should be considered null and without effect. Thus I command that the Code of Cuenca should put a stop to all the rest of your cases.

2. The term of those who appeal

Those who appeal to the king in the above cases should be summoned the third day [after their initial request] in front of the door of the *iudex*. This term allows that if, in the meanwhile, they want to agree between themselves, they should not appeal to the king. But if they are not mutually agreed, they should present themselves before the tribunal of the door of the *iudex* and the one who does not present himself should lose the case.

3. He who appeals can change his mind

When both present themselves, if he who has appealed changes his mind regarding the appeal and wants to receive the decision of the code, he should not appeal to the king.

4. The responsible intermediary who should be given to the appellants

The *iudex* should give to the appellants as a responsible intermediary any civic messenger [*andador*]. But the responsible intermediary should be such a person that they should both trust him and he should not be suspected by either of the litigants. The responsible intermediary being appointed, he who prosecutes should take the oath of *mancuadra* [no malicious intent], if he has not sworn it already, because with the term having lapsed, no one should have responded for the *mancuadra*. After the litigants accept the responsible intermediary, he should indicate to them the date that they will meet. And the litigant who is not present willingly on the indicated date should lose the case. The litigant who wants to name a lawyer in his place should name him in front of the door of the *iudex* in the presence of the responsible intermediary, and not in another place.

5. The appellant who says that he has enemies

The responsible intermediary being designated, if any of the litigants do not dare to go openly for fear of their enemies, he should swear that it is true that he has enemies and he should go to the king by the way he pleases.

6. The appellant who arrives first before the king

He who arrives first before the king should wait for his opponent three days, if before separating [the person separating who has not arrived] knew where [the first arrival] should meet the king. If [the person separating] did not know the correct place, he who arrives first before the king should wait for his companion six days. If an opponent presents himself before the king with the responsible intermediary and the other does not, once the term lapses [the non-presenter] loses the case by the testimony of the responsible intermediary. If one arrives first and the other does not present himself within the term indicated with the responsible intermediary, once the term lapses he should lose the case by the testimony of the responsible intermediary.

7. If the appellants are enemies

If the litigants who ought to appeal to the king are enemies, each one should give a surety bondsman to the *iudex* the day of the term and should present himself together with the responsible intermediary. After they undertake the journey with the responsible intermediary, they should walk and stop as the responsible intermediary commands, until they find the king within the bounds of his kingdom.

8. No one searches for the king outside the kingdom

No one should seek the king outside the kingdom, until [the king] returns. And when the king is in the kingdom, [the appellants] should summon themselves again and they should go to him, as has been stated.

9. He who hurts his adversary during the journey

If one injures, kills, or even insults his adversary on the route, he should pay double the penalty of the crime that he has committed.

10. If a litigant or the responsible intermediary becomes ill on the journey

If one of the litigants or the responsible intermediary becomes ill during the journey, those who are healthy should wait for him until he gets well or dies. If he gets better, they should proceed with their journey. If the responsible intermediary dies, the litigants should return and the *iudex* should designate another responsible intermediary for them. If it is one of the litigants who dies, the others should similarly return and the dead man's heir ought to substitute for the deceased.

11. The appellants whom the journey bothers

If the road becomes burdensome to the litigants or the designated responsible intermediary [mentioned] before, and both [litigants] want to wait for the arrival of the king, they should establish again another term in the presence of the responsible intermediary, two *alcaldi*, the *iudex*, and an *alcaldus*, or the sworn *alcaldi* of the king. And when it pleases one of them to go to the king, he should indicate again that term which has been said. He who does not want to go should lose the case. If they cannot retain the first responsible intermediary, the *iudex* should designate another and they should go as has been said. If the journey of the litigants becomes burdensome for them and they want to designate another instead of the king for judging them, whether in the city or outside it, they should name him without any penalty. When the litigants arrive together before the king, they should enter with their responsible intermediary as quickly as possible.

12. The fine of the responsible intermediary who changes the decision

The responsible intermediary, who receives his title through his fidelity, ought to guard nothing more [closely] than this; that he should not change the decision that has been given, he being present. For if he changes the decision and it is proved by the one who gave it, let him be hurled from the city cliffs or let his tongue be cut out as a faithless individual rather than a trusted one.

13. The pay of the responsible intermediary

The litigant who is defeated in the case should pay the expenses that his opponent had made by his going and return. He also should pay for some shoes worth two *solidi* and nothing more for the responsible intermediary who accompanied them. The litigants, moreover, should provide the responsible intermediary jointly [his costs of] going and returning.

CHAPTER XXVIII
The Collectors of Money for the Council

1. After a half-year of leaving office, officials of the council should not respond [to legal suits] by sureties, if they have inhabited houses

If the *iudex*, the *alcaldus*, the *notarius*, the collector [of fees], the *andador*, or the *almutazaf* have inhabited houses in the town after a half year of having left office, they should not respond by sureties. But if they do not possess inhabited houses, they should respond at all times.

2. He who holds declared money of the council

Whoever holds declared money of the council should respond for it at all times.

3. The election of the collectors

We order by the code that each parish should have its collector.

4. The bondsmen of the collectors

All collectors should provide two legal bondsmen who have houses abundant in sureties from which the *iudex* has the right to the money for the council. These bondsmen should not leave the bond until money of the council is paid. And while the *iudex* finds sureties in the houses of these bondsmen, he should not take sureties from any other house of the parish. But if he does not find sureties in these, he should take them in all the parishes, wherever he finds them.

5. The collectors will be responsible before the *iudex*

The above-mentioned collectors should be responsible before the *iudex* for money of the council, and they should constitute themselves debtors when the *iudex* orders them. And those to whom the collectors make themselves debtors should take sureties in their houses in the name of the *iudex*. When they do not find sureties, the *iudex* should take them on their behalf in all the parishes.

6. He who removes the sureties from the collector

Whoever deprives the collector of the sureties for money of the council, upon taking them should pay the collector an *aureus*. Whoever does not redeem the sureties from the power of the collector within the thirty-day term should lose them.

7. He who does not redeem his sureties

If the collector or his bondsman does not redeem the sureties from the power of the *iudex* within the term of thirty days, he should likewise lose them.

8. The collector who cares for the sureties badly or collects something wrongfully

If by the fault of the collector the sureties of the bondsmen are lost, the collector should pay them double. If the collector collects a tribute from someone who is not included in the census list, he should pay it double and, furthermore, he should pay an *aureus* as fine.

9. The collector who modifies the census list of the council

If the collector who has the census list of the council adds or changes something in it, he should pay ten *aurei* and double the damage caused.

10. Those who make the census list

If the sworn [recorders?] of the census list, both of the city as well as of the villages, are declared guilty of falseness, each one of them should pay ten *aurei* and, furthermore, they should be proscribed as liars and perjurers. The sworn who make the census list once should never make another.

CHAPTER XXIX
Cases Between Christians and Jews

1. Cases between Christians and Jews

If a Jew and a Christian litigate for something, two citizen *alcaldi* should be designated, one of whom should be Christian and the other Jewish. If one of the litigants is not pleased by the judgment, he should appeal to four citizen *alcaldi*, two of whom should be Christian and two Jewish. These four should have final judgment. Whoever appeals the judgment of these four should know that he will lose the case. These *alcaldi* should guard against judging anything else than what the Code of Cuenca prescribes.

2. Witnesses between a Jew and a Christian

The witnesses between a Christian and a Jew should be two citizens, one Christian and the other Jewish, and all the things denied by the testimony of these [two] should be confirmed and believed. Anyone who ought to testify should swear with double the sureties or on his feet, according to the Code of Cuenca. If it is the Christian who places his foot and is defeated in the case, the *iudex* should imprison him in the jail of the king until he pays.[1]

3. The Jew who testifies that his debtor was outside jail

If the Jew testifies that the prisoner is outside jail, the *iudex* should put him in the power of the Jew until he pays. Moreover, if it is the Jew who places his foot and is defeated in the case, the *albedí* [Jewish *iudex*, chancery official] should imprison him in the jail of the king.

4. The Christian who testifies that his debtor is outside jail

If it is the Christian who attests that the prisoner is outside jail, the *albedí* should place him in the prison of the Christians, from whence he should not leave until he pays.

5. The testimony for delivery of sureties

Be it known concerning witnesses, whether a Christian or a Jew, [if] he delivers double the sureties and he does not redeem them within the term of nine days, he should lose them completely.

6. If the *albedí* does not want to do justice

If the *albedí* does not do justice, he should pay ten *aurei* to the *iudex* and, furthermore, the plaintiff should take as sureties with impunity what he can seize of the things of the Jews outside of the *alcacería* [district of shops Jews rented from the king]. The *iudex* should divide the above-mentioned ten *aurei* with the plaintiff.

7. The *iudex* who does not want to do justice

If it is the *iudex* who does not do justice for a Jew, he should pay ten *aurei* to the *albedí* and, furthermore, the Jew should take as sureties all that he can seize of the things of the Christian.

8. The taking of sureties between a Jew and a Christian

If a Christian does not want to give judicial satisfaction to a Jewish plaintiff, he [the Jew] should take sureties in the house of the Christian with any citizen, as the Code of Cuenca prescribes. And if the Jew is a citizen who has real estate, he should retain the sureties; if he is not a citizen who has real estate, that citizen with whom he took them should retain them. If the Jew does not want to name *alcaldi*, the Christian should take sureties in the house of the Jew with any Jewish citizen and the Christian should keep the sureties if he is a citizen who has real estate in the town; if he is not a citizen who has real estate, the Jew with whom he took them should retain them.

9. He who delivers the sureties without the order of the plaintiff

If the Christian or the Jew who retains the sureties delivers them to their owner without order of the plaintiff, he should pay ten *aurei* to the *iudex* or to the *albedí* and to the plaintiff.

10. The citizen who does not want to take sureties with a Jew

If a Christian citizen does not want to take sureties with a Jewish plaintiff, he should pay five *solidi*, and the *iudex* should take sureties from him for this fine and should divide them with the plaintiff.

11. The Jew who does not want to take sureties with a Christian

If a Jewish citizen does not want to take sureties with a Christian plaintiff, he should pay five *solidi*, and the *albedí* should take sureties from him for this fine and should divide them with the plaintiff.

12. The Christian who prevents the taking of sureties

If a Christian prevents the taking of sureties by a Jew or does not want to open the door to him, the *iudex* should take sufficient sureties from him for the claim and for the fine of five *solidi* and should divide this fine with the plaintiff.

13. The Jew who prevents the taking of sureties

If it is the Jew who prevents the taking of sureties by a Christian or [the Christian] is deprived of them [in some way], the *albedí* should take sufficient sureties from him for the claim and for the fine of five *solidi*.

14. The *iudex* who does not want to take sureties with a Jew

If the *iudex* does not want to take sureties with a Jew, he should pay ten *aurei* to the *albedí* and to the plaintiff.

15. The *albedí* who does not want to take sureties with a Christian

If it is the *albedí* who does not want to take sureties with a Christian, he should pay ten *aurei* to the *iudex* and to the plaintiff.

16. The place and time of judgments

The cases between Jews and Christians should be before the gate of the *alcacería* and not at the synagogue. The time of the meetings of the court should be from the completion of matins in the cathedral church until terce. When they sound terce, they should conclude the judgments. He who does not present himself before the court should lose the case.

17. The oath of the Jew and of the Christian

For all claims, should they be Christian, should they be Jewish, up to a value of four *menkales*, the Christian should swear without the cross and the Jew without the Torah. If the claim is worth four *menkales* or more, the Christian should swear on the cross and the Jew on the Torah. And if the Jew or the Christian does not want to swear, he should lose the case.

18. Agreements between Jews and Christians

If the Christian receives a Jew as debtor through his money, and the Jew has a wife or children, he should make them all debtors with him, since, if they are not made debtors and the Jewish debtor dies or flees, his wife and his children would not answer in any other manner for that debt. If the Christian accepts them as debtors and the Jew dies or flees, his wife and children should pay that debt. If it is the Jew who receives a Christian as debtor through his money, and his wife or children are not made debtors with him, they would not answer to the Jew for that debt, if the Christian dies or flees. If they are made debtors, they should pay when it is necessary.

19. Agreements between Jews and Christians

All agreements that are made between Jews and Christians in the presence of witnesses should be legal and firm, except for the profit agreement, since the profit in some manner should increase more than double at the end of a year. And according to this proportion, the Jew should demand the one-month profit or that of another time, both long as well as short, during which he invests his money at interest.

20. Concerning usury money

After the money of the loan is doubled, it should not earn more.

21. The Jew who puts the sureties of a Christian on sale

If a Jew puts the sureties of a Christian on sale, and this can be proved in the *alcacería* or outside it, he should return double the sureties. Nevertheless, if there is an agreement between them to the fact that the Jew should put the sureties on sale, it can be done without any penalty, as long as the Jew can prove the agreement with the testimony of a Jew and of a Christian, as the code prescribes.

22. Money doubled from the sureties

The Jew should undertake to sell the sureties after he has doubled the money, and the *venditor* should hold them during three days. And if some money is surplus, it should be returned to the owner of the sureties.

23. The Christian who wants to sell his sureties

At any time that the Christian wants to sell his sureties, the Jew should deliver them to the *venditor* and the *venditor* should respond to the Jew that he has received his money. What remains should be delivered to the owner of the sureties.

24. The oath of the Jew concerning the sureties

If a Jew and a Christian litigate on something that cannot be proved with witnesses, [in cases involving] up to four *menkales* the Jew should swear holding sufficient sureties in his hand and he should be believed; for four *menkales* or more he should swear on the Torah that he has the sureties in his hand.

25. If a Christian does not want to testify with a Jew, or the reverse

If a Jew does not want to prove with a Christian that which he sees, he should pay double all the claim. The Christian should have this same judgment, if he does not want to prove it with the Jew.

26. Christians and Jews may have judicial appointments at the same time

When Christians do not have judicial appointments, Jews should not have them either. The Jews may have judicial appointments according to the Code of Cuenca, except on Saturday and on their feasts.

27. Those who testify in legal cases between Christians and Jews should be citizens

In Cuenca there will be no testifying about a Jewish citizen unless by Jewish and Christian citizens; nor about a Christian, unless by Christian and Jewish citizens.

28. Witnesses of Christians and Jews should not answer to a challenge [by combat]

The witnesses of Christians and Jews should not answer to a challenge [by combat].

29. No one may take weapons out of the town to sell them

For the advantage and defense of the city, we establish by the code that neither Christian nor Moor nor Jew should remove wooden or iron weapons from the city. And whoever removes them to sell them should pay twenty *aurei*. He who takes them for the purpose of fighting and making war should pay no fine because of this. Also, no weapon or vessels of gold or silver should be taken out of use in Cuenca.[2]

30. The judgment that is given in the court to the Christian and to the Jew

All judgments that are given in the court of the *alcaldi* to the Jew and to the Christian should be firm and legal, and they should not appeal.

31. The sureties that the Jew does not want to show

If the Jew has sureties and the Christian wants to redeem them and they are not shown immediately to him, the Jew should lose the profit of the money. However, he should agree that the Christian should show him money first. If the Christian does not show money, the Jew does not have to show the sureties, except when the Christian says that he delivered them to the *venditor*.

32. The Christian who injures or kills a Jew

If a Christian injures or kills a Jew, he should pay five hundred *solidi* to the king, if it can be proved, as the code between Jews and Christians prescribes. But if not, for injury he should clear himself with two of four designated [citizens] and for death with twelve citizens, and he should be believed. If it is the Jew who injures or kills a Christian, he should pay the penalty of the offense that has been assigned, if it can be proved, according to the Code of Cuenca. But if not, for injury he should be cleared with two of four designated Jews and should be believed; for death, he should be cleared with twelve Jewish citizens and should be believed.

33. All the pecuniary penalties of Jews belong to the king and not to another

Jews do not have any part in the pecuniary penalty of a Jew, because all belong entirely to the king, since, in fact, the Jews are serfs of the king and they are entrusted to his treasury. Equally, neither does the *iudex* have a right to a seventh part of the pecuniary penalty of a Jew, since he has not done any work to request it.

CHAPTER XXX

The Government of the Military Expedition

1. The government of the military expedition and the guarding of the city

When the council wants to make a military expedition [*exercitus*] against the enemy, before it departs, watchmen should be placed in each parish who should guard and keep watch over the city day and night. There should remain also two sworn *alcaldi* together with an acting *iudex*, whom the annual *iudex* leaves in his place. And these *alcaldi* together with this *iudex* should concern themselves with protecting the city, as has been said. Also it remains established in the code that once the council has departed [on expedition], all strangers should be expelled from the city. After sunset, if the guards find anyone walking in the streets without carrying a light, they should seize all his belongings and put him in confinement until the following morning. In the morning, he should be brought before the [acting] council, and if he was a citizen or the son of a citizen, he should be absolved;[1] but if he was a stranger, let him be hurled from the city cliffs. The guards abovesaid should guard the city against fire, warning the house-dwellers that they should be careful of fire and if, God forbid, a fire happens, everyone should hasten first to the gates and secure them, and only then should [they] return to extinguish the fire. This is stated because on many occasions some, wanting to betray the city, set a fire so that, while everyone was trying to extinguish the blaze, they were free to open the gates and receive the enemy. Furthermore, if someone is suspected of potentially endangering the town, the acting *iudex* together with the *alcaldi* should expel him from the city or hold him captive until the council returns. The same precautions should be taken to guard the city at harvest-time.

2. The pay of the guards of the city

Those [compelled to] remain in the town by the council [during a military expedition] should nonetheless have the same share of booty taken by the militia which is granted to any horseman [who did serve]. We establish this because those required to stay behind by the council's order had no opportunity to take any booty.

3. He who stays behind from the military expedition without the command of the council

All horsemen, whether from the city or from the villages, who stay behind from the military expedition without mandate of the council should pay two *aurei*. Also, foot soldiers in the same circumstance should pay an *aureus*, unless they were ill or absent from the district of Cuenca.

4. The *señor* of the house should go on the military expedition

The *señor* of each house should go on the military expedition and no other in his place. But if the *señor* of the house is old, he may send in his place his son or nephew who represents his house, and he should not be a salaried worker. Wage earners should not excuse their masters from going on the military expedition.

5. What arms are borne on campaign, and shares their bearers have

The horseman serving in militia expeditions who fails to bring a shield, lance, and sword should receive only one-half of his normal booty share. A foot soldier who failed to bring a light lance and a dagger or a club should receive no share. A foot archer bringing a crossbow with two bow strings and one hundred arrows should receive a half-share of booty for them; any substitution for this equipment should receive nothing. The horseman archer, trained in that skill, who brings a crossbow with two bowstrings and two hundred arrows should receive a full share of booty [for that equipment];[2] any substitution for this equipment should receive nothing. A person wearing a long-sleeved mail jacket with a helmet should receive a full booty share for them, as does a person with a short-sleeved or sleeveless mail jacket with a helmet. Mail jackets worn alone should receive a half-share of booty. Persons wearing only a helmet should receive a quarter-share. Persons who bring chains with twelve collars [for holding prisoners] should receive a full share. The share should be reduced proportionately for a chain with fewer collars.

6. Children and women should be prohibited from the military campaign

Women and children should not go on campaign with the town's militia, nor receive any shares of booty.

7. The election of camp guards

Where all the military expedition assembles together, there the *iudex* and the *alcaldi* should choose trustworthy watchers from each parish, from among those whom the people call *talayeros* [scouts], who have good horses. And if the *iudex* and the *alcaldi* learn that a scout does not have a good horse or that he himself is weak or a coward, he should be replaced and another should be put in his place.

8. The pay of scouts

Each scout should have an ox or four *aurei* as salary for his work, that which pleases him more. If the military expedition does not obtain so much booty that they [the scouts] can be paid fully, each one should receive two *aurei*. If the military expedition does not acquire anything, the scouts should receive nothing. The scouts ought to proceed according to the orders and the will of the *alcaldi*.

9. The scout who encounters some difficulty

The scout who does not fulfill his obligations every day should lose all his salary. The *Señor* of the city, together with the *iudex* and the *alcaldi*, should lead the military expedition. Also they [the command group] select the leaders.

10. The one who injures a guide

If someone injures a commander guiding the military expedition, he should lose his right hand.

11. Those who go to collect information

If the *Señor*, together with the *alcaldi*, orders someone to collect information, the one who goes should receive half of all that is gained thereby, and the council receives the other half.

12. Where they should record the encampments and other things in writing

Where the military expedition prepares its food to pass the night, there the *notarius*, together with the *iudex* and the *alcaldi*, should record in writing the encampments, the men, the animals, and the weapons. We command that these things be written at the beginning, because if someone deserts from the military expedition with something stolen or sends a message to the Muslims, one can know from the encampments. But, since it seems impossible that anyone could depart with something stolen or that he could send a message to the Muslims without the complicity of his encampment companions, by this we order that for offenses of this type, the companions who remain should suffer the penalty that this other one would have suffered, had he been made prisoner.

13. The dispatch of a mobile raiding force

When they want to dispatch a mobile raiding force [*algara*], half the group of each encampment should go in the mobile raiding force and the other half should remain in the rear guard [*açaga*]. And if any excess individuals are in half the encampment, because they should not be equal, they should remain with the rear guard as well.

14. The fifth part of the mobile raiding force

Those who go in the mobile raiding force should receive a fifth part from all the things that they obtain as booty.

15. The mobile raiding force indemnifies its animals

Members of the mobile raiding force should be compensated for all animals from the fifth part [of the booty] that they have obtained [as a part of that force], as the code prescribes.

16. The election of the *quadrellarii*

The day that the mobile raiding force departs, all the parishes should designate a *quadrellarius* [booty divider] for each parish, who should divide the booty on the day of the division, delivering to each one his share faithfully.

17. The recording of the booty of the military expedition

These *quadrellarii* should make a written record of the quantity of the total booty, and do it guaranteeing through such men that, if by chance something should be lost later, they should indemnify it for them. The *quadrellarii* should do the recording and the guarding of the Moors, the animals [horses, asses], the sheep, and the cattle. And any guard who does not deliver what he had in custody on the day of the division, as is written, should pay according to what the council prescribes.

18. Animals of the military expedition should be in the hands of the *quadrellarii*, the *iudex*, and the *alcaldi*

The mounts should be in the hands of the *quadrellarii*, the *iudex*, and the *alcaldi*, and if these [officials] observe that someone mistreats an animal, they should take it from him and should give it to one who will care for it well.

19. The *quadrellarii* should give animals to the injured and invalids

The *quadrellarii* should examine [those who are] injured, sick, the old, and invalid of the entire military expedition and should give them animals which should carry them until the day of the division. If the *quadrellarii* do not do this properly, the *iudex* and the *alcaldi* should take sureties daily of a *menkal* for each one, and with this money they should rent animals to carry the injured, sick, old, and invalid.

20. The day of the partition

When the day of the division arrives, in the first place they should compensate [for loss of] animals and injuries; after this, should give to the soldiers a sixth part [of the booty]. We said "to give the sixth part" because when horsemen and foot soldiers are together, they should not have to consider as rightfully theirs more than a sixth part. When the horsemen are alone without those on foot, one should give them a fifth part [of the booty]. When those on foot are alone, one should give them a seventh part [of the booty].

21. No one should be given a fifth part for the Moor whom they want to present in exchange for a captive Christian

Neither the horsemen nor those on foot, according to the code, should be given a fifth part of any Moor whom they will offer for a captive [Christian]. Nor should they be given a fifth part nor a sixth nor a seventh of the other things, but only of the Moors [not needed for prisoner exchange], the animals, and the sheep and cattle.

22. What animals should be compensated

[The owners of] animals that the Moors have beaten, killed or crippled should be compensated. [The owners of] animals that are lost in this way the mobile raiding force should similarly [as in 20] compensate from its fifth part [of the booty].

23. The price of the animals that should be compensated

The compensations should not exceed sixty *aurei*; and up to sixty *aurei*, each one should receive for his horse as much as he swears [in value] with two citizens [testifying]. Other animals should not exceed twenty *aurei*; and up to twenty, each one should receive as much as he swears with two citizens. The asses should not have any [separate] compensation, but should have their part just as the horses.

24. The price of treating injuries

The [victim of a] wound that has bone fracture should receive twenty *menkales*. The [victim of a] wound that passes from side to side [breaks the skin in two places] should receive ten *menkales*. For any other injury [the victim] should receive five *menkales*. These should be the compensations for injuries, as much for men as for animals that have been injured, as much within the city as outside of it.

25. The pay of the doctor

The surgeon should receive this price; be it known, for a wound that has a bone fracture from a blow, twenty *menkales*, and for this alone. For an injury that passes [breaks the skin] and requires two bandages, he should receive ten *menkales*. For any other injury that does not pass or have a bone fracture, the surgeon should receive not more than five *menkales*.

26. The salary of animal herders on the military expedition

Each animal herder, both of sheep and of livestock, should have a sheep, whichever he chooses. The guards of captives should receive [the same] as the animal herders; that is to say, a sheep for each one. And the animal herders as well as the guards of the captives should guard continually by day and by night until the day of the division.

27. Election of the animal herders

The animal herders and guards should be selected equally by each parish.

28. Bondsmen of the animal herders

The animal herders and guards first should give legal bondsmen from those [over] whom the council has jurisdiction, when it is necessary.

29. He who unhorses a horseman

If a horseman, or one on foot, unhorses a horseman at the gate of a castle or of a town, he [who unhorses him] should have his horse; and he who unhorses him in another place should receive the shield, the saddle, or the sword, whichever pleases him most of these things.

30. He who first enters into a castle

The horseman or one on foot who first enters into a castle or tower should have any Moor of those who are found there. And if there are two or more who enter at the same time, they should share that Moor in common.

31. The compensation of weapons

The horseman or one on foot who loses a lance with or without a standard in the body of a Moor at the gate of a castle or of a town should receive two *aurei* for the lance with a standard; for the lance without a standard, one *aureus*. All weapons that are lost on a battlefield should be indemnified.

32. He who is made captive on a military expedition

If a horseman or one on foot is made prisoner during a military expedition, his [family or heir] should be compensated for his weapons and his mount.

33. The redemption of a captive

If a horseman becomes captive, and in [among the captives of] the military expedition there is a Moor horseman who can be exchanged for him, he should be given for him. Equally a Moor foot soldier should be given for a Christian foot soldier.

34. The captive Moor who is an *alcayat*

If a Moor *alcayat* [warden or castellan] or *señor* [chief officer], who at that moment commands a castle, is seized, if the king wants to have him, he should redeem him with one hundred *aurei* and he should belong to the king. The other captives, both the rich as well as the poor, should belong to those who can acquire them.

35. The division of cattle

The *alcaldi* together with the *quadrellarii* should give to all in the military expedition, to all the parishes equally, and to the *Señor* of Cuenca, the meat of the booty cattle. If some take cattle in other ways, their ears should be cut.

36. What booty should be brought to partition and divided

When the day of the partition arrives, all the things that have been obtained, such as sheep, cattle, animals, garments, clothing, money, gold, silver, and weapons, except the living Muslims, should be brought to the division.

37. The encampment that is suspect

The *iudex* and the *alcaldi* should investigate all the encampments, if they have suspicion of theft. And whoever they find stealing something should be left without his share [of booty] and, furthermore, his hair should be shorn in the form of a cross, and his ears should be cut.

38. He who has written two times

The same penalty will be administered to the one who makes a writing two times [submits his name in writing for a double share of booty]; that is, [his hair] should be shorn in a cross, his ears should be cut, and he should lose his share.

39. The shares of the standard of the council

The standard of the council should have the right to two shares. The *iudex* should receive these shares for himself. Nevertheless, if the standard or *Señor* of another council should receive more shares, as many shares should be received by the standard of the council of Cuenca; and the *iudex* should retain two of these shares, and the other shares should belong to the council.

40. The shares of the *adalil* [battle commander]

All guides or battle commanders, if they are known, should receive two shares.

41. He who shouts "pillage"

Everyone who shouts "pillage" [*tala*] in the military expedition should be left without a share and should pay ten *aurei*.

42. He who does not present booty on the day of the division

Whoever has something from the military expedition and does not present it to the *quadrellarii* on the day of the partition, should pay it double as a thief.

43. The code of the auction

Whoever buys something at the auction and does not pay for it within the term of nine days should pay double its amount. And the nine days having elapsed, the plaintiff should take live and dead sureties until [the debtor] pays it double. And if that one denies the debt, the plaintiff should prove it with two companions from the mounted raiding party.

44. He who gives a bondsman for auction money

If someone who places a bondsman for auction money and does not relieve him within the term of nine days, and the bondsman pays double, the debtor should pay quadruple [four times the value] to the bondsman. And if the bondsman has paid only the quantity [owed], the debtor should pay him double. Furthermore, it should be known that the auction bondsman does not have any term in which to bring the indebted to judgment.

45. He who injures another in a military expedition

Whoever injures another in a military expedition with prohibited weapons should lose his right hand.[3]

46. He who injures another without forbidden weapons

He who injures him otherwise but not by forbidden weapons, should pay double the penalty of the offense, whatever it is, according to the Code of Cuenca.

47. He who kills another

He who kills another should be buried alive under the dead person.

48. He who commits a theft

He who commits a theft, and it cannot be proved against him, [of] up to five *menkales*, should clear himself with twelve citizens and should be believed. For five *menkales* or more, he should respond by judicial combat. If the theft can be proved against him, he should pay double the claim within the nine-day term, as the code prescribes.

49. He who wants to make a claim

He who wants to make a claim to the council, be it the *Señor*, the *iudex*, an *alcaldus*, or anyone else, should make it the first day of the division, when all the council is summoned by proclamation. And if the full council is in agreement in considering it, it should be held firm and legal. But if the council is not in agreement in considering it, because of someone being opposed, the claim should not be legal. The promise or donation of another day should not be legal.

50. He who gives something without the command of the council

If the *Señor* of Cuenca, the *iudex*, the *alcaldi*, the *quadrellarii*, or anyone else gives something to anyone that day or another [day] without the order of the council, he should pay double that thing, according to the code on theft, and he to whom it was given should be free without penalty. Whoever of the council in this case has made a claim and wins in the case against the one who gave it or received it, he [the claim maker] should cover the fine and keep it.

51. The pay of the chaplain and of the *notarius*

The chaplain of the council should be given any Moor as pay. The *notarius* who goes on the military expedition should be given equally a Moor; the chaplain and the *notarius* should not be given anything from the military expedition unless they had been a part of it.

52. The *quadrellarii* [should divide booty] evenly among the parishes

The *quadrellarii*, [assisted by] the *notarius*, should divide [the booty] equally among the parishes.

53. He who does not receive his part within a term of nine days

If the *quadrellarius* does not pay someone his corresponding share within a term of nine days, he should pay double to the plaintiff and also an *aureus* to the *iudex* and to the *alcaldi*. If this happens due to the fault of the *notarius*, the same *notarius* should pay double the share and the *aureus* fine, as has been said.

54. The plaintiff does not accept another debt

The plaintiff should not receive any other debtor after the nine days [during which] the *quadrellarii* should pay double, as has been said. They have to [acknowledge any debt] during [that] nine-day term.

55. The *quadrellarius* who commits a theft

The *quadrellarius* who commits a theft or defrauding in the division should pay as a thief if it is proven; and make it known that he should never have an office of the council nor should he be received as a witness.

56. The salary of the *quadrellarii*

The *quadrellarii* should receive as pay for their work a cavalry booty share each, in addition to their [normal] portions.

57. The pay of the *iudex* and of the *alcaldi*

The *alcaldi* and the *iudex* should receive four *aurei* each if the military expedition obtains good booty. However, if it procured little, each one of them should receive two *aurei* and nothing else. If the military expedition does not obtain anything, they should receive nothing.

58. They receive a fifth part there where they take provisions

The horsemen and those on foot that go in a raiding party should receive a fifth share, a sixth [share], or a seventh [share], according to what the code prescribes, at the place where they take provisions. The code orders that the horsemen alone [during a raid made up exclusively of cavalry forces] should receive a fifth share; the horsemen and those on foot [together] should receive a sixth part; and those on foot alone should receive a seventh share.

59. The leader who leads a raiding party

He who leads a raiding party should receive two shares, if he is the only leader; because, if there were more than one leader in the raiding party, they should have only one share each, unless they are given other portions voluntarily.

60. The others should answer to the leader for a fifth part

The leaders should take a fifth part and answer for them to the *iudex*. And whoever prevents the leader from taking a fifth, sixth, or seventh share should pay ten *aurei*.

61. The auction that is held without the *iudex* being present, and the *aurei* of the auction

The auction that is held without the *iudex* being present should not be legal. Whoever ought to pay auction money should pay at the rate of four *menkales* per *aureus*.

62. The renting of a horse

Whoever rents his horse as a participant in a raiding party for booty, after he has received the horse, even though he has not departed with the leader, nonetheless, if the horse is healthy, [the renter] should pay to the owner of the horse the quantity agreed according to the estimate of the leader. What we said of the horse, we say it also regarding the provisions, that is to say, of the supplies.

63. He who loses his horse in the raiding party

Whoever loses his horse in the raiding party, in the way that has been said above concerning the military expedition, should receive up to sixty *aurei* for it, swearing it with two citizens.

64. Leaders should distribute the shares of the participants in the raiding party

The leaders should distribute the shares of the raiding party members, and those same leaders should be the judges of those who litigate for something [gained in the raid].

65. The leader who does not pay within the term of nine days

All leaders who do not pay within the term of nine days should pay double the share. The nine days having elapsed, the plaintiff should not [advance any other claims], unless to [that person] who divided [the share] instead of the leader.

66. He who robs the house of participants in the raiding party

Whoever robs the house of participants in the raiding party should pay two hundred *aurei* and depart as an enemy forever, if he confesses it; if he denies it, he should clear himself as in the case of homicide.

CHAPTER XXXI
The Emergency Military Muster

1. He who does not go in the emergency military muster of the council

Whoever does not go in the emergency military muster of the council, if he is a horseman, should pay two *aurei*; if he is on foot, he should pay one *aureus*. Equally, if someone hears the call to the emergency military muster and he does not go immediately to seek the standard, day and night, at the place where it can be found, he should pay two *aurei* if he is a horseman; if he is a foot soldier, he should pay one *aureus*, as has been said. But if someone asserts that he walked a day and a night, and, nonetheless, he could not arrive before [the standard was carried from the vicinity], he should swear alone and should be believed.

2. He who says that he did not hear the proclamation

If anyone says that he did not hear the proclamation of the emergency military muster, he should swear alone and should be believed. He who finds himself outside the town when the call sounds for the emergency military muster, if when he returns he cannot find any company with whom to go, should not pay anything.

3. The horseman who does not have his horse and he who is ill should not go in the emergency military muster

Neither he who is ill nor the horseman who does not have his horse in the town should pay anything. Also the horseman whose horse is in the municipal fort or injured should not go in the emergency military muster. When the emergency military muster arrives at a village where there is no standard, the strangers should join themselves with the first that arrive; but if they do not join, they should pay as has been said. He who says that he could not arrive earlier, or that he did not find himself in the town when the call sounded, should swear alone, as has been said, and should be believed.

4. The first [members] of the emergency military muster who put enemies to flight

If the first [members] of the emergency military muster defeat enemies, the later members who did not intervene in the combat should not receive anything of the booty that the first members have obtained, if it is not by agreement with the first combatants.

5. The horse that dies in the emergency military muster

If someone's horse dies in the emergency military muster, the council should pay for it, if the owner of the horse can prove it with two citizens, as the code prescribes.

6. The witnesses concerning the death of the horse in the emergency military muster

The code prescribes that the witnesses should testify that they personally have seen the horse die, and that it was not by the will of its owner; and also that [its death] was to the advantage of the council, and that it was not engaged in a hunt.

7. The witnesses who are not believed

If the witnesses are not believed, they should respond to the challenge by judicial combat; and if not [challenged], they should not yield.

8. The witnesses who are believed

If the witnesses are believed, the owner of the horse should swear with two citizens [other than the witnesses] that the horse did not die through his fault. And in the oath he should include the price that it cost him, if a year has not passed since he bought it; however, if a year has elapsed, he can do it with two citizens [swearing] up to [a value of] sixty *aurei*, and should recover [the value of] his horse.

9. How the horse ought to be shown to the council

If someone's horse is crippled or some [other] injury happens to it, the owner of the horse should show it to the council, and the *iudex* should keep it for thirty days. If it heals, it should be returned to its owner; but if not, the council should pay for it.

10. He who does not show the horse until the third day

If the owner of the horse does not show it to the *iudex* or to two *alcaldi* until the third day after the return of the emergency military muster, he should lose [his right to compensation for the horse]. Sureties should be taken from those who do not go in the emergency military muster until the third day after the return, since, after the third day, no one has to respond.

11. He who pillages the battlefield in combat

If the council or the components of the raiding party or of the emergency military muster engage in a field battle, and before the standard returns from the conflict, someone pillages the battlefield or steals something, he should pay four hundred *aurei* and should be banished forever. And if he does not have it to give, let him be hurled from the city cliffs. If he is under suspicion and it cannot be proven about him, he should clear himself with twelve citizens.

12. Those who do not assist those who are fighting

This same judgment we give regarding those who are in sight and do not assist those who are fighting, [or who] hide in some place, or flee from the battle line. Whoever finds something from the battle up to nine days after [the battle] should present it for the partition and, by finding it, he should receive a fourth of all that he found.

13. He who gives advice to a gang

Whoever, be he a villager or a citizen, makes the council dishonor the *Señor* of Cuenca or any other without the command of the *iudex* and of the *alcaldi* or does violence to someone or for this same reason gives advice to a gang should pay five hundred *aurei*; and [the same penalty] to others when they were consenters, both in the council as well as in the [giving of] advice, the ones about whom the *iudex* and the *alcaldi* know to have conspired in this crime.

14. He who steals something in battle or in the military expedition

Whoever steals something from the things of the Muslims, and it is not demanded from him within the twenty-seven-day term from the day the standard enters the city, once these days elapsed, he should not respond.

15. The leader who leads the military expedition that takes a castle

Any Christian leader who leads the military expedition against a castle or a town, if he conquers it, should take the house that he wants with all the things that are there. [Likewise], if the leader is a Moor, he should take the house that he wants as well, together with the things that are there and, furthermore, all his relatives [in that town] should be safe.

16. Those of the emergency military muster who recapture cattle on this side of the boundary stones

The participants in a raiding party or an emergency military muster who recapture livestock of Cuenca from the Moors on this side of the boundary stones; that is to say, Villora, Iniesta, Tébar, Rus,[1] should receive a thirtieth part from the sheep and an equal amount from the cattle. If they recapture it beyond the boundary stones, they should receive a tenth part from any class of cattle. For the Moors that they bring back, from either this side or beyond the boundary stones, they should receive five *menkales* apiece, and for each horse or mule the same. For the cattle that they procure after entering a town or a castle, they should not answer; the same is true of the beasts and of the Moors [taken in a town or castle]. Of the cattle on this side of the boundary stones of the Tajo River, they should receive the same as from the Cuenca cattle. Of the cattle beyond the boundary stones of the Tajo, they should receive a fifth part where they want to recapture it, whether it be on this side or the far side of the above-mentioned boundary stones.

17. He who brings a message to the leader

Whoever brings a message of a Moorish military expedition or raiding party, if the council subsequently defeats them, should receive five *aurei*.

18. He who brings a Moorish leader or the head of a spy

Whoever brings a Moorish leader to the council should receive ten *aurei*, and he who brings the head of a known spy should receive five *aurei*, and these *aurei*, both for the leader as well as for the spy, should be given by the council.

19. The execution of Moorish leaders

The council should execute Moorish leaders in any way that pleases it.

CHAPTER XXXII
The Code of Purchase, of Sale, and of Collateral of Real Estate

1. The code of purchase, of sale, and of collateral

Whoever wants to sell his goods should [ordinarily] accept his buyer as bondsman and debtor, since if he accepts [a bondsman] from another, it would not be legal. Nevertheless, if the seller fears that the buyer is leaving or will not pay, he should demand a bondsman from him, according to the Code of Cuenca, who should pay the debt the day of the term, if the buyer has fled or has not paid.

2. He who wants to buy something

He who wants to buy something should buy it with a surety bondsman who frees him of all claim and fine, if it is necessary. If someone does not accept a bondsman in this way and after the other person [offers one] judicially for the purchase, he should lose it unless he gives an observer, according to the Code of Cuenca.

3. The validity of purchase and of sale

The sale, purchase, or exchange of something, be it real estate or furniture, should be ratified between everyone except monks, so that no one can back out after it has been made.

4. He who wants to sell real estate

He who wants to sell some real estate should proclaim it during three days in the city, and if some of his relatives want to buy it, he should sell it for as much as he who wants to buy it will pay. The three days having transpired, he should sell it to whom he wants.

5. No one should go back on the agreement of what is sold

The transaction being made, no one can go back on it. If the seller does not proclaim it and sells it, the relatives of the seller cannot claim it from the buyer, but only from the seller, because he sold the real estate secretly without his relations knowing of it; therefore, he should give them as large a piece of real estate and of the same quality and for the same price as he sold it. But if it was proclaimed, as has been said, he does not have to answer to anyone for it. If the code prescribed that no one could sell real estate to other than his relatives, the properties would be depreciated totally and their price would not be able to help captives or homicides.

6. He who pledges real estate or a Moorish servant

If a debtor pledges a vineyard or other property, or a Moorish servant, whether the property or the Moor can bring revenue or not, the lender should have the item unredeemed forever, having its usufruct, until he recovers all the money that he gave for it. And when the owner of the item wants to recover it, he should redeem it from January to January [within a year] and not after, if it is a vineyard. If it is arable land, he should redeem it from [the feast of] Saint Michael [29 September] to Saint Michael. If it is not either one thing or the other, he should redeem it when he has the money. In Cuenca, real estate can never be destroyed or lost.

7. He who wants to sell pledged real estate

He who possesses a pledged property or something else cited earlier and wants to sell [the pledged property] because of the wrath of the king [a kind of outlawry], for homicide or for captivity, should notify the owner of the sureties [given for the pledged property] so that he can redeem [the sureties]. But if [the owner of the sureties] does not want to or is unable to sell them, once [the seller of pledged property] has taken his money, he should deliver the rest to the owner of the sureties. If [the owner of the sureties] cannot sell them, he should pledge them to whomever he wants under the same conditions in which he has them. And such a sale should be legal. Moreover, it should be such a firm pledging so that neither the buyer nor the one who pledged should lose anything through this nor should they pay any fine. Nevertheless, if the one who sells the sureties cannot recover all his money, the one who pledged should not answer to him because of this, unless [the seller of the sureties] can prove with witnesses that both agreed to this, knowing that the owner of the property would deliver all the money to him, if the value of the property would not be sufficient to reimburse him.

8. Pledging made with conditions

A property, an animal, or something else that is pledged on a fixed date and is not redeemed within the indicated term should be sold, except real

estate, gold, silver, precious stones, and iron and wooden weapons. That
which the code permits to be sold should be given to the owner [of the
sureties].

9. He who rents houses for a year

Whoever rents a house or a shop for a year or for a month should hold it
until the last day of his term, and neither the lessor nor the lessee may go back
on the agreement or break the conditions. Nevertheless, if the lessee wants to
leave because of some need or mishap that happens to him, he should rent it at
the same time to another who should respond to the owner of the house in his
name and under the same conditions, together with the price of the rent;
otherwise, he should not leave the house.

10. The lessee who causes some damage to the house

If someone causes some damage to the house that has been rented to
him, he [the lessee] should compensate him [the lessor] according to the
estimate of two citizens.

11. The lessee who does some work on the house

He who does work on the house rented to him by order of the owner of
the house should calculate this expenditure and also the work that he has done
in the price of the rent, and the owner of the house should restore it.

12. The owner of a pledged house who wants to rent it [to his lender]

If someone pledges his house and wants to rent it to the holder of the
money, he should rent it to him, if it pleases him who has it in pledge,
otherwise not. If it does please him, he should pay the amount of the rent that
they have mutually agreed upon, and he should remain in it as long as it
pleases him who has it in pledge, and no longer.

13. He who [sub]lets a rented house without the owner knowing about it or without paying him

Whoever [sub]lets a rented house without the owner knowing about it or
without paying him should pay double the amount of the rent.

CHAPTER XXXIII
The Code of Pledging and of Sales

1. The code of pledging, and of the sale and of the renting of animals

Whoever sells an animal to a citizen, according to the Code of Cuenca, the buyer should hold it for nine days, during which time he should examine it to see whether it is healthy or not.

2. He who discovers that the purchased animal is injured

If the buyer indicates that the animal is injured within the term of nine days, he should return it to the seller and should recover the price that he gave for it. If he has it more than nine days, in no way should the seller yield to him in going back on the deal. Nevertheless, if the seller assures him that he sold him a healthy animal, [the seller] should swear with two citizens that he tells the truth and he should not accept the animal nor return the money. If he does not want to or cannot swear it, he should return the price and keep the animal.

3. The buyer who cannot show the injury

If the buyer says that the animal is injured, but he cannot show the injury, [the agreement] should not be undone. Regarding other defects, the buyer should not return the animal unless for injury solely, as has been said.

4. If a pledged animal dies by chance

If someone pledges a horse, an ox, or other animal to carry a load and it dies because of the excessive load or inordinate work, [the receiver of the pledge] should pay for it because it died by his fault. Moreover, the owner of the animal should receive for it as much as he declared by oath, receiving it on account from the price in money that, upon pledging it, was given to him. If he who has the animal says that it did not die due to the fault of anyone, but through a disease to which it succumbed, he should swear with any citizen that this is the truth and should be believed. In addition, the owner should lose the animal and should return the money that he has received for it.

5. If the pledged animal is injured

If an animal is living and is injured while in the power of him who has it in pledge, he should pay for it. If someone pledges an animal or whatever else belonging to another without the consent of its owner, he should lose the money and the sureties should be redeemed.

6. The agreement concerning the load

Whoever pledges his animal to another to carry loads stipulates with him how much load it should carry and on which road it should be led, and if thereafter the animal dies under that load and on the agreed road, [the other] should not pay anything.

7. He who bears a pledged animal beyond the agreed place

If the owner of the animal can prove with witnesses that the other made it carry more than he was aware of or carried it to another place, and that it died on that road, [the one who had it in pledge] should pay for it according to the oath with its owner. If [the owner] cannot prove it, he who has it in pledge should swear with a citizen that it did not die through his fault and that he did not load it to excess or bear it to another place, and he should be believed. The owner should lose the animal and should return the money that he had received to the pledge receiver.

8. He who takes something loaned

If anyone takes a loaned animal or something else and loses it, or injures it, or it dies under his control, he should pay for it according to the judgment of its owner. If someone bears an animal or something else that has been loaned to him beyond the place covenanted, or he does not return it to the house where he took it on the day established, he should pay double for it.

9. He who denies a loan

If someone takes a loaned animal or something else and for fear of the above-mentioned penalty denies the loan and says that he took it in security or in rent, and the other, on the contrary, can prove it, he [who borrowed the animal] should pay double the claim. If he [the plaintiff] cannot prove it, he who defends should swear alone and should be believed.

10. He who takes control of another's animal

Whoever takes control of another's animal, be it an ox, horse, any other animal, or something else, against the will of its owner or without his assent, should pay double for it and, furthermore, for each day that the thing is in his control, he should pay an *aureus*.

11. The renting of an animal

If someone rents an animal, he should not pay anything if it dies before he can return it to its owner; however, he must swear that it did not die due to anyone's fault, and he should be believed. Nevertheless, if he who has taken the animal in rent leads it beyond the agreed place, changes the road, or does not return it on the indicated day, and meanwhile it is captured, dies, or is lost, he should pay for it by the judgment of its owner and, furthermore, he should give daily to the owner of the animal the amount of the rent until he pays it.

12. The rented animal that is injured

He who takes in rent a healthy animal and before he returns it to its owner, it is nailed, is watered, has harness sores, or has some other injury, he who takes it in rent should keep it for thirty days.[1] And if in this time period he cannot cure it, he should pay for it by the judgment of its owner. Nevertheless, during these days which he holds it to cure it, until he pays the owner [for the unhealed animal], he should not pay the amount of the rent [for that period].

13. The situation of lessee and of lessor

The renter and he who gives a healthy animal in rent cannot go back on the deal.

14. He who hires a man who works badly

If someone hires a servant or another man to work the land and he does not work at the rate of the other hired workers, he who hired him should dismiss him, giving to him the amount that he deserves.

15. The hiring of a Moor or of a servant

He who hires a Moor or a servant should watch him until he is returned to his owner, because if he escapes, he is obligated to pay his price by the judgment of his *señor*. Also, if he kills him or injures him, he should pay for it. If he flogs or injures him, he should pay the fine of the offense that he has committed, according to the Code of Cuenca.

16. He who kills another's animal

If someone kills another's animal or injures it, he should pay for it by the judgment of its owner, if the plaintiff can prove it; but if not, the suspect should swear with a citizen and should be believed.

17. He who beats another's animal

If someone beats another's animal, he should pay five *solidi*, if the plaintiff can prove it; but if not, [the suspect] should swear alone and should be believed.

18. He who injures another's animal

He who injures another's animal should pay five *aurei*, if it can be proved of him; but if not, he should swear alone and should be believed.

19. He who pulls out the hair from the tail of another's animal

He who pulls out the hair from the tail of another's animal should pay five *solidi* for as many hairs as he pulled out, if it can be proved of him with witnesses; but if not, he should clear himself, swearing alone, and should be believed.

20. He who pricks another's animal

Also, who pricks [punctures its flesh] another's animal should pay or clear himself.

21. He who mounts another's animal

He who mounts another's animal against the will of its owner should pay ten *solidi*, if it is proved of him with witnesses; but if not, he should swear alone and should be believed.

22. He who loads another's animal

He who loads another's animal against the will of its owner should pay double and, furthermore, he should pay ten *aurei* for as many nights as it remained in his control, if it can be proved of him; but if not, the suspect should swear and should be believed.

23. He who places a horse next to a mare

Everyone who puts a horse next to a mare against the will of the owner of the horse should pay two *aurei* every time or should give half of the colt to the plaintiff; but this remains the choice of the plaintiff, if he can prove it; but if not [the accused] should swear alone and should be believed. This precept is said as much of the greater animals as of the lesser, so much of the large as of the small; no one has to swear but he alone, except for [the following] small animals, such as pigs, sheep, goats and others like them,.

24. He who takes the products of another's livestock

Whoever takes the products [presumably milk, fleece, and so on] of another's livestock against the will of their owner, should pay double for all the products according to the judgment of their owner, and also should pay double [the value] of the livestock which die of natural causes or by another manner while in his control.

CHAPTER XXXIV
Dogs

1. He who kills a tracking dog

Anyone who kills a mastiff, a bloodhound, or a greyhound should pay five *aurei*, if it is proved of him with witnesses; but if not, he should swear with any citizen and should be believed. He who kills another's hound should pay ten *menkales*, if it can be proved of him with witnesses; but if not, he should swear alone and should be believed.

2. He who kills a herding dog

If someone kills a herding dog that is capable of killing a wolf or keeping it from the livestock, he should pay fifteen *menkales*, if it can be proved of him with witnesses; but if not, he should swear with one citizen and should be believed.[1]

3. He who kills a *carauus*

Who kills a *carauus* [small dog, probably a type of terrier] that can enter and leave by drains should pay five *menkales*, if it can be proved of him; but if not, he should swear alone and should be believed.

4. He who injures a tracking dog

Anyone who injures a mastiff, a bloodhound, a greyhound, a herding dog for wolves, or a hound should pay as though he had killed it, or he should clear himself in the same way.

5. He who kills a dog in self-defense

If someone kills a dog to defend himself from it, he should not pay anything, if he can prove it; but if not, the owner of the dog should swear that the former did not kill it in self-defense, and the owner should receive the fine noted above for dogs.

6. The dog that bites someone

If a dog bites someone and that person cannot kill it, the owner of the dog should put the animal in the power of the plaintiff so that he can do what he pleases to it, if the plaintiff can prove it; but if not, the owner of the dog should swear with two of four designated individuals and he should be believed. For all other damage that a dog causes, both in the house of another and outside of it, his owner should pay or should place the animal in the power of the plaintiff, as has been said, if the plaintiff can prove it; but if not, the owner of the dog should swear alone and should be believed.

7. The cat

Anyone who kills another's cat should pay twelve *denarii*, if it can be proved of him with witnesses.

8. The hen

Anyone who kills another's hen should pay eight *denarii*.

9. Geese and other domestic fowl

He who kills a goose should pay a half *menkal*; for a duck, twelve *denarii*; for a peacock, an *aureus*. For other domestic fowl or animals he should pay by the oath of its owner.

10. He who says that he did not knowingly kill a domestic fowl

If he who has killed [a domestic fowl] says that he has not done it knowingly, he should swear and he should pay half the fine, and the owner should be quit of him. If he who has killed it confesses it and the plaintiff wants to bring him to judgment, the accused should pay double the fine that has been noted above.

11. He who injures a domestic fowl

If someone injures a hen, a goose or other domestic fowl, he should pay according to the oath of its owner, and the perpetrator should pay [that price] for it.

12. He who steals another's hen or other domestic fowl

If someone steals another's hen or other domestic fowl and the owner proves it, he should pay for it as a thief. If he denies it and it cannot be proved of him with witnesses, he should clear himself as in the case of theft.

13. He who kills a dovecote dove.

He who kills a dovecote dove, both in the town or outside of it, or traps it in a snare or in another trap should pay five *solidi*. For a domestic dove, ten *solidi*.

14. The dovecote

Anyone who put nets or snares on the windows of a dovecote or penetrates within it should pay three hundred *solidi*. He who burns or destroys it should pay the same, if it can be proved of him with witnesses; but if not, he should clear himself with twelve citizens and should be believed. He who kills another's cat in his dovecote should not pay anything.

CHAPTER XXXV
The Code of the Hunters

1. The *fuero* of the hunters who on military expeditions or on other occasions injure a game animal or kill it, and those who start the hunt in the first place

If someone from the beginning starts a game animal such as a boar, deer, wild goat, hare, rabbit, partridge, etc. with his dogs, it should be his, even though someone else, the dogs of another, or another's hunting bird kills it, or it falls into another's trap, except in his hunting house.[1]

2. He who builds a house [type of trap] for wild goats

If someone makes a house trap to hunt prey and someone else seizes it in that trap, that hunter should give half to the owner of that house trap and the rest should belong to the hunter.

3. He who violates [the rights of] a hunter

He who violates the rights of a hunter who started the hunt, as has been said, should pay him ten *menkales* for a wild goat; for a deer, five; for a boar, six; and, furthermore, he should pay ten *aurei* for the violation that he made against [the hunter], if the hunter can prove it; but if not, the suspect should clear himself with any citizen and should be believed.

4. Also concerning one who violates a hunter's rights

Also, he who violates a hunter's rights to a hare, a rabbit, a partridge, another item of game, or a fowl of this class should pay double the item of game and the above-mentioned fine of ten *aurei*, if the plaintiff can prove it; but if not, the suspect should clear himself with any citizen and should be believed.

5. He who kills a dog or hunting bird of a hunter

Whoever kills another's tracking dog or hunting bird for the prey should pay double for it according to the oath of its owner. If someone injures a dog or a hunting bird, he should similarly pay according to the oath of its owner.

6. He who deprives a dog or hunting bird of its prey

If someone deprives a dog or hunting bird of its prey, he should pay an *aureus* and double the value of the prey. If the dog or the hunting bird is lost for that reason, he should pay for it according to the oath of its owner.

7. He who first wounds [a hunted animal] during a military expedition and what he should receive

He who first wounds a hunted animal during a military expedition or on another occasion should receive the head back to the ear if it is a boar; if it is a deer, he should receive the hide; if it is a wild goat, he should receive a strip from the loin and his part from the meat. And he who prevents him should pay double for it.

8. The hunt that arrives at a populated area

If hunted game arrives at a populated area without dogs and dies there, as many as arrived there [of the local population] should receive their corresponding parts [unspecified], and the wife who is pregnant should receive two parts. He who first wounded it should receive as the code prescribes.

9. The hunt that brings the dogs to a populated area

If the dogs chase the hunted game to a populated area, and the hunter is absent, those who arrive at the place with the game should feed the dogs and should keep the prey for three days. After the third day they should divide the meat and should reserve the skin for the hunter, and they should also keep the dogs for their owner.

10. The game of the hunter that falls into another's snare

If someone is pursuing game with dogs or a hunting bird and the prey happens to fall into another's snare, the pursuer should seize it and reset the trap. If he does not do this, he should pay the fine that has been established for releasing a trap.

11. He who finds a tired or dead item of game

Whoever finds a tired item of game, without dogs, should not answer for it. If he finds it dead and some hunter says that his dogs killed it or it was killed with an arrow, the hunter should swear with any citizen, for a deer, wild goat, boar, or doe. For other kinds of game, he should swear alone and should be believed, and he should keep the game. If he does not want to swear it or he cannot, it should not be given it to him. What we said of the arrow, we say of a javelin and of any other class of weapon.

12. He who finds game in another's trap

Whoever finds game in another's trap or escaped from the trap with a broken foot, an injury, or a cut should render it to the owner of the trap. If he does not do so, he should pay as it has been said above.

13. The equipment of fishermen

If someone steals the net of a fisherman or the fish from his net or trammel, he should pay the damage as a thief, if he is declared guilty; but if not, he should clear himself as in the case of theft.

14. He who breaks another's fishing weir

If someone breaks another's fishing weir and takes something from it, he should pay ten *aurei* and double the damage caused.

15. He who fishes with a forbidden net

The fisherman who fishes within a radius of nine paces around a mill or from the channel of Villalba to Belvis with a trawling net or with a trammel should pay twenty *aurei*.

16. He who springs another's trap or snare

If someone springs another's trap, a snare, or tile trap, he should pay five *solidi* and double the damage according to the oath of the plaintiff, if he can prove it; but if not, the suspect should swear and should be believed.

17. He who seizes game in another's trap

We give this same judgment for the one who seizes another's trapped game and does not deliver it to its owner.

18. The animal or other thing that releases another's trap

If someone's animal or something else springs a trap, snare, or tile trap, the owner of that which springs the trap should reset it. If he does not do so, he should pay five *solidi*.

CHAPTER XXXVI

The Code of Hired Workers

1. The code of hired workers and the penalty of those who do not pay the merited wage

If someone hires workers and does not pay them their wage the same day, on the following day the *iudex* should take from him sureties for the double fine and for the wage, and should make those sureties available at interest for the double fine of the wage, since the worker is worthy of his wage. Those sureties should not be used for a feast, a fair, or for any other reason.

2. The pay of the salaried servants and what they ought to receive, if they leave before the stipulated term

The salaried servant, if he agrees with someone to stay with him from the beginning of March until the feast of Saint John [24 June], and before concluding the term leaves his *señor*, should receive half the pay he would merit. He who leaves his *señor* from the feast of Saint John until that of Saint Michael [29 September], the month of August having elapsed, should receive two parts from the pay that he would have gained. If he leaves him before the month of August, he should receive half of the pay that he would have gained. If he leaves his *señor* from the feast of Saint Michael until the beginning of March, he should receive a third part of the pay that he would have gained. If the *señor* releases his employee before the day of the term, he should give him all that he had gained.

3. When a servant wants to take leave of his *señor*

When the servant or salaried person wants to take leave of his *señor*, he should take leave of him in a settled place. And then if the *señor* has some complaint of him, [the *señor*] should demand a bondsman from [the servant] within a term of nine days from his leaving. And after the bondsman is received, [the *señor*] may make demands when it pleases him. However, if the *señor* of the salaried person is in a military expedition, in a defensive muster, or outside of the district of Cuenca, so that he cannot return before nine days, on his return he should demand a bondsman from him where he wants to find him and he should receive satisfaction from him. If the *señor* is found within the district of Cuenca and does not demand a bondsman of him within nine days, these [days] having elapsed, [the salaried person] is not legally required to respond.

4. When the servant should receive his pay

The *señor* should pay [the servant] within the term of nine days from the day of [his] leaving; if contrary to that, he should pay double.

5. The salaried person who does not leave

If the salaried person does not leave [after having agreed to do so, from the *señor*'s property], he should lose his pay and, furthermore, when the *señor* finds out, he should receive judicial satisfaction from him.

6. The condition of housekeepers and of wet nurses

This same we say of housekeepers and of wet nurses whom someone has in his house, except that she who merited it should receive the pay when she wants to leave, since she worked for the entire time. The servants or salaried persons do not work for the entire time, since in periods of snow and in other similar periods they do not do any work.

7. He who injures or kills his *señor*

If the salaried person or the servant injures his *señor*, he should lose his right hand and his pay. If he kills him, let him be hurled from the city cliffs or burned as a traitor; and this should remain the choice of the relatives of the deceased.

8. This same we say of the housekeeper

This same we say of the housekeeper and of the wet nurse who injures or kills her *señora*.

9. Who *señores* are

We call *señores* the fathers and the mothers of the family and their sons and daughters.

10. The *señor* who injures his servant

If the *señor* injures or kills his servant, he should pay the penalty that has been assigned, since another's children are not injured with impunity. Therefore, anyone who injures them should be punished in accordance with the laws and customs of Cuenca. If the salaried person or the servant argues with his *señor* or he does not work according to his pleasure, the *señor* should dismiss him from his house, giving to him the pay he has merited; the *señor* is never permitted to whip or beat him.

CHAPTER XXXVII
The Code of the Herders

1. The code of the herders, both of sheep and of cattle, and the time that the herder ought to keep the sheep

The sheep herder should keep the herd of his *señor* from the feast of Saint John [24 June] until the same day of the following year.

2. The period in which the *señor* can release the sheep to the herder

If the *señor* wants to [release] the sheep to [the care of] his herder, he should release them before they begin to lamb and he should pay [the herder] as much as he has earned in accordance with the contract that they have established by common agreement; after [the sheep] begin to lamb, the herder should not be dismissed. But if the *señor* wants to dismiss him, he should give the pay for an entire year and [the herder] should go. If the herder leaves the sheep of his *señor* to their own will, without intervention for any need, he should receive nothing. If a clear need [to be absent] befalls the herder, such as enmity [of a legal enemy], disease, or captivity, he should receive as much as he earned and go forth in peace.

3. The pay of the herder

The pay of the herder should be this: a seventh part of the lambs and of the cheeses; a seventh part of the wool of the sterile ewes and of the rams; a seventh part of the milk of the goats, and a seventh of the kids. The *señor* should give to the herder, to the chief shepherd, and to the drover eight *kaficii* for payment, half of one grain and half of another. The *señor* should feed their dogs. The chief shepherd and the drover should receive the pay they have agreed on with their *señores*. The *señor* should give to all the herders their payment by the feast of Saint Martin [11 November]. If [the herder] is not given it, the herder should buy his shares and later the *señor* should guarantee them according to the oath of the herder, if he does not believe his simple word. The herder should receive also two *solidi* to buy himself sandals and four sheep skins to make himself a garment.

4. The herder who does not obey the command of his *señor*

The herder should keep the sheep in accordance with the mandate of his *señor*. If he presents the branded fleece or the [cropped] ears of [any] sheep that get killed or die [he does not have to pay]. If he does not do it, he should pay all the damage [the value of the sheep] according to the oath of his *señor*.

5. The suspected herder

If the *señor* has a suspicion that the herder or his men have [wrongfully] killed [the sheep], he should swear it [that this has occurred] and the herder should pay. If the *señor* does not want to swear it, the herder should swear and should be believed. If the herder does not want to swear it, he should pay [the value of the sheep].

6. The herder who does not obey the command of the council

If the council for fear of war commands that the herders not go beyond a given boundary stone, and a herder passes it, he should pay any damage that happens from thieves or the *montaticum* of that council or of another castle according to the oath of his *señor*. Because of this, we order by the code that the herders should abide by the law of the council. And if one of them trespasses [and goes beyond] the prohibited boundary stone, he should pay ten *aurei* to the *iudex* and the *alcaldi* and the *señor* of the livestock, and although the herder did not incur any damage, nevertheless, he should pay because he was contumacious and disobedient to the council. Concerning this fine, anyone who accuses a herder should receive an *aureus* from the community [presuming he can sustain the charge].

7. The herders place animals to lead the herds

The herders, both of sheep and of cattle, should provide the animals to lead the herds. Anyone who disrupts the herd should pay the fine as for [breaking into] an inhabited house.

8. The sheep herders and those of cattle have the same law

The code regarding cattle herders and their *señores* is the same [as that for the sheep herders] and they should be held equally to the law of the council. And he who trespasses the boundary stone should pay the above-mentioned fine.

9. The pay of cattle herders

The cattle herder should receive a calf of two years as pay annually; and the calf herder a calf of one year.

10. The allotment of the products from the cattle

Each one of the *señores*, both of sheep and of cattle, should receive from the yield of the cheeses and of the butter in accord with the expense they have given; therefore, we say that each one should provide salt and payment according to the quantity of sheep or of cattle.

11. The butter that the herders make after the feast of Saint John

The herders should take a seventh part of the butter that they make after the feast of Saint John. The rest should belong to their *señores*. But if they do not do it thus, they should pay for it according to the oath of their *señores*.

12. The pay of goatherds

The goatherd who leaves his house and returns to it, if he receives payment, should receive a seventh part of the milk and of the kids. If he does not receive payment, he should receive a fourth of the kids and a seventh of the milk and four *denarii* for each four sterile goats.[1]

13. The suspected goatherd

The goatherd who presents a known *parapera* should be believed.[2] If the *señor* doubts the *parapera*, he should swear [to its lack of authenticity] and the herder should pay [the value of a goat]. If the *señor* does not want to swear, the goatherd should swear and should be believed. If [the goatherd] does not want to swear it, he should pay. If the goatherd says of a lost goat that it was not included in the herd, the owner should swear that the same animal or another in its place was included, and the goatherd should pay for it.

14. The goatherd who leaves the goats before the term

If the goatherd leaves the goats before the term, if it is not for one of the three above-mentioned reasons, he should receive nothing of the pay that he has earned. If it is the owner of the goats who leaves them after they begin to bear young, he should give the [goatherd his] pay for the entire year. Before, then, should [the goats] begin to bear young, [the owner] can leave them, paying [goatherd] what he has earned.

15. The condition and pay of the swineherd

The swineherd should have the same condition and code that the goatherd has. The pay of the swineherd for the whole year will be six *denarii* for each pig or an *almud* of wheat, whichever pleases the owner more.

16. The guarantee of the pastureland keeper

If the pastureland keeper wants to keep the animals of the council, he should first give to the *iudex* legal bondsmen, who would indemnify any damage that is caused or that happens through his fault.

17. The pay of the pastureland keeper

The pay of the pastureland keeper for the entire year is twelve *denarii* for each animal, and for a colt of one year, the same.

18. Where animals should be delivered to the pastureland keeper

Whoever delivers his animal to the pastureland keeper should present it at the Valencia Gate and in the afternoon should recover it there.

19. The animal that the pastureland keeper loses

If the pastureland keeper loses an animal, he should pay for it. But if he says that it was not included, the owner should swear with two citizens for a horse; for another animal, he should swear with one citizen alone; and the pastureland keeper should pay for it. The owner should include in his oath the price of the animal or the horse.

20. The animal that falls into a river

If an animal falls into a river or into a ravine whence the pastureland keeper cannot draw it [out], he should call out and request aid so that all help him. If [the pastureland keeper] does not do this, he should pay for it if [the animal] dies or receives some injury.

21. The animal that the pastureland keeper kills

If the pastureland keeper kills or injures some animal, he should pay for it. If he says that it was some other person who killed or injured the animal, the pastureland keeper should swear with any citizen and should be believed, and he who the pastureland keeper names in his oath should pay this.

22. The cattle herder

The cattle herder should have the same code and condition that the pastureland keeper has. The pay of the cattle herder should be at the will and agreement of the owners and of the cattle herder.

CHAPTER XXXVIII

The Loyalty of All Wage Earners

1. The loyalty of all wage earners and servants

Every salaried servant, be he a herder, swineherd, or gardener, ought to keep this loyalty to his *señor*; to know that he should be faithful to him in all that is entrusted to him and given to him in deposit and as secret. He should be faithful in keeping all his goods, so that he does not cause damage to them nor consent that someone else might do it. And he should not have relations with the wife of the *señor*, nor with his daughter, nor with the wet nurse, nor with the housekeeper.

2. He who commits adultery with the wife of his *señor*

If a hired servant, be he a herder, a swineherd, or a gardener, commits adultery with the wife of his *señor*, [the *señor*] should kill him together with his wife, as the *Fuero* prescribes, or should kill him publicly, if he can prove it with witnesses. If he cannot prove it with witnesses, [the *señor*] should accuse him of perfidy and [the accused servant] should answer by a judicial challenge. If he is defeated [in the challenge], it remains to the judgment of his *señor* to do what he pleases with him. If he wins, he should be believed and rehabilitated by the field of judicial combat. Furthermore, the *señor* should give him the pay that he has merited.

3. He who has carnal relations with the daughter of his *señor*

If a salaried servant has carnal relations with the daughter of his *señor*, he should lose the pay that may have earned if the *señor* can prove the fact with witnesses; and, furthermore, he should depart forever as the enemy of all the relatives of the *señor*. If [the *señor*] cannot prove it with witnesses but he suspects him, he [the servant] should answer to the challenge [of judicial combat]. If he is defeated, he should be considered a traitor and should leave as an enemy forever. If he wins, he should be believed and rehabilitated by the field of judicial combat, and he should receive his pay.

4. He who has carnal relations with the wet nurse of his *señor*

If the salaried servant has carnal relations with the wet nurse of his *señor* and for this reason her milk is spoiled and the child dies, he should be an enemy forever and he should pay the pecuniary penalties for homicide. If he is only suspect, he should be challenged and fight in judicial combat. If he is defeated, he should pay the pecuniary penalties for homicide and depart as an enemy forever. If he wins, he should be believed and rehabilitated in the field and, furthermore, he should receive his pay.

5. He who has carnal relations with the housekeeper of his *señor*

If the salaried servant has carnal relations with the housekeeper of his *señor* and the *señor* can prove it with witnesses, the servant should lose the pay that he had earned and he should be expelled from the house without any penalty.

6. Concerning all the damage that the wage earner does to his *señor*

If the wage earner steals something from his *señor*, he should pay for it according to the oath of his *señor*. If the herder, the servant, the wage earner, the swineherd, or the gardener has caused the damage, theft, or loss to [his *señor*] by his fault, the guilty person should pay for it according to the oath of his *señor*, and the *señor* should include in his oath that he does not do it for greed, or for hatred that he has against the servant. Nevertheless, if the servant can prove with the testimony of citizens prior to the oath that the item the *señor* claimed from him neither was lost nor died through his fault, he should be believed and should not answer to the *señor* for it.

7. The herder who denies an animal

If the herder denies that the animal the owner claims from him was placed in the herd, the *señor* should prove it together with his associates or with citizens, as the code prescribes, and the herder should pay for it. If the *señor* cannot prove it, the herder should swear and should be believed.

8. The herder should not answer to his *señor* for damage caused by thieves

The herder should not answer to his *señor* for things that thieves rob from him, unless the wage earner, because of his foolishness, leads or drives the things of his *señor* to a place where he ought not to go, or, against the command of his *señor*, he has gone to the site where his things were lost. Since if the servant goes to some site against the command of his *señor*, even though the servant might be made a prisoner, nonetheless his *señor* ought not lose his things, but should demand them from his [servant's] bondsman, from his father, from his mother, or from his wife, if he has one.

9. The treasure that a servant finds

Anything that a servant finds in a raiding foray, in a military expedition, or in a defensive muster belongs to his *señor*, whose bread he eats and whose orders he obeys. Also, if he finds some treasure or something else, all of it will belong to his *señor* whom he cares for and attends.

CHAPTER XXXIX
The Code of the Guards Who Watch the Livestock

1. The code of the guards who watch the livestock

The *sculca* [livestock herders organization] designates its *alcaldi* and the *sculcarii* [livestock herders] abide by their statute; and those *alcaldi* do justice and judge the litigators before the *sculca* dissolves, since, after separation, no one should respond for a complaint or claim that may have happened during the *sculca*.

2. He who does not abide by the statute of the *sculcarii*

If someone does not abide by the statute of the *alcaldi* of the *sculca* or by its council meeting, he should pay what they establish as a fine.

3. Who should hold the *sculca*

Thus the *sculca* ought to be held. The owners of the livestock should hold the *sculca* in the months of December, January, February, and the first half of March, providing one horseman for each two herds of cattle, and one horseman for each three herds of sheep. From the first half of March until the feast of Saint John [24 June], the council [of Cuenca's *sculca*] should hold it. From the feast of Saint John until the feast of Saint Michael [29 September], it should be held so that there will be an *Alcayat* of Cuenca, of Beteta, of Poveda,

Armallones, Zahorejas, Huertapelayo, Cañizares, and Recuenco. These villages should provide sixty men on foot from the feast of Saint John until the feast of All Saints [1 November], so that [the herders] can go to the mountains with the cattle. These villages should not have the *sculca* with the council, nor pay [fees] in the council's *sculca*. The *miles* who has more than one hundred sheep should have the *sculca*. Thus, as each one gives the sheep to the herder on the feast of Saint John, it should be for all year. He who does not do this should be fined for the *montaticum*. The *miles* who goes in the *sculca* should be a citizen or villager and should have a horse which is worth more than twenty *aurei*.

4. The code of the company of hunters

The company of hunters designates its *alcaldi* and abides by its statute; and these *alcaldi* should judge all the cases that occur in the company. And if someone injures another during [the meeting of] the company, he should be given judicial satisfaction according to the judgment of those *alcaldi*, before the company separates; because after the separation of this group, no one should respond for injury by the company. If someone from the company or from its *alcaldi* fails to carry out the command of the council, he should pay the fine that it imposes on him.

CHAPTER XL
Those Who Find Something Should Proclaim It, and the Corroborators

1. Those who find something should proclaim it, and the corroborators

Whoever finds an animal or something else in the city and does not proclaim it on the same day, and it passes a night in his control, should pay double for it, as in the case of theft. If he finds it outside the town, within the district [of Cuenca], and he does not bring it to the city within the term of three days and does not proclaim it, he should pay for it equally, as in the case of theft.

2. Something proclaimed and claimed falsely

After something has been proclaimed and no one has claimed it honestly, he who found it should hold it until its owner appears. If, when the owner presents himself, it has been lost or has died, the one who found it should not pay anything, if he wants to swear that it did not die nor become lost through his fault. If he does not want to swear that, he should pay for it.

3. He who falsely claims a found thing

Whoever deceitfully makes a found thing his own should pay double for it. The owner of what is found should refund to him who found it, according to his oath, all that he spent on the found thing.

4. If an animal becomes pregnant in the house of him who found it

If an animal becomes pregnant in the house of him who found it, he should receive half of the value of the suckling, if the owner claims it later. If it was found pregnant already, the one who found it should not receive anything from the suckling.

5. He who loads a found animal

He who finds an animal and loads it in such a way that diminishes its value should pay double for it when its owner reclaims it.

6. He who takes a claimed thing

Whoever takes an animal, or anything else, after it has been claimed, and thereafter is defeated in that legal case, he should pay double for it.

7. One who says that a claimed thing has been given to him

Whoever says that a claimed thing has been given, sold, or entrusted to him should present a corroborator. And the corroborator should present a bondsman who fulfills the Code of Cuenca. In like manner, this corroborator, if he says that he will give another corroborator and gives him, in agreement with the Code of Cuenca, he [the second corroborator] should be accepted if he presents a bondsman who fulfills the Code of Cuenca. And with this third corroborator the judgment should conclude.

8. The code concerning corroborators

The code prescribes that the judgment should not pass beyond the third corroborator. If some corroborator or defender says that the [found] entity has been born and has been fed or made in his power, and the entity is worth more than twenty *menkales*, he should swear with two citizens and should be believed. If it is worth less than twenty *menkales*, he should swear with any citizen and should be believed equally. If someone cannot fulfill this, he should pay double the claim.

9. Another *fuero* concerning corroborators

Whoever promises to provide a corroborator should be given until the third day following from [the hearing] before the door of the *iudex*, to the beginning of the meeting of the [Friday] court of the [*alcaldi*].

10. He who says that the corroborator is outside the district

If he says that the corroborator is presently outside the district, he should swear that he says the truth, and then he should be granted a twenty-seven-day term, so that, if he can, he should bring him [the corroborator] within the first nine days; but if not, within the second nine days; and if he cannot within the second [either], at least he should bring him in the third. If he cannot bring him at all, he should lose the case and should pay double the claim.

11. He who promises that he will present a corroborator

Whoever promises to present a corroborator, at that point he should give the latter's name, since otherwise, it should not be legal.

12. The term [in which to] present a corroborator

He who has a twenty-seven-day term to present a corroborator and cannot present him in the first or second nine days, if in each one of those terms he has not come to swear that he sought him in all possible ways and that, despite this he could not find him, should lose the case and pay double the claim, as has been said. Nevertheless, if the claimant says that the corroborator has gone to the king, on pilgrimage, in the *requa*, in a raiding party, in a hunting party, or in the *sculca*, or that he is ill, the plaintiff should wait for him, as has been said concerning the designation of witnesses. Although the claimant is present each nine-day term to swear, if he does not bring the claimed thing in any of the periods, he should lose the case.

13. He who says that he purchased the thing at the fair

If the claimant says that he purchased the claimed thing at the fair, he should prove with two citizens that he purchased it at the fair and during the day, and he should be believed. If he says that he purchased it at the fair, but not during the day, it should not be valid for him, because this is the code of the fairs: that all that is purchased should be in the presence of witnesses and during the day.

14. He who says that he purchased the thing from the Muslims

If the claimant says that he purchased the thing in the land of the Muslims, he should prove it with the *exea* or with two citizens of that *requa*. If he proves it with the *exea*, he should be believed. If he proves it with two citizens, [for the item valued] up to twenty *menkales*, he should be believed; above twenty *menkales*, the plaintiff should challenge by judicial combat, if he wants to.

15. He who says that he drew the thing at auction

If he says that he drew the thing at auction, he should prove it with the leader [of the raid] and one citizen, or with two participating in the raiding party, and he should be believed.

16. He who says that he purchased the thing from the *venditor* of the council

If he says that he purchased it from the *venditor* of the council, he should present him as a corroborator. If the *venditor* appears as the corroborator, the plaintiff should have his case with the corroborator, as it has been said above. If the *venditor* denies it, the claimant should pay double the claim. Later, if he can win in the case with the corroborator, he should receive restitution for all he may have paid to the plaintiff, together with all the expenses.

17. He who says that he purchased the thing in the market

If the claimant says that he purchased the claimed thing in the market, he should present a corroborator, as has been said above, since the conditions of the market and of the fair should be the same.

18. Another *fuero* concerning corroborators

Whoever ought to present a corroborator according to the Code of Cuenca, should present him in Cuenca, as has been said above. Despite the fact that it should have been said that it is not valid if the corroborator has not been presented in Cuenca, nonetheless, there are cases among those which are valid which will not be brought to Cuenca. For example, if someone comes from another place to live in Cuenca and he has received in his homeland the price for the property that he may have sold, if someone claims from him that price on the site where he sold the property and where he collected his price, he should present a corroborator in the following way: that is to say, the plaintiff and the claimant should find a responsible intermediary. And if the thing is such as the claimant asserts, the plaintiff should pay for the footwear costs and the expenses of the responsible intermediary and he should lose the case. If the thing is not such as the claimant was saying, he [the claimant] should pay the amount of the footwear costs and the expenses of the responsible intermediary and he should lose the case.[1]

19. Clothing claimed

If someone claims a piece of clothing, and the one who possesses it defends it, saying that he purchased it already sewn, and promises to present a corroborator for this, [the possessor] should bring it [the garment] to the city as the code prescribes. And if [the possessor] does not do it, he should lose the case. If [the possessor] says that he purchased it from an unknown person, he should swear whether the claimant purchased it from an unknown person, and the plaintiff [claimant] should swear in like manner that he never sold that piece of clothing, nor gave it away, nor took it, but lost it by chance or through theft, and the plaintiff should recover his clothing. If the [possessor] presents the clothing that is claimed by him in good condition, he should not pay double; but if he retains the claimed thing and he is defeated in the case by right, he should pay double for it. However, if the plaintiff says that many other things together with the item in question were robbed, taken from him or lost by him, [the plaintiff] should claim that he considers it suspicious, according to the code of the city, and the other should respond to him judicially. In the same way, if he from whom the clothing is claimed says that he purchased the clothing from a known draper, both should find a responsible intermediary so that he can ascertain the truth of the matter from that draper. And if the draper confirms [that the possessor purchased the object from him], the plaintiff should lose the case and should pay the footwear costs and the expenses of the responsible intermediary. If the draper denies [that the possessor purchased the object from him] or he is not capable of elucidating the truth of the matter, the possessor should lose the case and should pay the footwear costs and the expenses of the responsible intermediary. Moreover, because drapers can with difficulty recognize clothing when it has grown old, we command that no one should answer after a half year for clothing that was purchased from the draper uncut, if he can confirm with his citizens that this much time has already elapsed.

20. The bedding that is claimed

If someone claims another's bedding, he who says that he purchased it at the fair should prove it, as the code of the fairs prescribes, and he should be believed. If he says that he purchased it in the market or at some other place, he should present a corroborator, as the Code of Cuenca prescribes. Otherwise, he should lose the case. If he says that it has been woven in his house, he should prove it with three citizens or with the weaver and two women citizens, and he should be believed. If he cannot prove it, he should lose the case.

CHAPTER XLI
The Code of Guests [and Other Matters]

1. The code of guests

If a guest buys bread, wine, or cereals in the house of his host, he should not pay for lodging. But if he does not buy anything in the house of his host, he should pay for lodging: be it known, he should pay a fee each night for each animal. For all that the merchant buys in the presence of his host, the merchant should prove it with [his host], and [the merchant] should be believed and not answer to the challenge. Wherever the merchant wants to stop, there he ought to pay for lodging, [even] though he has his things in another house. If the merchant wants to sell something of which the owner of the house wants to buy a portion, if the owner of the house is not present, he should receive half the merchandise; if it is sold to a citizen [as against a person not a citizen of Cuenca], he should receive nothing because of this, if he is not present; if he is present, he should receive half the merchandise, paying the cost. If the owner of the house injures his guest, he should pay double the penalty of the offense that he has committed. If it is the guest who injures the owner of the house, he should pay the penalty for the offense that he has committed, according to the code of the city. If the owner of the house kills his guest and he is declared guilty, he should be buried alive beneath the dead person. The owner of the house should not answer for his guest regarding lost things that may not have been entrusted to him; but he should answer for entrusted items. If the guest has suspicion of the owner or of someone attached to him, the owner should give legal satisfaction, according to the code of the city.

2. The code of *exeae*

All *exeae* should present legal bondsmen in the council for the fact that the *requa* that each leads should be secure, both for the departure and for the return. Thus, he ought to pay for any damage that happens during the *requa*, except for theft, evil actions, or the debt of someone else. The *exea* should judge the muleteers who quarrel during the *requa* and should do justice among them. If any *exea* is proved to have been disloyal to the council, let him be hurled from the city cliffs. The *exea* should receive an *aureus* for the livestock fee for one hundred ewes or rams. For each cow, he should receive a *menkal*. For a captive who is freed by [payment of] money, he should receive a tenth part from the redemption fee. For the Moor who is redeemed in exchange for a Christian, he should receive only an *aureus*. The *exea* provides for a captive in his house only until he brings him to his own people. And for that food he should receive an *aureus*, both for feeding him a single day and for additional time.

3. He who sets fire to another's haystack

Whoever sets fire to another's haystack should pay five hundred *solidi* and double the damage caused, if he is declared guilty; but if not, he should clear himself with twelve citizens and should be believed. Whoever steals straw should pay for it as a thief, or he should clear himself as in a case of theft.

4. Bees

If a swarm of bees leaves a beehive and is housed in another's hive in which there are bees, the owner of this beehive should buy that swarm for a *menkal* or he should share it half and half. If it houses itself in an empty beehive, the owner of the swarm should buy the beehive for four *denarii* and should take it away. If someone's bees alight on a wall or another's house, or in another's tree, their owner should take them, but in such a way that he should not do any damage. If some bees alight in someone's house, within or without, they should belong to the owner of the house, if they do not have another owner. If someone finds unclaimed bees in an open field, he should keep them without any penalty. If someone breaks or damages a beehive containing bees, he should pay an *aureus*. If he steals it, he should pay for it as a thief or he should clear himself as in the case of theft. He who injures or steals another's bees, both in an open field as well as in town, should pay for them as has been said. If someone violates another's apiary, he should pay as for a dwelling violation or he should clear himself, if it cannot be proved of him, just as in a dwelling violation. If the bees kill or sting a person, [the bees' owner] should not have any penalty because of this.

5. The cereals purchased in August

If someone offers money to pay for the crop when it is harvested in August, he should obtain an *almud* for each *menkal* and no more. Whoever collects more, should he be Christian, Jewish, or Muslim, should pay ten *aurei* to the *iudex* and to the *alcaldi* and to the plaintiff. These cereals, if they are not paid for from the month of August until Christmas day, should not be given until the following August. The other foods should be saved according to other needs.

6. The sureties for bread and wine

Whoever does not want to accept sureties of double value for bread, wine, meat, or cereals should pay an *aureus* to the *almutazaf* and to the plaintiff. Nevertheless, if he who provides the sureties does not present them within a term of nine days, [the person who does not want to accept the sureties] should present them to the *venditor* without any penalty. And what is more, once [the person who does not want to accept the sureties] pays the price, he should give it to the owner of the sureties.

7. He who takes sureties outside the district without authority of the council

Whoever without mandate of the council, of the *iudex*, or of the *alcaldi* takes sureties outside the district should pay sixty *menkales* to the *iudex*, to the *alcaldi*, and to no other.

8. The gift that the council gives

All gifts that the council gives, proclaimed by the voice of the town crier on Sunday or on Monday after any Easter, should be legal, if no one contests them; no gift of the council will take effect when five or more members of the council contest it. The objection of less than five of the council should not be valid.

9. Pacts and agreements

Pacts and agreements should be legal, except those that violate the code. Whoever infringes on the code should be stoned without any penalty [to the stone thrower].

10. The untruthful witnesses

Whoever confirms or swears falsely should pay double the claim, if he is declared guilty with witnesses, and, furthermore, he should not be received in the future as a witness and his name should be proscribed, so that the turpitude of his falseness should be made public more and more, unless he should be affirmed or judged with the accord of a confraternity or a parish. He who accuses another of falseness in what is sworn or asserted and cannot prove it should pay sixty *menkales* to the *alcaldi* and to the plaintiff. The *alcaldi* should also receive half the double fine for untruthful testimony.

11. What is deposited and entrusted

For all that is deposited or entrusted [with the defendant] that the plaintiff cannot prove with witnesses, no one is cleared except by his own testimony. Nevertheless, if after the judgment it can be proved that the thing denied is found in [the defendant's] power, [the defendant] should pay double its value to its owner, and the ninth part to the Palace as a thief.

CHAPTER XLII
Craftsmen

1. Craftsmen

If a master craftsman starts some work such as a tower, church, book, bridge, windmill, vineyard, or any other work, he should finish it according to the contract that he has made; if [he does not], he should pay double the money that he received for the task. If before finishing the work, the craftsman dies, his heir should receive as much as the master had finished. And if he has received more, he should return it. Having done this, the owner of the work should seek another master. If [the master craftsman] does not have an heir, his bondsmen should repay the money that he did not earn. The master craftsman who does not complete the work within the term established should pay double the money that he has received. In the same way, the owner of the work should pay double the money that he has not paid in the periods established.

2. Carpenters

If a carpenter, a metal founder, or a roofer does bad work in another's undertaking, he should correct it and if by this some damage occurs, he should pay double for it.

3. Smiths for animals

If the blacksmith puts horseshoes on an animal and nails it [penetrates its hoof to the flesh], he should pay for it, if because of this some injury occurs. If the horse loses the shoe before nine days, the blacksmith should replace it; after nine days, he should not answer for it. The blacksmith should receive one *solidus* for each equine animal, whatever type it is; for the mule, the fourth part of a *solidus*; for a jackass, six *denarii*. If the owner of the animal possesses the horseshoe, the blacksmith should put it on for a *denarius*; if he does not want to do it, he should pay an *aureus* to the *almutazaf* and to the plaintiff.

4. Smiths for tools

If the blacksmith sells a hoe, a plowshare, a pruning hook, a sickle, an ax, or another tool that breaks according to the oath of the buyer, the blacksmith should repair the tool that same day or return his money. If the blacksmith does not want to do either one or the other, the *almutazaf* should take sureties from him in the amount of five *solidi*, until he pays; and the *almutazaf* should divide these *solidi* with the plaintiff, as the code prescribes. The blacksmith who does not deliver the completed work by the established date should pay double the deposit he received for the thing. If he changes the steel or the iron, he should pay five *solidi*; if [he disputes the accusation], he should swear and should be believed.

5. Goldsmiths

The goldsmith should receive gold and silver for weighing, and after weighing should return it. And if he mixes something with the gold and the silver, he should pay for it as a thief, if he is declared guilty; but if not, he should clear himself according to the estimate of the damage that had been done. And if he does the work badly or breaks the precious stones or changes them, he should pay similarly. All goldsmiths should work with the mark [a half pound, c. 230 grams] of silver at four *menkales* and in [proportion to] this agreement should work what will be greater or smaller.[1]

6. The code of the cobblers

The cobbler who sells shoes of sheepskin as if they were of goatskin, or goathide for cowhide, or dressed sheepskin for leather should pay an *aureus* to the plaintiff and the *preposito* [head] of the cobblers,[2] if the plaintiff can prove it; but if not, he should clear himself as the code prescribes. Anyone who trims the sandals or the soles also should pay an *aureus* to the head [of the cobblers]. Any cobbler who does not deliver his work completed on the established day should return double the deposit. The buyer who does not pay the price at the established time should lose the deposit, and the cobbler should sell his work to whomever he pleases. The cobbler should sew the shoe in such a way that the seam does not fail until the sole is broken; if he does not want to do it, the head [of the cobblers] should take sureties from him in the amount of an *aureus* and should oblige him to sew it. If the head [of the cobblers] does not want to do justice, the *almutazaf* should take sureties from him in the amount of two *aurei*. In the same way, the *almutazaf* should take sureties from him whom the head orders.

7. The code of the tanners

If a tanner switches one hide [for another], he should pay for it as a thief. He who works on or prepares the skins badly should pay double the damage. If the seam of a hide fails before the hide is broken, the tanner should sew it again free of charge. If he does not want to do it, he should pay five *solidi* to the *almutazaf* and to the plaintiff. If the tanner does not deliver the completed work on the day established, he should return double the deposit; if he has not received a deposit, he should pay an *aureus*. If the buyer does not pay the tanner on the day established, he should pay double the price. And be it known that the tanner should not have to be left with nothing but the stomach hides or other remnants.

8. The code of the tailors

If a tailor changes or steals something from that which has been delivered to him to make, he should pay for it as a thief, since some tailors occasionally tend to remove something from the hides; others from the back; others from the cloth. If the owner cannot prove the damage, the tailor should clear himself as in the case of theft, according to the calculation of the damage. If he damages the cloth upon cutting it, he should pay for it. If he makes the clothing badly or stains it, he should pay for it. If the tailor loses or removes something from that which has been delivered to him to make, he should pay for it. The tailor should not be left with nothing to use [with which to make garments] but the remnants, either of the borders of fabrics, or of the hides, or of the backs, since all of it belongs to the owners of the garments. If the tailor does not present the finished clothing on the established day, he should pay an *aureus* to the *almutazaf* and to the plaintiff.

9. The code of the weavers

If a weaver changes another's thread and the plaintiff can prove it, he should pay double for it and lose the amount of the weaving. After the garment is woven, he should return it to the owner dry and clean and with the same weight of thread that he gave him. And if the cloth has been reduced in measurement or in weight, he should pay double for the entire decrease. If he weaves the cloth badly or does not present it on the day established, he should pay double for it. The owner of the fabric should pay double the price if, after being warned by the weaver, he does not pay him that same day. The fuller should receive two *menkales* for woven fabric, dyed and beaten. The fabric piece should have a length of twenty *cannas* [1 rod = 16.5 feet] and of breadth, two *cannas*. The nap of the cloth shearing should belong to the owner of the fabric. The fuller who does not present the woven fabric on the day established, dyed, beaten, and prepared, should pay ten *aurei*. The same fuller should pay everyone who beats the fabric with a club or [stretches it with] a pulley. The fuller who dyes cloth more than three items at a time should pay two *aurei*; we say this because, when many fabrics are dyed together, they are totally ruined. The fuller who changes or ruins the fabric should pay ten *aurei* and double the damage. He ought to warp at the rate of ten strands, and the warp should have seventy-eight ends; the end should have one hundred threads; there should be as many threads in one tooth of the comb as in any other. It should be woven with four treadles to a loom.

10. Cloth shearers

Concerning the cloth shearers we do not say anything at the moment, because they should have to answer to the weavers for the damage that they cause the fabrics, such as if they break them, beat them badly, or make them greater [stretch them] or against what is established in the code; and the weavers should have to answer to the owners of the fabrics. The *almutazaf* has to take sureties for all these pecuniary penalties.

11. Vintners

The vintners or those who may have a tavern should sell wine according to the law of the Council. And if someone violates it, he should pay two *aurei*. Everyone who sells watered wine should pay two *aurei* if it can be proved of him; if not, he should clear himself with twelve citizens. The tavern keeper who measures with other than the round measure, that is, without a spout, should pay two *aurei*. If the tavern keeper does not pour the measure to the brim, making it firm and straight, he should pay two *aurei*. The buyer should receive any overflow from the wine. The measurer who puts his thumb within the measure should pay two *aurei*. The tavern keeper or vintner who does not want to sell wine by this precept, in spite of having wine in his house, should pay two *aurei* and, furthermore, it should be proclaimed that he should not have a tavern for one year, or he should be punished at the will of the *almutazaf*.

12. Woodcutters

The woodcutters and those who carry loads in the streets and plazas should give their cries so as not to cause damage. If they cause damage by breaking or pushing something, they should pay for it. Nevertheless, if the woodcutter can prove that [as] he was walking, [he was] giving cries in such a way that they should have been heard, he should not pay anything.

13. Brickmakers and tilemakers

The brickmakers and the tilemakers should make tiles that have two palms in length, a palm and a half in width at the head, and a palm and a hand at the other end, and have a thickness as much as the knuckle of the thumb has length. And they should be baked in such a way that they should not be broken by ice or by rain. And if they are broken within a year by ice or by rain, the tilemaker should pay for them. A thousand tiles should sell at five *menkales*.

14. The form of the bricks

The form of the bricks should have a large palm of width, a palm and a half of length, and two fingers of thickness, and they should be well baked. And if within a year a brick is broken by lack of baking, the brickmaker should pay for it. A thousand bricks should sell for four *menkales* and not more. If one of the brickmakers breaks this precept, he should pay ten *aurei* to the *almutazaf* and to the plaintiff. The brickmaker who does not present the bricks or the tiles on the day established should pay double for them.

15. Potters

If the potters bake the pots or the other jars badly and they are broken by lack of baking, they should pay for them. A pot, a pitcher, or a jar should sell for as many *denarii* as it has pints of capacity, and no more. In the same way, he who sells pots in exchange for food should sell them in agreement with the above-mentioned calculation of *denarii*.

16. The potter who does not want to keep this precept

The potter who does not want to sell in accordance with this precept should pay an *aureus* to the *almutazaf* and to the plaintiff.

17. The code of the butchers

If a butcher sells decaying meat or meat from sick animals or pigs, or mixed meat, that is, goat meat with sheep meat, or fetid meat with fresh meat, he should pay ten *aurei*.

18. He who sells game outside the market

Whoever sells game such as hares, rabbits, partridges, or river fish in any house outside the market or in his own house should pay five *aurei* to the *almutazaf* and to the plaintiff, if it can be proved of him.

19. He who sells river fish outside the district

Whoever carries fish to sell from the district of Cuença to another place should pay five *aurei* or should swear with two citizens and should be believed.

20. Shopkeepers and retailers

I command that the shopkeepers and the retailers should sell and buy their commodities in conformance to the law of the council. Any shopkeeper, retailer, butcher, fishmonger, vintner, tailor, cobbler, tanner, weaver, or any other craftsman who does not want to keep the law of the council should pay two *aurei*, if it can be proved of him; if not, he should clear himself with two citizens and should be believed.

CHAPTER XLIII
The Equalization of the Parishes

1. The equalization of the parishes

For the honor and enlargement of the city we order that, when it pleases the council, all the villages should be equalized into parishes. Only the rural villages should be equalized; those of the city should never be equalized. What is more, each parish should pay [taxes] in accordance with the number of citizens.

2. How the houses of the city ought to be covered

He who has a house in the city covered by straw should cover it with tile; if [he fails to do so], he should pay all his taxes as if he does not dwell in the town. And if there is someone so obstinate that he will not cover his house with tiles, he should give it to another settler who will cover it with tile; and the former owner should pay his taxes before everyone. This should be done from the tower of Malvecino up to the new work on the wall of the Arrabal, in such a way that it should enclose the wall on the side of the Júcar and the wall on the side of the Huécar.

3. Drainage channels and the pecuniary penalties of those who do not want to make them

Drainage channels should be made in all the villages where water flows through and streams join. He who does not do it should lose there his share of the arable land. And hereafter, whatever destroys drainage channels and whenever [they are destroyed], the owners of those properties that are in the fields with the drainage channels should repair them; those who do not want to repair and rebuild them should lose the properties that they possess there, and the councils of the villages should give them to other settlers who should make drainage channels, repair them, and rebuild them as often as they are destroyed, in perpetuity.

4. The tile works, the sand bank, and the millstone quarry

I command that no one should buy a sand bank, a millstone quarry, or a tile works for work on the walls, nor should the council buy such properties where these things are found; and this precept should be observed in perpetuity.

5. Pastureland of the council and who ought to hold it

No one should have a grass pasture except he who possesses an inhabited house in Cuenca with his wife and children. Two *arançatas* should be marked off for the entire year, setting five grass plots on the headland at five paces. If someone wants to mark off more, he should surround it with a fence or with palisades. He who does not fence it thus should not receive tax resources for that.

6. What village ought to have pasture land

The village that does not possess at least three horses should not have pastureland. The statute of all pastureland should be the same as that of the pastureland of the council.

7. How the river fish ought to be sold

The river fish should be sold in accordance with a pound of meat. The pound should consist of forty-eight ounces. A pound of trout from finger-length up to a *mazales* [forearm-length fish] should be sold for no more than a *solidus*. A pound of trout from the smallest up to the finger-length [ones] should be sold for up to ten *denarii*. The pound of barbels from the finger-length until the forearm-length should be sold for up to eight *denarii*. A pound of small fish [probably carp] from the smallest to finger-length should be sold for up to six *denarii*. Forearm-length [and greater] trout and barbels should be sold for the price that the fisherman can get.

8. What fish are *mazales*

We call fish *mazales* that should be trout or barbels, referring to those which measure in length from the elbow to the closed fist, without counting the head and the tail.

9. Fish that are not from the river should be sold with the arbitration of the council

Sea fish and eels should be sold for the price that the council determines. He who does not want to weigh a fish as has been said should lose it and pays five *aurei*.

10. The truce of the king or of the council

If someone breaks the truces of the king or of the council, let him be hurled from the city cliffs, if one can seize him. If he escapes, he should lose all that he possesses, in real estate as well as in movable goods, and the proceeds [from the sale of his belongings] should be assigned to the construction of the walls.

11. He who sells more expensively than is customary because of the coming of the king

Whoever sells at a higher price than is customary because of the coming of the king should lose the item thus sold and should pay ten *aurei* to the *alcaldi* and to the plaintiff.

12. The penalty for those who conspire against the king

If someone harms the king, let him be hurled from the city cliffs. If he wishes the king's death, he should be burned together with all his family and with all his accomplices. And also, so that in the territory there should not be walls that have heard of so great a crime, his house should be demolished down to the foundations.

13. The custody of fishing on the river Júcar

Whoever fishes from the narrows of Villalba up to Belvis with some clever device, except with a fishhook, should be seized and lose all that he has. Half should be assigned for the work on the walls and the other half for the needs of the guards of the mountains and of the waters.

14. How long it is forbidden to fish

This precept should be observed rigorously from the Pentecostal feast until the feast of All Saints [1 November].

15. How long it should be forbidden to hunt

In the same way anyone should be punished who hunts rabbits or hares from the Easter feast until the feast of Saint Martin [11 November]. If the council does not designate guards to enforce this observation, it should pay one hundred *aurei* to the king as a fine.

16. What time hired workers ought to stop work

Hired workers should work until the bell of the workers sounds in the church of Holy Mary. Whoever leaves before the [end of] work should lose his wage for that day. This is established on the fasting days; on other days, they should work until the bells should sound vespers in the parochial churches.

17. The code of the conclusion of the struggle

If, God forbid, the council or others are defeated by the enemy and during the flight or in another manner they procure something [booty], absolutely all of it should be common to all the companions, as if they had gained it victoriously, since this seems just and equitable. For when they leave in a military expedition or in a raiding party, being ignorant of whether they will return defeated or victorious, notwithstanding, they should promise and intend to obtain [booty]. However, he who brings back the horse or the mule of a citizen should receive an *aureus* from the owner of the animal, and he should return it to the citizen or his heirs and not keep for himself either the saddle or anything else. The one who brings back the horse of an enemy should receive its saddle or two *aurei*, whichever is more pleasing to him. He who brings back a work horse or a mule should receive an *aureus* and should give it over, as well as everything else, for the partition.

18. The house which has to be examined for theft

He who suspects that someone is concealing something stolen in his house should, with the *iudex* and an *alcaldus* or with two *alcaldi*, tell the owner of the house that he should permit them to search his house; and if [the house owner] does not want to [permit the search], then he should pay for however much the plaintiff says is hidden in that house. Nevertheless, let it be known that whoever requests that a house be searched ought to request it by day; at night no one should request it, nor should the owner offer the house for search. However, [the plaintiff] can watch the surroundings of the house at night, so that neither the thief nor the stolen item should be brought out from there. The one who wants to search it ought to say what there is and how much there is that he [believes to have been stolen from him], and if he finds what he said within, he should take it; if he finds something else, although he says that it was taken from him, he should not take it because he did not say before what it was nor give a description of the thing.

19. He who conceals a thief from the *iudex*

Whoever conceals or does not present a prisoner, a stolen thing, or something robbed during a truce to the *iudex*, to an *alcaldus*, or to the *andador* should pay four hundred *solidi*, if it can be proved of him; but if not, he should clear himself with twelve citizens and should be believed. If he does not present what he carries to the *alcaldi*, to the council, or to the king on the indicated day, according to what had been fixed, he should suffer the penalty that he would have suffered for not delivering it. If the thing taken is something other than a human, he should present for that thing as much as the *alcaldi* confirmed in their oath.

20. The concealer of a theft

To the resolution stated above it is added that in any house where a stolen thing has been discovered, the owner of the house in which that thing is, should he be a lessee or another, should answer because of this; that is, he should present the perpetrator of the crime or he should pay the fine with the ninth part [of the value of the object], as the code states concerning theft. Nevertheless, he should not have a judgment of death, unless he is proscribed or an infamous person, or was seized some other time for the same offense; if he is such, let him be hurled from the city cliffs as if he had committed that same theft.

End

Notes

Introduction

1. Joseph F. O'Callaghan, *A History of Medieval Spain* (Ithaca, N.Y. and London: Cornell University Press, 1975), 172, 240, 270–72; María Pilar Aparicio-Llopis, "Fuero," *Dictionary of the Middle Ages,* gen. ed. Joseph R. Strayer, 13 vols. (New York: Charles Scribner's Sons, 1982–89), 5:308–10.

2. James F. Powers, *A Society Organized for War: The Iberian Municipal Militias in the Central Middle Ages, 1000–1284* (Berkeley, Los Angeles, and London: University of California Press, 1988), 48–49; Julio González, *El reino de Castilla en la época de Alfonso VIII,* 3 vols. (Madrid: Sucesores de Rivadeneyra, 1960), 1:924–27.

3. Heath Dillard, *Daughters of the Reconquest: Women in Castilian Town Society, 1100–1300* (Cambridge and New York: Cambridge University Press, 1984), 8.

4. George H. Allen, ed., "Forum Conche, fuero de Cuenca: The Latin Text of the Municipal Charter and Laws of the City of Cuenca, Spain," *University Studies Published by the University of Cincinnati* ser. 2, 5, 4 (Nov.–Dec. 1909): 5–92; 6, 1 (Jan.–Feb., 1910): 3–134. The following English scholars generally accepted Allen's views: H. W. C. Davis, review of *Colección para el estudio de la historia de Aragón,* vol. 2, *Fuero del [sic] Teruel, transcripción y estudio preliminar de Francisco Aznar y Navarro* (Zaragoza: Gasca, n. d.), *English Historical Review* 23 (1908): 766–72; Davis, review of *Forum Conche (Fuero de Cuenca),* ed. George H. Allen (Chicago: University of Chicago Press, 1909–10), *English Historical Review* 26 (1911): 168–72; Adolphus Ballard, ed., *British Borough Charters, 1042–1216* (Cambridge: Cambridge University Press, 1913), cxxxii–iv.

5. Jean Gautier-Dalché, "Sur quelques clauses du Fuero de Cuenca (Forma Sistemática): aménagement de l'espace, population et institutions," *Cuadernos de Historia de España* 74 (1997): 124–25.

6. María del Carmen Carlé, *Del concejo medieval Castellano-Leones* (Buenos Aires: Instituto de Historia de España, 1968), 109–31.

7. Carlé, *Concejo medieval,* 111–12, 125. "Fueros de la villa de Palenzuela, 1074," *Colección de fueros municipales y cartas pueblas de los reinos de Castilla, León, Corona de Aragón y Navarra; coordinada y anotada,* ed. Tomás Muñoz y Romero (Madrid: Don José María Alonso, 1847), 275–76. "El rey de Castilla, don Alfonso VI, confirma el fuero concedido a Nájera por los reyes Sancho el Mayor y García el de Nájera," in *Colección diplomática medieval de la Rioja (923–1225),* ed. Ildefonso Rodríguez de Lama, 3 vols. (Logroño: Gonzalo de Bercero, 1976–79), 2:79–85. "Fuero latino de Sepúlveda, confirmado el 17 de noviembre de 1076 por Alfonso VI," *Los fueros de Sepúlveda,* critical edition and documentary appendix by Emilio Sáez (Pamplona: Editorial Gómez, 1953), 47–48.

8. *Fuero de Calatayud*, ed. Jesús Ignacio Algora Hernando and Felicísimo Arranz Sacristán (Zaragoza: Talleres Gráficos La Editorial, 1982), 35, 36, 47. "Fuero de Daroca, 1142," in *Estudio histórico-político sobre la ciudad y communidad de Daroca*, ed. Rafael Estebán Abad (Teruel: Consejo Superior de Investigaciones Científicas, 1959), 364–69. *El fuero de Molina de Aragón*, ed. Miguel Sancho Izquierdo (Madrid: Impresa Clásica Española, 1916), 89–92. *El fuero de Estella según el Manuscrito 944 de la Biblioteca de Palacio de Madrid*, ed. Gustaf Holmer (Göteborg, Stockholm, and Uppsala: Almqvist and Wiksells, 1963), 36–37, 41, 53, but only the *alcalde* is cited here. *Fuero de Alfambra*, ed. Manuel Albareda y Herrera (Madrid: Tipográfico de la Revista de Archivos, Bibliotecas y Museos, 1925), laws 3, 7, 13, 16, 17, 21, 25, 27, 33, 35 (describing the process of the election of the *iudex* much in the manner of Cuenca), 45, 55–57, 71, 76, 77, 80–81, 87, 91, 97, 99, 104, 106. None of these cite the *sayón*, however.

9. *Fuero de Daroca*, *andador*, 365, 367, 369, *escribano* and *almotaçaf* (*almutazaf*), 367. *Fuero de Molina*, *andador*, 93–94. *Fuero de Estella*, *alcaide* (military commander), 56, *vendador* (*vendidor*), 44. *Fuero de Alfambra*, *andador*, laws 25, 51, 87, 99, *corredor* (Romance version of *vendidor*), 49, *notario*, 106, as a signatory to the charter.

10. Clay Stalls, *Possessing the Land: Aragon's Expansion into Islam's Ebro Frontier Under Alfonso the Battler, 1104–1134* (Leiden, New York, and Köln: E. J. Brill, 1995), 280–97.

11. Powers, *Society*, 162–87.

12. Gautier-Dalché, "Sur quelques clauses," 127. Gautier-Dalché argues that the text of the code suggests a distinction between lands acquired at the time of conquest (*quiñones*) as against land divided later (*quadriella*).

13. Powers, *Society*, 203–4.

14. Frank Henderson Stewart, *Honor* (Chicago and London: University of Chicago Press, 1994), 81–85.

15. Dillard, *Daughters*, passim.

16. Archivo Capitular de Catedral de Cuenca, *cajones* 1–2, nos. 8, 14–16, 18–20, 22.

17. Dillard, *Daughters*, 160–67.

18. James F. Powers, "Frontier Municipal Baths and Social Interaction in Thirteenth-Century Spain," *American Historical Review* 84 (June 1979): 663–64.

19. For the origins of this debate among Hispanic scholars, see Powers, "Frontier Municipal Baths," 660–61. For a more recent overview, see Robert I. Burns, "The Significance of the Frontier in the Middle Ages," in *Medieval Frontier Societies*, ed. Robert Bartlett and Angus MacKay (Oxford: Oxford University Press, 1989), 307–30.

20. Powers, "Frontier Municipal Baths," 664–67.

21. Powers, *Society*, 115–17.

22. Powers, *Society*, 52, 55, 58–60.

23. Powers, *Society*, 162–87.

24. Powers, *Society*, 219–29.

25. *Forum Conche*, Ms. Q, iij, 23, Biblioteca de San Lorenzo el Real, El Escorial, Spain. *Forum Conche*, Ms. Lat. 12.927, Bibliothèque Nationale, Paris. *Fuero de Cuenca, Codice Valentino*, Ms. 39, sig. 88-5-21, Biblioteca Universitaria de Valencia, Spain. *Fuero de Cuenca, Fragmento Conquense, Legajo* III, *expte.* nº I, Archivo Municipal de Cuenca, Spain.

26. *Forum Fari*, Ms. N. iij, 14, Biblioteca de San Lorenzo el Real, El Escorial, Spain.

27. *Les fueros d'Alcaraz et d'Alarcón*, ed. Jean Roudil, 2 vols. (Paris: Librairie C. Klincksieck, 1968). *El fuero de Baeza*, ed. Jean Roudil (The Hague: G. B. Van Zonen, 1962). *Fuero de Béjar*, ed. Juan Gutiérrez Cuadrado (Salamanca: Calatravas Libreros, 1974). Jean Roudil, ed., "El manuscrito español 8331 de la Biblioteca del Arsenal de París," *Vox Romanica* 22 (Jan.–June 1963): 127–74; 22 (July–Dec. 1963): 219–380. *Los Fueros de Villaescusa de Haro y Huete*, ed. María Teresa Martín Palma (Málaga: Imprenta de la Universidad de Málaga, 1984). *Fuero de Úbeda*, ed. Juan Gutiérrez Cuadrado (Valencia: Artes Gráficas Soler, 1979). *El fuero de Zorita de los Canes*, ed. Rafael de Ureña y Smenjaud (Madrid: Establecimiento Tipográfico de Fortanet, 1911). *Fuero de Plasencia*, ed. Jesús Majada Neila (Salamanca: Gráficas Cervantes, 1986). The Fuero de Iznatoraf was published as part of the *Fuero de Cuenca* edition of Ureña cited below. See also Alfonso García-Gallo, "Aportación al estudio de los fueros," *Anuario de Historia del Derecho Español* 26 (1956): 437–40.

28. *Fuero de Cuenca*, ed. Rafael de Ureña y Smenjaud (Madrid: Tipografía de Archivos, 1935). Allen, ed., "Forum Conche, fuero de Cuenca," *El fuero de Cuenca*, ed. Alfredo Valmaña Vicente, 2nd ed. (Cuenca: Editorial Tormo, 1978).

29. *El fuero latino de Teruel*, ed. Jaime Caruana Gómez de Barreda (Teruel: Concejo Superior de Investigaciones Científicas, 1974). *El fuero de Teruel*, ed. Max Gorosch (Stockholm: Almqvist and Wiksells, 1950).

30. I summarized the Castilian and Aragonese arguments and offered my initial version of this debate in James F. Powers, "Frontier Competition and Legal Creativity: A Castilian-Aragonese Case Study Based on Twelfth-Century Municipal Military Law," *Speculum* 52 (July 1977): 483–87. Since then others have argued independent cases rather similar to mine, but at greater length. See Powers, *Society*, 219–29; Alberto García Ulecia, *Los factores de diferenciación entre las personas en los fueros de la Extremadura castellano-aragonesa* (Seville: Gráficas del Sur, 1975), 355–488; Ana M. Barrero García, *El fuero de Teruel: su historia, proceso de formación y reconstrucción crítica de sus fuentes* (Madrid: Artes Gráficas y Ediciones, 1979), 53–137.

31. *Fuero de Plasencia*, ed. Majada Neila, 383–84. *Los fueros d'Alcaraz et d'Alarcón*, ed. Roudil, 1:7–11. *Fuero de Zorita de los Canes*, ed. Ureña y Smenjaud, xii–xxi. *Fuero de Baeza*, ed. Roudil, 20–25. *Fuero de Úbeda*, ed. Gutiérrez Cuadrado, 22–23. Roudil, "El manuscrito español 8331," 127.

32. *Fuero de Úbeda*, ed. Gutiérrez Cuadrado, 32–37. "Carta de fueros otorgada al concejo de Zorita por el rey Don Alfonso VIII, juntamente con el Maestre de Calatrava Don Martin de Siones, en Pinella a 8 de abril de la era de 1218 (año 1180), según aparece de la confirmación de Fernando III, dada también en Pinella a 6 de mayo de la era de 1256 (año 1218)," *Fuero de Zorita*, 417–23.

33. José Martínez Gijón, "La familia del Fuero de Cuenca, estado de una investigación científica," *Atti del Secondo Congresso Internazionale della Società Italiana di Storia del Diritto*, vol. 1, *La crítica del testo* (Florence: L. S. Olschki, 1971), 415–39. García Ulecia, *Los factores de diferenciación*, 355–488. Powers, *Society*, 219–29.

34. Powers, *Society*, 219–29. Gonzalo Martínez Díez, "Los fueros de la familia Coria Cima-Coa," *Revista Portuguesa de Historia* 13 (1971): 343–73. James F. Powers, "The Creative Interaction Between Portuguese and Leonese Municipal Military Law, 1055 to 1279," *Speculum* 62 (1987): 53–80.

35. Ureña y Smenjaud, *Fuero de Cuenca*, viii–xi. Rafael Gibert, "El derecho

municipal de León y Castilla," *Anuario de Historia del Derecho Español* 31 (1961): 741, also accepts this time period of c. 1190.

36. González, *Alfonso VIII*, 1:207.

37. Ureña y Smenjaud, *Fuero de Cuenca*, xi. The document has been published in González, *Alfonso VIII*, 2:925–26.

38. González, *Alfonso VIII*, 1:197–98; 2:857–63. Peter Rassow, *Der Prinzgemahl: Ein Pactum Matrimoniale aus dem Jahre 1188* (Weimar: Hermann Bohlaus Nachfolger, 1950), 72–73.

39. González, *Alfonso VIII*, 1:707–8.

40. Rodericus Ximenius de Rada, "Historia de Rebus Hispaniae," *Opera*, ed. María Desamparados Cabanes Pecourt (Valencia: Anubar, 1968), 166–67. Rassow, *Der Prinzgemahl*, 72–87. González, *Alfonso VIII*, 1:417, 2:25–26, 3:40–41, 920. O'Callaghan, *Medieval Spain*, 243.

41. Gutiérrez Cuadrado, *Fuero de Úbeda*, 32–37.

42. Joseph F O'Callaghan, "The Beginnings of the Cortes of León-Castile," *American Historical Review* 74 (1969): 1503–37.

43. I am indebted to Dr. Theresa Vann, whose paper at the meeting of the American Historical Association in New York in 1990 on the impact of the *Forum Conche* on the practices of the town led me to consider the possibilities of this line of argument.

44. José Luís Martín, *Orígenes de la Orden Militar de Santiago* (Barcelona: Selecciones Gráficas, 1974), documents 166, 191, 194, 204, 215, 216, pp. 348–96.

45. Archivo Capitular de Catedral de Cuenca, *cajones* 1–2, nos. 14–15, 18–22, 22.

46. *Cajón* 1, no. 15, 28 June 1193, on the vigil of feast of Saints Peter and Paul, may have affected the move to Monday; *Cajón* 2, no. 21, 2 November 1194, is adjacent to All Saints' Day, 1 November although on a Wednesday. For the listing and impact of feast days in the *Forum Conche*, see Chapters I, XXVI, XXXVI, XXXIX, and XLIII.

47. *Cajón* 1, no. 14.

48. Gutiérrez Cuadrado, *Fuero de Úbeda*, 148–49. Alfonso García-Gallo, "Los fueros de Toledo," *Anuario de Historia del Derecho Español* 45 (1975): 355–488 and "Nuevas observaciones sobre la obra legislativa de Alfonso X," *Anuario de Historia del Derecho Español* 46 (1976): 620–29.

Poem and Prologue

1. For this kind of document to contain prefatory poetry at the outset of the text is unique, and a word of explanation is in order. One can only surmise why this miniature song of deeds has been inserted. While the Alfonso referred to in the poem is not specifically identified as a king, since it is attached to a law code granted by him, the author clearly assumed the literate audience knew that he was the king of Castile. As for the inspiration for the poem itself, the likely explanation may be advanced that Alfonso VIII had achieved what he thought to be important victories in the comparatively recent past as the *Forum Conche* was being redacted. The Castilian king did

defeat the neighboring monarchs cited in the poem between 1195 and 1197, after they attacked his lands in the wake of the battle of Alarcos in 1195. The poet may have thought its insertion timely and proper in so important a legal document, an addition that could be considered as yet one more piece of evidence placing the code in the last decade of the twelfth century.

2. This prologue is most unusual. Except for paragraphs three and nine, the king is referred to in the third person, far from the norm of ordinary chancery style. It is possible that paragraph nine, the final paragraph, constituted the original prologue, possibly accompanied by some of the material from paragraph three. But, as seems to have been the case with the poem, the circumstances of the *Forum Conche* and its exceptional form and length caused interpolations of later material to mark the occasion in a proper fashion. As noted in the Introduction, the references to factual circumstances suggest that the interpolations in the prologue had to have been written by 1196, roughly contemporary to the victories cited in the poem.

Chapter I

1. *Potestates* are top level nobles, *milites* are knights or lower level aristocracy, and *infançones* constitute the middle ranking nobles.

2. Special taxes paid to the royal officials known as the *mayordomo* and the *merinius*.

3. Not to be confused with the *alcaldus*, a city official, both of which derive from Muslim officialdom.

Chapter II

1. Despite the ambiguity here, other charters using the Cuenca formulary divide the ten-*aurei* fee among the parties.

2. The meaning here is that if either Christians or Jews enter on the wrong day they do so at their own risk. The result of such action will not be eligible for any judicial process.

Chapter III

1. This law seeks to rule out groundless, frivolous litigation, possibly undertaken for purposes of harassment.

2. Probably paid to the field owner, under the laws of theft.

3. An *almud* constitutes approximately 1.6 modern bushels, probably measured here half in wheat, half in barley or rye. A *kaficius* constitutes approximately 12 modern bushels.

Chapter V

1. Presumably here the damage indicates whatever crop or plant damage those suffer who do not receive the water to which they are entitled.

Chapter VII

1. Possibly a stone bench or a kind of kiosk.
2. In Latin, but the Romance version suggests grass instead of fish.

Chapter VIII

1. Presumably the first fifteen and the first twenty days of the month respectively.

Chapter X

1. The Era calendar was at this time thirty-eight years in advance of the Year of Our Lord version.

Chapter XI

1. The Romance version of the charter (2, 1, 35) makes laws 42 and 43 one law, making it clear that "the other case" refers to the preceding law.
2. Law 46 raises real questions regarding a woman's eligibility for the ordeal of hot iron, limiting its application in such a way as apparently to contradict Laws 39–42 and 47, although larceny, homicide (except for husband killing), and arson are not considered in those laws. Both Latin and Romance texts contain the contradictions, leaving one to conclude that levels of proof must have varied in certain ways to allow for some free play in the interpretation of the sentencing process. Possibly the religious nature of the ordeal has some role to play here. The text is unclear, nonetheless, save to indicate that a woman considered to be a prostitute has her civil rights substantially restricted. For a fuller discussion of such accusations against women and their context, see Heath Dillard, *Daughters of the Reconquest: Women in Castilian Town Society, 1100–1300* (Cambridge and New York: Cambridge University Press, 1984), 196–204.

Chapter XII

1. The Latin version suggests the shin.

Chapter XIV

1. Which is to say, he will pay the penalty of a guilty party.

2. Meaning here accepted as a citizen with all privileges of citizenship, having overcome some challenge to his honor.

3. He has presumably changed his mind regarding presenting himself after the first two have been sentenced.

Chapter XVI

1. While neither the Latin nor the Romance versions state who the taker of the securities might be, presumably the annual *iudex* is somehow responsible, since he pays the resulting fine.

2. The Book in this case is the *padrón*, the census and tax list for the city.

3. Roman measure, approximately twelve ounces.

Chapter XIX

1. That is to say, the bondsman has twenty-seven days to produce the debtor; failing that, he has another nine days to pay the bond.

Chapter XXI

1. It was the custom to cast lots to determine whether a challenged person would have to participate in a judicial duel to settle his case, should the trial procedure reach that point.

Chapter XXII

1. Here the reference is to municipal officers, who act as umpires in such a duel.

Chapter XXIII

1. A peaceful expedition to Muslim lands.

2. Leader of the *requa* expedition.

Chapter XXIV

1. An oath swearing no malice in pursuit of the claim.

Chapter XXIX

1. The expressions "on his feet" and "places his foot" probably means to undertake judicial combat.

2. The Latin uses *mortificentur,* or amortized.

Chapter XXX

1. The Romance version notes that he is to be stripped and beaten.

2. The Romance version adds a conventional bow as an option to the crossbow for both horseman and foot soldier.

3. In this law and the two that follow, given the mixed nature of the forces that constituted the average expeditionary force, the presumption here must be that the victim of the injury or death at the hands of the perpetrator is a member of the same allied forces on campaign as the perpetrator.

Chapter XXXI

1. These are all place names of locations within the *alfoz* or governing area of Cuenca.

Chapter XXXIII

1. Nailed probably refers to a nail penetrating the hoof to the flesh of the animal; watered probably indicates an animal swollen from retained water.

Chapter XXXIV

1. The Romance version adds, "For all other dogs, large as well as small, he does not pay more than two *menkales.*"

Chapter XXXV

1. A category of trap, possibly a kind of cage.

Chapter XXXVII

1. The leaving of his house presumably means he leaves his property to herd the goats, rather than graze them on his own land. The text could suggest that he is paid in

part for sterilizing the goats in lots of four, or that he is paid for each sterile goat that he may or may not have sterilized. The closely related code of Teruel expresses this in much the same way. See Jaime Caruana Gómez de Barreda, ed., *El fuero latino de Teruel* (Teruel: Talleres Gráficos, 1974), law 486.

2. The *parapera* is a mark placed on an animal hide by the herdsman after the animal's death, rather than the brand on a live animal. It was a way of accounting for a missing member of a herd. It appears to differ from the brand placed on a living animal, and possibly involves cutting the hide in some way. See the vocabulary in Max Gorosch, ed., *El fuero de Teruel* (Stockholm: Almqvist and Wiksells, 1950), 588–89.

Chapter XL

1. Footwear expenses sometimes occur in connection with persons who must travel in connection with a legal case; usually this means purchasing a pair of shoes for the involved party. See also the instance of the responsible intermediary in XXVII, 13.

Chapter XLII

1. This equivalent in grams is established on the modern avoirdupois scale. It contrasts to the weight of meat and fish employed in the next chapter (XLIII, 7).

2. A medieval corruption of the Latin *praepositura*.

Glossary of Latin and Romance Terms
Used in the Code

açaga (Romance **zaga**). The rear guard of a military expedition.

adalil (Romance **adalid**). Military commander, from the arabic *dalil*.

albedí. Chancery official who handled legal cases for Jews; Jewish equivalent of the *iudex*.

alcacería. District of shops and residences Jews rented from the king in Cuenca.

alcayat (Romance **alcaide**). Warden of castle or castellan, derived from the Arabic *al-qāid*.

alcaldus (pl. **alcaldi**) (Romance **alcalde**). Elected alderman and judge in a parish, derived from the Arabic *al-qādī*

algara. A mobile raiding force, attached to a campaign army, derived from the Arabic *al-gara*.

almud. A measure of grain, usually a mixture of wheat and barley or rye, used as payment and equal to approximately 1.6 bushels.

almutazaf (Romance **almotacén** derived from the Arabic *al-muhtasib*). The chief official of the city market, inspector of weights and measures.

andador. [The Romance term is used here, since this officer in Latin is called primarily *apparator*, although by the later Romance edition the position had apparently subsumed two lesser functionary offices, *quaestor* and *deambulator*, from the Latin version.] An officer whose tasks included those of court clerk, city functionary, and collector of surety pledges.

apellitum (Romance **apellido**). Defensive muster of the city militia.

arançada (**arançata**) (Romance **aranzada**). A land measure of approximately 447 square meters or a tenth of an acre.

attemplantes (Romance **atenplantes**). Members of a resident class lacking full citizenship.

aureus (pl. **aureii**). Latin form of *maravedí alfonsi*, gold money created by Alfonso VIII of Castile, modeled after the Almoravid Muslim *dinar*, the value of which varied in time and place.

butello. Along with *cucumere* (Romance *cohombro* or a *pepino*), two kinds of cucumber.

canna (pl. **cannas**). The same in medieval Latin and Romance, a rod (16.5 feet or 5 meters) in length, used in textile measurement.

carauus (Romance **cáravo**). A small dog, probably a type of terrier.

collacio (Romance **colaçion**). Basic governmental regional district, usually thought to derive from the ecclesiastical parishes of the town, not unlike the modern *barrio*.

concilium (Romance **concejo**). The municipal council of householders, the largest civic body in the town, which could pass laws and act as a level of judicial appeal.

corredor (Latin **venditor**). A licensed public seller of commodities in the city market, a broker for sureties, also a term for the auctioneer of combat booty. See also **venditor**.

denarius (pl. **denarii**) (Romance **dinero**). Copper coin valued at one-twelfth of the *solidus* (Romance *sueldo*).

escribano (Latin **notarius**). Clerk of records, kept the census list (*padrón*) and the city's tax records.

exea. Leader of the *requa*, an expedition or caravan into Muslim lands for commercial purposes, involved in prisoner trading.

exercitus (Romance **hueste**). Offensive military service of the city militia, often with the king.

expeditio (Romance **hueste**). Offensive military service of the city militia, often with the king.

fanega. Unit of dry measure equal to approximately one bushel or thirty-five liters of grain.

fazendera. Tax in behalf of public works

forum (Romance **fuero**). Initially a grant of immunities given to nobles and ecclesiastical organizations; when used in connection with towns it means the town charter, even when that extends to a complete municipal code. The word is occasionally employed in the code to refer to smaller bodies of custom within the body of law.

host (Romance *hueste*). Offensive military service of the city militia, often with the king, used less frequently in text than *exercitus* or *expeditio*.

infançones. Middle level nobles.

iudex (Romance *juez*). Chief elected civil officer in the city, both a mayor and a justice at the first level of appeal in court.

kaficius (pl. **kaficii**) (Romance **cahiz**, pl. **cahices**). A measure of grain, approximately twelve bushels.

mancuadra. An oath swearing to nonmalicious intent in the pursuit of a claim.

mazales. Trout or barbels (a kind of carp).

menkal. A coin of copper or copper and silver mixed, valued at approximately one-fourth of an *aureus*.

merino. Royal territorial administrator who received the king's rents from the city council.

miles (pl. **milites**). (Romance **caballero** pl. **caballeros**). Horse owner who rendered combat on horseback, the bottom rank of the nobility roughly equivalent to the term *knight*.

montaticum (Romance **montazgo**). Royal woodland usage tax.

notarius (Romance **escribano**). Clerk of records, kept the census list (*padrón*) and the city's tax records.

obolus (Romance **meaja**). Older money of uncertain value; varying between one-half and one-sixth of a *denarius*.

padrón. Census and tax list

parapera (Romance **papapera**). A mark on an animal hide by which the herder records the fact of its death for accounting purposes to the owner of the animals.

pedaticus (Romance **portazgo**). Royal and city market toll payment.

podium (Romance **poyo**). Possibly a stone bench or a kind of kiosk built into the wall of a house but on the street.

potestates (Romance **potestades**). The top rank of the nobility.

quadrellarius (Romance **cuadrillero**). An officer who divided booty, elected by each parish during military expeditions.

requa (Romance **recua** or **recloa**). An expedition or caravan into Muslim lands for commercial purposes.

sagio (Romance **sayón**). City bailiff, town crier, and executioner.

saints' days. The following feast days of saints are mentioned in the code: Saint John, June 24; Saint Peter, probably August 1, marking his freedom from prison; the Assumption of the Virgin Mary, August 15; Saint Michael, September 29; Saint Martin, November 11. Also the Circumcision of our Lord, January 1; Feast of All Saints, November 1.

sculca (Romance **esculca**). Organization of livestock herders, who held periodic meetings to determine grazing practices and the maintenance of livestock trails.

sculcarii (Romance **esculqueros**). Members of the livestock herders organization.

señor (pl. **señores**). When capitalized in the text, it refers to the royal representative in the city. In lower case it refers to the male head of a family or household or an owner, employer, or master.

señora. Female head of a household, married to a *señor*.

solidus (pl. **solidi**) (Romance **solido** or **sueldo**, pl. **solidos** or **sueldos**). Twentieth part of a silver pound. Contained twelve *dineros*.

stadium (Romance **estado**). A measurement of length, approximately seven feet. It also served as a measurement of surface, equal to approximately forty-nine square feet.

talayero. Military scout, used on the march in expeditions.

telonearius (Romance **portazguero**). Collector of the *pedaticus/portazgo* tax.

vecinus (Romance **vecino**). A citizen of the town, registered in the *padrón*, the municipal tax list.

venditor (Romance **corredor** or **vendedor**). A licensed public seller of commodities in the city market, a broker for sureties, also a term for the auctioneer of combat booty.

Select Bibliography

Manuscripts

Forum Conche. Ms. Q, iij, 23, Biblioteca de San Lorenzo el Real, El Escorial, Spain.
Forum Conche. Ms. Lat. 12.927, Bibliothèque Nationale, Paris.
Fuero de Cuenca. Codice Valentino. Ms. 39, sig. 88-5-21, Biblioteca Universitaria de Valencia, Spain.
Fuero de Cuenca. Fragmento Conquense. Legajo III, *expte.* no. I, Archivo Municipal de Cuenca, Spain.

Published Editions of the *Forum Conche* and the *Fuero de Cuenca*

Allen, George H., ed. "Forum Conche, fuero de Cuenca: The Latin Text of the Municipal Charter and Laws of the City of Cuenca, Spain." *University Studies Published by the University of Cincinnati* ser. 2, 5, 4 (Nov.–Dec. 1909): 5–92; 6, 1 (Jan.–Feb. 1910): 3–134.
Ureña y Smenjaud, Rafael de, ed. *Fuero de Cuenca*. Madrid: Tipografía de Archivos, 1935.
Valmaña Vicente, Alfredo, ed. *El fuero de Cuenca*. 2nd ed. Cuenca: Editorial Tormo, 1978.

Published Editions of Primary Sources

Albareda y Herrera, Manuel, ed. *Fuero de Alfambra*. Madrid: Tipográfico de la "Revista de Archivos, Bibliotecas y Museos," 1925.
Algora Hernando, Jesús Ignacio and Felicísimo Arranz Sacristán, eds. *Fuero de Calatayud*. Zaragoza: Talleres Gráficos "La Editorial," 1982.
Caruana Gómez de Barreda, Jaime, ed. *El fuero latino de Teruel*. Teruel: Talleres Gráficos, 1974.
Esteban Abad, Rafael, ed. "Fuero de Daroca, 1142." In *Estudio histórico-político sobre la ciudad y communidad de Daroca*. Zaragoza: Talleres Gráficos "La Editorial," 1959. 361–72..
Gorosch, Max, ed. *El fuero de Teruel*. Stockholm: Almqvist and Wiksells, 1950.
Gutiérrez Cuadrado, Juan, ed. *Fuero de Béjar*. Salamanca: Calatravas Libreros, 1974.
——. *Fuero de Úbeda*. Valencia: Artes Gráficas Soler, 1979.
Holmer, Gustaf, ed. *El fuero de Estella según el Manuscrito 944 de la Biblioteca de*

Palacio de Madrid. Göteborg, Stockholm and Uppsala: Almqvist and Wiksell, 1963.

Majada Neila, Jesús, ed. *Fuero de Plasencia.* Salamanca: Gráficas Cervantes, 1986.

Martín Palma, María Teresa, ed. *Los Fueros de Villaescusa de Haro y Huete.* Málaga: Imprenta de la Universidad de Málaga, 1984.

Muñoz y Romero, Tomás, ed. "Fueros de la villa de Palenzuela, 1074." In *Colección de fueros municipales y cartas pueblas de los reinos de Castilla, León, Corona de Aragón y Navarra; coordinada y anotada.* Madrid: Don José María Alonso, 1847. 273–78.

Rodríguez de Lama, Ildefonso, ed. "El rey de Castilla, don Alfonso VI, confirma el fuero concedido a Nájera por los reyes Sancho el Mayor y García el de Nájera." In *Colección diplomática medieval de la Rioja (923–1225).* 3 vols. Logroño: Gonzalo de Bercero, 1976–79. 2:79–85.

Roudil, Jean, ed. *El fuero de Baeza.* The Hague: G. B. Van Zonen, 1962.

———. *Les fueros d'Alcaraz et d'Alarcón.* 2 vols. Paris: Librairie C. Klincksieck, 1968.

———. "El manuscrito español 8331 de la Biblioteca del Arsenal de París." *Vox Romanica* 22 (Jan.–June 1963): 127–74; 22 (July–Dec. 1963): 219–380.

Sáez, Emilio, ed. "Fuero latino de Sepúlveda, confirmado el 17 de noviembre de 1076 por Alfonso VI." In *Los fueros de Sepúlveda.* Critical edition and documentary appendix. Pamplona: Editorial Gómez, 1953. 43–51.

Sancho Izquierdo, Miguel, ed. *El fuero de Molina de Aragón.* Madrid: Impresa Clásica Española, 1916.

Ureña y Smenjaud, Rafael de, ed. *El fuero de Zorita de los Canes.* Madrid: Establecimiento Tipográfico de Fortanet, 1911.

Ximenius de Rada, Rodericus. "Historia de Rebus Hispaniae." In *Opera*, ed. María Desamparados Cabanes Pecourt. Valencia: Anubar, 1968. 5–208.

Secondary Works

Aguadé, Santiago and María Dolores Cabañas. "Comercio y sociedad urbana en la Castilla Medieval: La comercialización de la carne en Cuenca (1177–1500)." *Anuario de Estudios Medievales* 14 (1984): 487–516.

Alonso Pedraz, Martín. *Diccionario medieval español: Desde las Glosas Emilianenses y Silenses (s. X) hasta el siglo XV.* 2 vols. Salamanca: Kadmos, 1986.

Aparicio-Llopis, María Pilar. "Fuero." In *The Dictionary of the Middle Ages*, Joseph R. Strayer, gen. ed. 13 vols. New York: Charles Scribner's Sons, 1982–89. 5:308–10.

Ballard, Adolphus, ed. *British Borough Charters, 1042–1216.* Cambridge: Cambridge University Press, 1913.

Barrero García, Ana M. *El fuero de Teruel: Su historia, proceso de formación y reconstrucción crítica de sus fuentes.* Madrid: Artes Gráficas y Ediciones, 1979.

Barrero García, Ana María. "El proceso de formación del fuero de Cuenca (notas para su estudio)." In *Cuenca y su territorio en la Edad Media.* Madrid and Barcelona: Consejo Superior de Investigaciones Científicas, 1982. 41–58.

Bishko, Charles Julian. "The Castilian as Plainsman." In *The New World Looks at Its History*, ed. Archibald R. Lewis and Thomas F. McGann. Austin: University of Texas Press, 1963. 47–69.

——. "The Frontier in the Middle Ages." Paper given at the American Historical Association Meeting, Washington, D.C., 29 December 1955. Available on the World Wide Web, home page of the American Academy of Research Historians on Medieval Spain, http://kuhttp.cc.ukans.edu/kansas/aarhms/mainpage.html.

——. "The Spanish and Portuguese Reconquest, 1095–1492." In *A History of the Crusades*, ed. Kenneth M. Setton et al. 6 vols. Madison: University of Wisconsin Press, 1962–89. 3:396–456.

Brodman, James W. "Municipal Ransoming Law on the Medieval Spanish Frontier." *Speculum* 60 (1985): 318–30.

Burns, Robert I. "The Significance of the Frontier in the Middle Ages." In *Medieval Frontier Societies*, ed. Robert Bartlett and Angus MacKay. Oxford: Oxford University Press, 1989. 307–30.

Carlé, María del Carmen. *Del concejo medieval Castellano-Leones*. Buenos Aires: Instituto de Historia de España, 1968.

Caruana Gómez de Barreda, Jaime. "La auténtica fecha del Fuero de Teruel." *Anuario de Historia del Derecho Español* 31 (1961): 115–19.

——. "La prioridad cronológica del Fuero de Teruel sobre el de Cuenca." *Anuario de Historia del Derecho Español* 25 (1955): 791–97.

Concejos y Ciudades en la Edad Media Hispanica. Móstoles: Unigraf, S. A., 1990.

Corominas, J. *Diccionario crítico etimológico de la lengua castellana*. 4 vols. Madrid: Gredos, 1954–57.

Davis, H. W. C. Review of *Colección para el Estudio de la Historia de Aragón*. Vol. 2. *Fuero del [sic] Teruel*, transcription and preliminary study by Francisco Aznar y Navarro. (Zaragoza: Gasca, n.d.). *English Historical Review* 23 (1908): 766–72.

——. Review of *Forum Conche (Fuero de Cuenca)*. Edited by George H. Allen (Chicago: University of Chicago Press, 1909–10). *English Historical Review* 26 (1911): 168–72.

Diccionario de historia de España, desde su orígenes hasta el fin del reinado de Alfonso XIII. 2nd ed. 3 vols. Madrid: Ediciones de la Revista de Occidente, 1968.

Dillard, Heath. *Daughters of the Reconquest: Women in Castilian Town Society, 1100–1300*. Cambridge and New York: Cambridge University Press, 1984.

García-Gallo, Alfonso. "Aportación al estudio de los fueros." *Anuario de Historia del Derecho Español* 26 (1956): 387–446.

——. "Los fueros de Toledo." *Anuario de Historia del Derecho Español* 45 (1975): 355–488.

——. *Manual de historia del derecho español*. 10th ed. 2 vols. Madrid: Artes Gráficas y Ediciones, 1984.

——. "Nuevas observaciones sobre la obra legislativa de Alfonso X." *Anuario de Historia del Derecho Español* 46 (1976): 609–70.

García Ulecia, Alberto. *Los factores de diferenciación entre las personas en los fueros de la Extremadura castellano-aragonesa*. Seville: Gráficas del Sur, 1975.

Gautier-Dalché, Jean. *Historia urbana de León y Castilla en la Edad Media: (siglos IX–XIII)*, trans. Encarnación Pérez Sedeño. Madrid: Siglo Veintiuno Editores, 1979.

——. "Sur quelques clauses du Fuero de Cuenca (Forma Sistemática): Aménagement de l'espace, population et institutions." *Cuadernos de Historia de España* 74 (1997): 121–45.

Gibert, Rafael. "El derecho municipal de León y Castilla." *Anuario de Historia del Derecho Español* 31 (1961): 695–753.

González, Julio. *Reinado y diplomas de Fernando III.* 3 vols. Córdoba: Graficromo, S.A., 1980–86.

——. *El reino de Castilla en la época de Alfonso VIII.* 3 vols. Madrid: Sucesores do Rivadeneyra, 1960.

——. *Repoblación de Castilla la Nueva.* 2 vols. Madrid: Artes Gráficas, 1976.

Lewis, Charlton T. and Charles Short. *A Latin Dictionary: Freund's Latin Dictionary Revised, Enlarged, and in Great Part Rewritten.* Oxford: Oxford University Press, 1879, reprinted 1986.

López, D. Mateo. *Memorias históricas de Cuenca y su obispado.* 2 vols. Madrid: Concejo Superior de Investigaciones Científicas y Ayuntamiento de la Ciudad de Cuenca, 1949–53.

Luís Martín, José. *Origenes de la Orden Militar de Santiago.* Barcelona: Selecciones Gráficas, 1974.

Martínez Díez, Gonzalo. *Las comunidades de villa y tierra de la Extremadura castellana (Estudio histórico-geográfico).* Madrid: Editora Nacional, 1983.

——. "Los fueros de la familia Coria Cima-Coa." *Revista Portuguesa de Historia* 13 (1971): 343–73.

Martínez Gijón, José. "La familia del Fuero de Cuenca, estado de una investigación científica." In *Atti del Secondo Congresso Internazionale della Società Italiana di Storia del Diritto.* Vol. 1.. *La crítica del testo.* Florence: L. S. Olschki, 1971, 415–39.

Martínez Llorente, Félix Javier. *Régimen jurídico de la Extremadura Castellana Medieval: Las comunidades de villa y tierra (S. x–xiv).* Valladolid: Universidad, Secretariado de Publicaciones, 1990.

Moxó, Salvador de. *Repoblación y sociedad en la España cristiana medieval.* Madrid: Ediciones Rialp, S.A., 1979.

Niermeyer, J. F. *Mediae Latinitatis Lexicon Minus: A Medieval Latin-French/English Dictionary.* 2 vols. Leiden: E. J. Brill, 1976.

O'Callaghan, Joseph F. "The Beginnings of the Cortes of León-Castile." *American Historical Review* 74 (1969): 1503–37.

——. *A History of Medieval Spain.* Ithaca, N.Y. and London: Cornell University Press, 1975.

Pérez-Bustamante, Rogelio. *El gobierno y la administración de los reinos de la Corona de Castilla, 1230–1474.* 2 vols. Burgos: Imprenta de Aldecoa, 1976.

Powers, James F. "The Creative Interaction between Portuguese and Leonese Municipal Military Law, 1055 to 1279." *Speculum* 62 (1987): 53–80.

——. "Frontier Competition and Legal Creativity: A Castilian-Aragonese Case Study Based on Twelfth-Century Municipal Military Law." *Speculum* 52 (July, 1977): 465–87.

——. "Frontier Municipal Baths and Social Interaction in Thirteenth-Century Spain." *American Historical Review* 84 (June, 1979): 649–67.

——. *A Society Organized for War: The Iberian Municipal Militias in the Central Middle Ages, 1000–1284.* Berkeley, Los Angeles and London: University of California Press, 1988.

Rassow, Peter. *Der Prinzgemahl: Ein Pactum Matrimoniale aus dem Jahre 1188.* Weimar: Hermann Bohlaus Nachfolger, 1950.

Sánchez-Albornoz, Claudio. "The Frontier and Castilian Liberties." In *The New World*

Looks at Its History, ed. Archibald R. Lewis and Thomas F. McGann. Austin: University of Texas Press, 1963. 27–46.

Stalls, Clay. *Possessing the Land: Aragon's Expansion into Islam's Ebro Frontier Under Alfonso the Battler, 1104–1134*. Leiden, New York, and Köln: E. J. Brill, 1995.

Stewart, Frank Henderson. *Honor*. Chicago and London: University of Chicago Press, 1994.

Valdeavellano, Luís G. de. *Curso de historia de las instituciones españoles de los orígenes al final de la Edad Media*. 3rd ed. Madrid: Ediciones de la Revista de Occidente, 1973.

Index

Abortion, 84

Adultery, 82, 85, 198

Alarcos, battle of 1195, 13, 20, 223 n. 1

Albedí (Jewish *iudex*), 13, 160

Alcaldes. See *Alcaldi*

Alcaldi: election of, 109; Jewish, 160; rights to fine shares, 33–35, 113, 121–22, 130, 132, 139, 142; 145, 195, 207, 208; role of, 5, 8, 38, 109–14; salary of, 114; as witnesses, 130–34, 149; as militia commanders, 167; of the *sculca*, 200–201

Alcayat, 32; Muslim captive, 171

Alfambra, *fuero* of, 6

Alfonso II, king of Aragon, 1, 17, 18–19

Alfonso VIII, king of Castile, 1, 2, 15, 17, 18–21, 29

Alfonso IX, 19–21, 28

Alfonso X, 22–23

Alfonso XI, 23

Alfoz, 7, 13, 20

Allen, George H., 18

Almohads, 1

Almoravids, 1

Almotacén. See *Almutazaf*

Almud (measure of grain), 41, 46, 197, 207, 223 n. 3

Almutazaf (market official), 6, 7, 8, 49, 57, 158, 207–8, 209–13; election, 109; role, 114–15; salary, 115

Alphonsipolis, 20, 28

Andadores (court official and sureties collectors), 5, 111–12, 138, 146, 158, 217; as responsible intermediaries for royal appeals, 156–58; election, 109; role, 116–17; share of penalties, 113; salary, 117, 158

Andalusia, 4

Animals: treatment of, 4, 183–89, 206, 209; compensation for those injured or lost on military campaigns, 168–69, 175, 177–78; sale of, 183; renting of, 184–85; as collateral,

183–84; unauthorized use or treatment of, 185–87; herding of, 194–98, 200–201; found, 202

Apparitores. See *Andadores*

Appeal, judicial, 4

Aragon, kingdom of, 1

Attemplantes (resident noncitizens), 132

Auctions, 118, 172, 175, 204

Aureus, 9

Baking in municipal ovens, 40

Bathhouses, 11–12, 13, 35, 40–41, 62–63

Bees, 7, 207

Berenguela, daughter of Alfonso VIII, 20–21

Bigamy, 83

Bishop of Cuenca, 3

Boars, 189–91

Bondsmen, 3, 8, 31, 32, 34, 54, 80, 93, 104–7, 112, 125–31, 139, 142–43, 158–59, 172, 200, 202; in real estate sales, 59–60, 180, 192–93, 209

Booty, 7, 15, 217; responsibility for the royal fifth share of, 111; shares of for citizens, 165–66, 168, 171–72, 174–77, 179; shares for equipment and weapons provided, 166; compensation for losses, 168; partition of, 169; special awards, 170; shares for officials and commanders, 172, 175; withholding booty, 172, 179; reward for capturing a town or castle, 179

Boundary stones of urban jurisdiction, 6–7, 195–96

Bows and crossbows, 29, 166

Brickmakers and tilemakers, 212–13

Burial alive, 11, 34, 79, 173, 206

Burial, privilege of, 31

Burning alive, 10, 34, 75, 79, 80–81, 84–85, 91, 216

Butchers, 213

Butter, 196

Acknowledgments

Thanks are due to a number of people who have contributed to this work. Julian Bishko, professor emeritus of the University of Virginia, read the entire translation and offered innumerable suggestions to the efficacy and readability of the text. Four of my students at the College of the Holy Cross, Audrey J. Blair, Clare L. Brewster, David M. Palumbo, and William J. Phoenix, have worked with the text in Latin and in translation as a part of senior theses, enhancing my awareness of textual possibilities and spurring my interest with their enthusiasm. Christian G. Samito, a former student, acquired some material for me from the Harvard Law Library while completing his law degree there. I have received supporting funds from the Committee on Research and Publication and the Perkins-Honeywell Scanning Grant at Holy Cross. The faculty and my fellow members at the Institute for Advanced Studies, especially Giles Constable and Bernard Bachrach, rendered invaluable assistance during my stay there in the spring of 1998. Research assistance was also rendered by the Archivo Municipal de Cuenca and especially by Dr. Antonio Chacón Gómez-Monedero, archivist of the Archivo Capitular de Catedral de Cuenca. I also must thank the readers of the manuscript for the University of Pennsylvania Press, and their diligent editors, for scrutinizing the translation with such care. My wife and colleague, Professor Lorraine C. Attreed of the College of the Holy Cross, offered her editorial and historical skills and unflagging support for my efforts throughout the enterprise. It is safe to say that I could not have completed this task without her encouragement, and it is to her that I dedicate this book. None of these generous individuals are responsible for any unintended errors; I must claim those.